Der.   .a

Democracy Realized

The Progressive Alternative

ROBERTO MANGABEIRA UNGER

VERSO

London • New York

First published by Verso 1998
© Roberto Mangabeira Unger 1998
First published in paperback 2001
All rights reserved

3 5 7 9 10 8 6 4 2

Verso
UK: 6 Meard Street, London W1V 3HR
US: 180 Varick Street, New York, NY 10014–4606

Verso is the imprint of New Left Books

ISBN: 978-1-85984-009-2

British Library Cataloguing in Publication Data
A catalogue record for this book is available from the British Library

Library of Congress Cataloging-in-Publication Data
A catalogue record for this book is available from the Library of Congress

Typeset by SetSystems Ltd, Saffron Walden
Printed by R.R. Donnelley & Sons, USA

CONTENTS

II   A MANIFESTO   261

I
AN ARGUMENT

DEMOCRATIC EXPERIMENTALISM
IN TROUBLE

The focus of ideological conflict throughout the world is changing. The old contest between statism and privatism, command and market, is dying. It is in the process of being replaced by a more promising rivalry among the alternative institutional forms of economic, social, and political pluralism. The basic premise of this new conflict is that market economies, free civil societies, and representative democracies can assume many different institutional forms, with radically different consequences for society. The political, social, and economic institutions established in the rich industrial countries represent a small part of a much larger range of possibilities. The existing distinctions among these possible forms – the differences, for example, among the corporate institutions of Germany, Japan, and the United States – amount to limited and ephemeral instances of much broader potential variations.

Everywhere in the world, however, there is today an experience of exhaustion and perplexity in the formulation of credible alternatives to the neoliberal program and to its defining belief in convergence toward a single system of democratic and market institutions. Having abandoned statist commitments and witnessed the collapse of communist regimes, progressives look in vain for a direction more affirmative than the rearguard defense of social democracy.

Confusion and disappointment are not confined to the left; they have become the common stigmata of the politically conscious. Even in the hegemonic country, the United States, living

3

through a triumphal moment in its relations with the rest of the world, ordinary working citizens are likely to feel themselves angry outsiders, part of a fragmented and marginalized majority, powerless to reshape the collective basis of the collective problems they face. They find the routes to social mobility for themselves and their children blocked in what is supposedly a classless society. They believe the people who run the country and its big businesses to be joined in a predatory conspiracy. They despair of politics and politicians, and seek an individual escape from a social predicament.

The public intelligentsia of the country deride ideological politics, large-scale projects of institutional reform and popular political mobilization as romantic and impractical. They insist upon the supremacy of technical policy analysis and practical problem-solving by experts. Yet this programatically empty and deenergized politics fails to solve the practical problems for whose sake it renounced larger ambitions. It slides into drift and impotence because it allows itself to degenerate into short-term and episodic factional deals, struck against a background of institutions and assumptions that remain unchallenged and even unseen.

Meanwhile, in every rich industrial democracy, beginning with the United States, a vigorous underground experimentalism has begun to change production and learning, informing and inspiring firms and schools. The contrast between the definition and the execution of tasks, supervisory and executory jobs, softens. Cooperation and competition combine in the same activities rather than remaining relegated to separate domains. Permanent innovation becomes the touchstone of success; successful firms must become more like good schools. However, this experimentalism in the little worlds of the firm and the school ends up hitting against the limits imposed by the untransformed public world, still exhausted and perplexed.

Democracy Realized reinterprets this exhaustion and responds to this perplexity. It does so in two steps: first and at length, through an argument; second, through a summary manifesto.

WHAT IS DEMOCRATIC EXPERIMENTALISM?

Practical progress and individual emancipation

The conception animating the arguments and the proposal of this book is **democratic experimentalism**. Democratic experimentalism is an interpretation of the democratic cause, the most influential set of ideas and commitments at work in the world today. It combines two hopes with a practice of thought and action.

The first hope of the democrat, according to democratic experimentalism, is to find the area of overlap between the conditions of practical progress and the requirements of individual emancipation. Prominent among such conditions and requirements are the institutional arrangements of society. Practical or material progress includes economic growth and technological or medical innovation, supported by scientific discovery. It is the development of our power to push back the constraints of scarcity, disease, weakness, and ignorance. It is the empowerment of humanity to act upon the world. Individual emancipation refers to the freeing of individuals from the hold of entrenched social roles, divisions, and hierarchies, especially when this social machinery draws force from inherited advantage, shaping the life chances of individuals.

Many of the great political doctrines and evolutionary social theories of the nineteenth century subscribed to the optimistic belief in a preestablished harmony between practical progress and individual emancipation. Liberal and socialist thinkers alike saw in the program of institutional reform they defended the necessary and even sufficient basis for both freedom and prosperity. We can no longer credit the functionalist and necessitarian assumptions about social change that made such a view intelligible and persuasive.

The idea of preestablished harmony has lost its authority. Many, however, are now tempted to replace this dogma with an equally unwarranted dogma of ineradicable conflict between the goods of prosperity and freedom. Each good would depend upon arrangements, and yield consequences, destructive of the other.

Even those who refuse to embrace this tragic view may suffer its influence. They may reduce the democratic cause to a moral and political conception justifying constraints upon practical forces over which democracy has no purchase. They may see economic life, and technological or scientific progress, as external to democratic advance, a source of problems more than of solutions.

By his first hope, the democratic experimentalist affirms that the conditions of practical progress and individual emancipation can intersect. A subset of the institutional conditions of practical progress also serves the purpose of individual emancipation. A subset of the institutional conditions of individual emancipation also promotes the goal of practical progress. The democratic experimentalist wants to find this zone of overlap and to go forward within it.

What makes this hope of finding and using the zone of overlap reasonable? Both practical progress and individual emancipation depend upon the capacity to transform social effort into collective learning and to act upon the lessons learned, undeterred by the need to respect a preestablished plan of social division and hierarchy or a confining allocation of social roles. Such constraints are particularly subversive of collective discovery and invention when they reflect inherited advantage, for they then fall like a blind and irresistible fate upon all forms of individual striving.

The intuitive idea at the core of the conjecture of possible overlap is that both practical experimentalism and individual emancipation require arrangements minimizing barriers to collective learning. They minimize such barriers by combining strengthened individual security and capacity with broader opportunities to try out different ways of associating with other people in every realm of our practical and moral experience.

This view is in turn connected with a thesis about our relation to the institutional and discursive structures we build and inhabit. We develop our faculties and powers by moving within these structures, but also by resisting, overcoming, and revising them. We may even make them more hospitable to the exercise and strengthening of our capacity to defy the limits of our social and cultural contexts.

The best way to work out the idea of an affinity between practical progress and individual emancipation is to develop our understanding of the internal structure of each of these two families of interests. At the heart of each lies a conflict of requirements. By modifying and moderating these conflicts we enhance the range and force of human powers, deepening our central experience of freedom.

Practical progress, of which economic growth and technological innovation are the most important species, counts for a democratic experimentalist in more than one way. Economic growth, with its reinforcing arm of technological development, lifts from human life the burden of drudgery and infirmity. We cannot be free when we are weak. The perversion of economic growth and its fruits begins when we attempt to make up for the scarcity of public goods by producing more private ones, and to find in private consumption a barren solace for social frustration.

The material benefits of economic and technological progress are, however, only part of the story. We have a stake in opening the business world more fully to the moral experiences upon which both democracy and experimentalism must draw. People spend much of their lives at work, engaged in practical economic activities. It matters whether people's workaday lives are shaped so as to tap and sustain the common element in democracy and experimentalism.

Central to all aspects of material progress is the relation between cooperation and innovation. Innovation requires cooperation. Nevertheless, every real form of cooperation remains embedded in arrangements generating settled expectations and vested rights of different groups relative to one another. People regularly resist innovation because they correctly believe it to threaten such rights and expectations.

Some ways of organizing cooperation are more friendly to innovation than others. They anchor security more in individual endowments than in group privileges. By preferring and developing such forms of cooperation – at the workplace, in each sector of production, and in the economy as a whole – we moderate the tension between cooperation and innovation, and enable them to reinforce each other.

By such means, we broaden the scope of experimental innovation in economic activity. We also nourish some of the core experiences sustaining a democratic culture: the ascendancy of individual endowments and capacities over group privileges as well as the ability to cooperate across the boundaries of preset, especially inherited, social divisions and hierarchies.

Consider now the internal structure of the good of individual emancipation. The development of individuality demands a cumulative thickening of our practical, cognitive, and emotional ties. Such a thickening, however, forever threatens us with the double risk of subjugation to other people and depersonalization under the weight of frozen social roles. We deepen freedom – the most basic freedom, which is the capacity for self-possession and self-development – by moderating the conflict between these twin needs of personality.

Preset schemes of social division and hierarchy, shaping the life chances of individuals on the basis of inherited resources and opportunities and subordinating the opportunities of cooperation to the interests of privilege and control, aggravate the conflict between the requirements of self-assertion. The freeing of individuals from the grip of these background structures diminishes the price each of us must pay for participation in group life, and helps reconcile the basic conditions of self-possession and self-development.

The major issue raised by such a reconciliation is one that has been central to the religions of the Bible: the relation between resistance or transcendence and solidarity or love. The secular content of the religious idea of transcendence is the inability of our created contexts of society and discourse fully to contain us, exhausting our powers of insight, experience, emotion, connection, invention, and production. There is always more in us than there is in our contexts. They are finite. We, relative to them, are not.

We can hope to diminish this disproportion between circumstance and personality by building institutional and cultural worlds that become more supportive of our context-transcending powers. Such contexts may fortify our resources and powers of resistance, even as they invite their own revision.

Our capacity for love and solidarity grows through the strengthening of our ability to recognize and to accept the otherness of other people. It is in love, the love least dependent upon idealization or similarity, that we most radically accept one another as the original, context-transcending beings we really are, rather than as placeholders in a social scheme, acting out a script we never devised and barely understand.

However, we are not fully these beings able to turn the table on their contexts and to accept one another for who we are and might become. We must make ourselves into such beings. The deepening of democracy, reconciling the opposed requirements of self-assertion, is one of the ways in which we do so. To this extent, democratic experimentalism draws energy and meaning from concerns outreaching politics and economics.

Thus, the conditions of individual emancipation and of practical progress are both structurally analogous and causally connected. This connection and this analogy make reasonable the first defining hope of the democrat. They lend credibility to our efforts to work in the zone of overlap between the conditions for the flourishing of these two families of goods.

Democractic experimentalism and ordinary people: insight and agency

If the first hope of the democrat is the hope of building in the zone of overlap between the conditions of practical progress and of individual emancipation, the second hope is that this work respond to the felt needs and aspirations of ordinary men and women. Democracy cannot go forward as the unrecognized gift of a cunning history to a reluctant nation.

People may be mistaken about what they need, but they cannot, if the factual assumptions of democratic experimentalism are true, be incorrigibly mistaken. The advances of democracy – its institutional innovations and its spurs to practical progress and individual liberation – must move toward fulfilling people's interests and realizing their ideals as they themselves see their ideals and interests.

If this second hope were unreasonable, democratic experimentalists would incessantly excite the demons of politics: the tendency of means to create their own ends, and of self-appointed vanguards to enshrine their power interests at the cost of their professed commitments. Ordinary people could not, except by accident, become the agents as well as the beneficiaries of their society-building work.

What makes this second hope reasonable is a feature of agency that I shall call **duality**. According to the **duality thesis** there are alternative persuasive ways to define and defend group interests.

Some of these ways are conservative and exclusive. They are conservative because they take the established institutional arrangements and the existing social and technical division of labor for granted. They are exclusive because this institutionallly conservative assumption leads each group to identify its interests with the preservation of its niche, and to see the immediately contiguous groups, in its social space, as its greatest enemies. Thus, to introduce an example developed later in this book, unionized workers in capital-intensive industry may see temporary workers or subcontractors as threats, and seek in plant-level or firm-level collective bargaining agreements security against the encroachments of these rivals.

Other approaches to the definition and defense of group interests and ideals are transformative and solidaristic. They propose a way of realizing the interests and ideals through the step-by-step change of a set of arrangements. Those unionized workers, for example, may find common cause with the temporary workers and subcontractors in supporting a scheme for more decentralized access to venture capital. The result of the change of arrangements over time is to revise the content as well as the context of recognized interests and professed ideals.

Ideals and interests draw much of their substance from their implicit institutional setting. By shifting the institutional ground from under them, we put pressure against our understanding of their content. We expose ambiguities of meaning and alternatives of development that lay hidden and invisible so long as this ground remained unshaken.

The conservative and exclusive strategies in the definition and defense of group interests may often be self-defeating but they almost always seem safe. They enjoy the advantages of tangibility. By contrast, the transformative and solidaristic approaches may seem leaps in the dark. The claim that a solidaristic strategy is more sustainable in the long run may ordinarily prove insufficient to outweigh the power of immediacy the exclusive strategy enjoys. That is why the argument for a transformative and solidaristic project may need additional help.

The visionary element in politics provides such help. The intimation of a different world, in which we would become (slightly) different people, with (slightly) revised understandings of our interests and ideals, supplements the cold appeal to group interest and familiar conviction. Thus, in transformative politics we must speak in the two languages of interest calculation and political prophecy.

Return to the earlier example. A program for the reconstruction of industry, to be sustained by a broadened popular alliance, will appear far more risky than a dogged defense of the prerogatives of mass-production industry and of the workers employed in it. The judgement of greater risk may be, to some extent, an illusion, elicited by a failure adequately to imagine the probable consequences of each approach. However, given the discontinuity between the biographical and the historical perspective (who wants to serve as an instrument of historical progress?), it is also a tenacious illusion. The visionary intimation of a reordered social world, with its poetic and prophetic attempt to connect present personal experiences to hidden social possibilities, helps right the scales of risk by enlarging the imaginative terrain on which the debate takes place. As the consequences of reforms for the understanding of interests and ideals become manifest, the boundary shutting the instrumental off from the visionary begins to open. Then history makes more room for imagination.

The availability of the solidaristic and transformative ways of championing recognized interests and professed ideals is the basic premise justifying the second hope of the democrat. **Correspondence** and **asymmetry** complement dualism as features of agency in the understanding of social change upon which democratic experimentalism relies.

According to the **correspondence thesis** group alliances and antagonisms are always just the reverse side of a set of institutional arrangements and a sequence of institutional reforms. Whether a certain alliance among social groups can be developed and sustained over time depends upon whether there is an institutional situation, or a trajectory of institutional reform, enabling the interests and ideals of the participant groups to converge. The more far-reaching is the program of reform, the tighter and more apparent does the link between the logic of alliances and the direction of institutional change become.

Whether it makes sense, for example, for organized workers in capital-intensive industry to ally with temporary workers and subcontractors depends upon whether there is a program of institutional reform and economic policy nourishing their combination. To the extent such a program succeeds, what began as a tactical partnership may turn into a lasting convergence. It may ultimately become a union of collective identities as well as of group interests.

The correspondence thesis reverses a characteristic tenet of Marxist theory. According to orthodox Marxism, there is an objective logic of class interests, rooted in the institutional positions of each mode of production and in the unyielding laws governing the crisis and succession of these production systems. The broader the scope and the greater the intensity of class conflict, the more transparent will the logic of class interests, class alliances, and class oppositions become. Those who mistake the content of this logic suffer the punishment of political defeat, reminding them of what they had tried to forget.

By the light of the correspondence thesis the clarity and fixity of group interests are specious and conditional. They depend upon failure to challenge and shake the arrangements that make the established understanding of interests seem self-evident. Social and ideological conflict wear away the patina of naturalness and necessity surrounding our views of agency and alliance. As such conflict broadens in scope and esclates in intensity, the question – What are my interests? – begins to get combined with other queries. What social worlds may arise from this one? To what groups would I belong in those subsequent worlds? What would my interests and my identity then become?

According to the **asymmetry thesis** the relation between political alliances and social or group alliances is asymmetrical. A set of group alliances presupposes a political alliance, in the broad sense of a shared project for developing and sustaining the institutional arrangements that would support the convergence of group interests. No alliance of group interests is natural or necessary except in relation to the arrangements sustaining it.

The struggle to establish such arrangements, followed by their piecemeal realization, are the basic requirements for the advancement of a social alliance. The contest over the mastery and use of governmental power is not the only tool of such an effort. It is simply its most prominent and familiar form, alongside all the other ways by which, outside government, people may seek to change the shape of their relations to one another.

Political alliances, however, do not presuppose social alliances in the same sense. They take the building of social alliances as a task and a horizon rather than as an antecedent condition. The project of reform and alliance must live in thought and action before it can be lived out as an acknowledged joinder of interests.

The asymmetry thesis may seem counterintuitive. If, however, it did not hold, deliberate, discontinuous, structural change in history would be impossible. Divisions of political force and opinion would simply map and reinforce the underlying class and community divisions, based in turn upon the established institutional arrangements.

Politics is the alternative to chance and necessity. If political and social alliances were not asymmetrical, chance and necessity would foreclose the space of intentional transformation.

Thus, the maxim of the unevenness of social and political alliances is a postulate of practical political reason. The evidence of historical experience may be insufficient to either confirm or disconfirm this postulate. We, however, have a stake in its being true. We even hope to make it more true by acting as if it were true.

The duality, correspondence, and asymmetry theses do rest upon certain assumptions about how society changes. They are indeed incompatible with much in the major traditions of classical European social theory as well as with many ways of thinking current in the contemporary positive social sciences. They nevertheless presuppose no strong, well-defined social theory. They are compatible with a family of views I have explored in other books.*

We cannot wait until we agree upon the truths of a new social theory to think and act as democratic experimentalists. We must find the ideas our efforts and commitments require, and try to make no assumptions that the facts of social reality and historical experience invalidate.

Democratic experimentalism needs the tools of the institutional imagination. In particular, it relies upon a practice of legal and economic analysis that takes institutional constraints and alternatives seriously.† It even requires a larger vision of society and history that can help inform and inspire its work. However, it cannot stop until it gets what it needs. It must find, justify, and develop its own presuppositions, forcing self-reflection upon its

---

* See Roberto Mangabeira Unger, *Politics: The Central Texts*, edited and introduced by Zhiyuan Cui, Verso, London, 1997.

† See Roberto Mangabeira Unger, *What Should Legal Analysis Become?*, Verso, London, 1996.

imagined or actual experiments to advance ahead of organized theoretical insight.

Institutional innovation

Democratic experientalism combines its two defining hopes with a practice: motivated, sustained, and cumulative tinkering with the arrangements of society.

A premise of this practice is the **internal relaton between understandings of ideals or interests and thinking about practices or institutions.** We should not regard the reform of institutional arrangements as an exercise in social engineering, appended as an instrumental afterthought to the definition of interests or ideals or to the formulation of principles of justice.

Our interests and ideals draw meaning from a double reference. They refer to aspirations and anxieties that the prosaic language of economic description and the familiar pieties of political discourse fail fully to exploit. With at least as much force, however, they also refer to the arrangements that we tacitly accept as their more or less natural expressions. When, for example, we invoke our ideals of democracy, we are likely to rely at least as much upon a background picture of what the contemporary North Atlantic industrial democracies look like as upon the pregnant and ambiguous rhetoric of our constitutional religion.

The double reference lends drama and movement to the language of politics. As soon as we begin to question the institutional assumptions of our interests and ideals, we expose fault lines that remained previously hidden from view.

What, for example, is more important about private property once we begin to experiment with its legal-institutional forms? The unqualified character of the power each owner enjoys over the resources at his command? Or the absolute number of economic agents able to use some part of these resources for their own initiative and on their own account? Some alternative arrangements for the decentralized allocation of access to productive resources may broaden private property in the second sense while limiting it in the first sense.

Our institutional choices do not merely execute the predefined program of our interests and ideals. They work out that program. It is, in large part, by enriching the institutional possibilities, and by pushing them in one direction rather than another, that we make them – and therefore ourselves – into one thing rather than another.

The dominant styles of normative political philosophy today, particularly in the English-speaking countries, treat the formulation of normative principles and ideals as an activity separate from, and prior to, the design of institutional arrangements. First, we establish principles of just distribution of rights and resources. Then, we design the arrangements most effectively realizing these principles in practice. The pieces of social engineering remain external and subsidiary to the work of prescriptive guidance.

Similarly, this reigning practice of political philosophy treats wants, moral intuitions, and perceptions of individual or group interest as a raw material to which normative theory can appeal. The elements of this material may be continuously refined in the light of theoretical reflection. They may, at least at the margin, be corrected, as we reject, for example, moral intuitions that fail to fit with others within a scheme of principle. They nevertheless enjoy a substantial independence from both beliefs and institutions.

Theorists often suppose that the separation of institutional design from prescriptive principles, on one side, and from raw wants and intuitions, on the other, is necessary to ensure the transcendence of normative theory over historical context. Yet by failing adequately to acknowledge the shaping of ideals by institutional preconception these rationalistic political philosophers deliver themselves all the more completely into the hands of their historical setting. No wonder so much of their speculation remains a philosophical gloss upon the distinctive practices of redistributive tax-and-transfer and individual-rights protection in the postwar industrial democracies. We must win our independence from the context, not assume it by a conceptual sleight-of-hand. One way in which we must win it is by probing the different directions in which we might develop our ideals, our interests, our intuitions, and even our wants as we begin to reshape their familiar institutional and ideological ground.

Therefore, a programmatic imagination useful to democratic experimentalism must also escape the false divisions to which speculative political philosophy remains bound. Institutional debates and experiments are not a separate and subsidiary exercise; they represent our most important way of defining and redefining the content of our ideals and interests.

In this activity the basic philosophical questions are how much guidance we are entitled to expect and where we can expect to find it. In seeking such guidance, we can never move from something that is merely contextual – the ideals and the institutions, the intuitions and the practices of our situation – to another thing that is beyond contexts. We can merely hope to broaden the range of experience, and to deepen the distance of judgement, from which we evaluate the living possibilities of the present.

A more focused factual assumption of the practice of instutional experimentalism is the idea of the primacy of **radical reform** as a species of transformative politics.* Reform is radical when it addresses and changes the basic arrangements of a society: its

---

* See Roberto Mangabeira Unger, *Social Theory: Its Situation and Its Task*, Cambridge University Press, Cambridge, 1987, pp. 163–5, and *False Necessity: Anti-Necessitarian Social Theory in the Service of Radical Democracy*, Cambridge University Press, Cambridge, 1987, pp. 172–246.

formative structure of institutions and enacted beliefs. It is reform because it deals with one discrete part of this structure at a time.

The idea of institutional tinkering, or part-by-part change, has often been associated with the abandonment of challenge to the fundamental institutions of a society, or even with a repudiation of any attempt to distinguish formative structure from formed routines. Conversely, the conception of such a challenge has just as often been connected with the idea that our institutional structures exist as indivisible systems, standing or falling together.

The point of acknowledging radical reform to be the dominant mode of transformative politics is to associate the idea of discontinuous, structural change with the practical attitudes of the person who forever asks: What is the next step? There are basic institutional arrangements and enacted beliefs in a society. They demonstrate their special power by their ability to shape the recurrent routines of political, econonomic, and discursive conflict, the limits within which the society-making resources of political power, economic capital, and cultural authority are put to use, and the assumptions about society taken for granted by collective agents in the understanding and pursuit of their interests. Although these formative arrangements are connected, and although some arrangements cannot be stably combined with others, the institutional order of society changes part by part and step by step.

It is the combination of parts and the succession of steps, reaching far beyond the starting point, and changing along the way our understanding of our interests, ideals, and identities, that makes a reform project relatively more radical. It is the direction in which the steps take us that make it more or less democratic.

The idea of revolution, when used to denote the total substitution of one indivisible system by another, describes nothing but a dangerous limiting case of transformative politics, seen under the lens of an illusion about how history happens. When reality resists the illusion, the would-be revolutionaries may resort to violence, seeking in physical force the means to make good on the hypertrophy of the will. They want to take from social reality what it stubbornly refuses to give them.

Today the idea of revolution has become a pretext for its opposite. Because real change would be revolutionary change, and revolutionary change is unavailable, and would be too dangerous if it were feasible, we are left to humanize the inevitable. Such is the project of a pessimistic reformism resigned to soften, especially through compensatory redistribution by tax-and-transfer, what it despairs of challenging and changing. Such is the program of gradual adjustment instead of "shock therapy," of a modicum of social protection rescued from the inevitable weakening of workers' rights, of a softer version of the other side's political project.

Thus did the disillusioned ex-Marxist become the institutionally conservative social democrat. He threw out the good part of Marxism, the transformative aspirations, and kept its bad part, the historical fatalism, changing its political significance. Lack of ideas soon made room for lack of character. He prostituted himself to fate, and betrayed his country by his way of accepting it.

False necessity and alternative pluralisms

The assumptions about social change that these ideas require are minimal, but they are not trivial. They exclude much: much in the ideas about the limits to the political transformation of society that are accepted in practical politics as well as much in the most famous traditions of social theory and the most influential versions of positive social science.

The practical imagination of institutional alternatives enables us to recognize transformative opportunity and to act on it. We remain crippled in our capacity to prosecute the cause of democratic experimentalism by the poverty of our institutional ideas, especially our ideas about the alternative institutional forms of representative democracy, the market economy, and a free civil society.

All over the world educated and politicized people claim to be interested in alternatives, and decry parties and politicians for the failure to produce them. It therefore seems surprising that so little by way of ideas, comprehensive or fragmentary, speculative or practical, comes from the widespread profession of interest in programmatic proposals. Practical constraints are insufficient to explain this emptiness. Dominant styles of thought stand in the way.

To work out alternatives such as the one outlined here, a way of thinking about society and politics must have two sets of minimal characteristics. The minimalism of these attributes leaves open a vast range of possibilities in both the form and the content of explanatory and programmatic ideas. It is therefore all the more striking that these two minimalist standards exclude many of the most influential contemporary discourses of social science, political economy, and political philosophy. They also rule out much of the approach to social realities and ideals that is implicit in the ordinary language of political and policy debate. It will take some doing – practical doing and intellectual doing – to break the programmatic silence that these influential narratives have helped induce.

The thinking we need to inform the imagination of structural transformation must recognize the crucial significance in any society of its formative context of institutions and beliefs. This recognition stands opposed to the idea, dominant in the positive social sciences, that practices and institutions require no special explanation and present no special problem. Either they represent the residue of past acts of problem-solving and interest accommodation (humdrum empirical social science), or they offer better or worse approximations to a democratic and market framework that is neutral with respect to the choices made by political and economic agents (rightwing, ideologically aggressive political science and political economy).

However, the style of social thought we need must also repudiate the necessitarian assumptions traditionally accompanying a structural focus. Three such assumptions have played an especially important role in the development of classical European social theory.

The first of these assumptions has been the closed-list idea. According to this idea, there is a closed, small list of possible institutional systems, such as feudalism, capitalism, and socialism, or the regulated market economy and the command economy. Each of these systems has predefined conditions of actualization. Often, the members of the closed list are held to form a predefined evolutionary sequence.

The second assumption is the indivisibility idea: the institutional systems composing the closed list form, according to this assumption, indivisible wholes. Each stands or falls as a single piece. Consequently, all politics is either revolutionary, substituting one indivisible system for another, or merely reformist, humanizing or reconfiguring a system that it has ceased to challenge.

The third assumption is the determinist idea. Necessary and sufficient conditions govern the actualization of the indivisible institutional systems. Lawlike forces determine their evolution.

The varieties of social thought that deny the central significance of formative structures and of structural discontinuity rob programmatic thinking of its proper target. In some versions, they support the view that institutional arrangements tend to converge, through trial-and-error, upon a set of best available practices. In other versions, they inspire the fetishistic idea that abstract institutional conceptions, like the market economy or representative democracy, have a single natural and necessary content, with variations relegated to minor status.

For their part, the traditional forms of structure-oriented thought, with their baggage of necessitarian assumptions about a lawlike history of indivisible institutional systems, drastically confine the terrain on which programmatic thought can operate while mythologizing its subject matter. The standard mode of transformative politics and therefore also of programmatic thought – revolutionary reform, understood as the part-by-part substitution of a society's formative context of institutions and beliefs – becomes impossible. Historical necessity displaces intentional agency.

The effective practice of the programmatic imagination requires us to retain the idea of structural change while affirming the basic contingency of institutional histories, the divisibility and part-by-part replaceability of institutional systems, and the legal indeterminacy – the multiple possible forms – of abstract institutional conceptions like the market economy and representative democracy.

Such a practice of social and historical explanation may fully acknowledge the tenacity of institutional orders; it need not degenerate into a voluntarist fantasy about the unlimited malleability of social arrangements. For even when we affirm the ramshackle character of institutional arrangements, we can also acknowledge how, once established, they gain a second-order necessity. The conceptions of group identity and group interest that they sustain begin to reconfirm them. Organizational and technological styles that cannot readily be changed, without risks and costs of transition, take them for granted. Influential doctrines, expounded as scientific insight in the universities of the leading powers, lend them a semblance of naturalness and necessity. Nevertheless, they remain, in the end, neither natural nor necessary.

The trouble is that such a practice of social and historical explanation, sensitive to structure but aware of contingency, is not yet at hand. We must build it as we go along, by reconstructing the available tools of social science and social theory. Its absence denies us a credible account of how transformation happens.

These enabling ideas come under the heading **false necessity**. They teach that the institutional arrangements of contemporary society are the outcomes of many loosely connected sequences of social and ideological conflict rather than of irresistible and determinate functional imperatives, driving forward a succession of indivisible institutional systems.

Nevertheless, certain qualities of combined institutional arrangements may indeed support the development of our collective practical capabilities, whether productive or destructive, better than others. Practical capabilities need to develop in a setting favorable to collective learning. Collective learning requires freedom to recombine people, practices, and resources, unfettered by the prescriptions of rigid systems of social roles and entrenched social divisions and hierarchies, especially when reproduced by the hereditary transmission of social advantage.

A strong causal connection exists between the power of institutional arrangements to generate such divisions, hierarchies, and roles and the relative insulation of such arrangements against effective challenge and revision. Institutions subversive of such limiting social bonds invite their own piecemeal and ongoing reform.

The possession of such qualities, in a higher degree than the immediate rival arrangements, may thus help explain the emergence, diffusion, and survival of certain practices and institutions. In that sense, there is something to the idea of functional imperatives helping account for the institutions we now have or might establish.

However, such imperatives do not select from a closed list of institutional possibilities. The possibilities do not come in the form of indivisible systems, standing or falling together. There are always alternative sets of arrangements capable of meeting, successfully, the same practical tests.* The selection and competition operate with the contingent fund of institutional arrangements and ideas that happens to be at hand, in a place or in the world. This fund is in turn the product of many loosely woven histories of conflict and invention. Functional constraint and historical contingency work together. Against this background, we can better understand the features of agency discussed earlier: duality, correspondence, and asymmetry.

The democractic experimentalist wants to put both functional constraint and historical contingency on his side. He wants to deploy the available stock of arrangements and ideas, and to add to it, in ways enabling him to advance along the zone of overlap between the conditions of practical progress and the requirements of individual emancipation.

From false necessity we learn to see through institutional fetishism and structure fetishism, two limits upon our ability to imagine and change society.

Institutional fetishism is the identification of institutional conceptions, such as a representative democracy, a market economy, and a free civil society, with a single set of institutional arrangements. Such abstract institutional conceptions lack natural and necessary institutional expressions. We can develop them in different directions, drawing upon the internal relation between our thinking about practices or institutions and our thinking about interests or ideals.

Structure fetishism presents at a higher level the same defect as institutional fetishism. It denies our power to change the

* See Roberto Mangabeira Unger, *Plasticity into Power: Comparative–Historical Studies on the Institutional Conditions of Economic and Military Success*, Cambridge University Press, Cambridge, 1987.

quality as well as the content of our practices and institutions: the way in which they relate to our structure-defying and structure-changing freedom. Structure fetishism finds expression and defense in an idea, hallowed in the history of social thought, that opposes interludes of effervescence, charisma, mobilization, and energy to the ordinary reign of institutionalized routine, when, half asleep, we continue to act out the script written in the creative intervals. An extreme version of structure fetishism is the political *via negativa* that celebrates rebellion against routinized institutional life as the indispensable opening to authentic freedom while expecting that institutions will always fall again, Midas-like, upon the insurgent spirit.

Like institutional fetishism, structure fetishism represents an unwarranted denial of our power to change society and, therefore, ourselves. The quality of social arrangements as well as their content are up for grabs in history. We have already seen that the variable relation of our institutions to our experimental freedom, including our freedom to experiment with our institutions, is of great practical interest.

In the economy, some sets of arrangements may favor the reconciliation of cooperation and innovation more than others, in part because they empower us more readily to grasp and to change, little by little, the organizational setting of production and exchange. In politics, some combinations of practices and institutions may be more supportive than others of sustained political mobilization. Contrary to the prejudices of conservative political science and of their mirror image, in the illusions of political romanticism, there is no fixed inverse relation between political institutionalization and political mobilization. We do not need to choose between a low-energy institutionalized politics and a high-energy extra-institutional or anti-institutional politics of personal leadership and energized crowds. The political thinking of democratic experimentalism begins in the rejection of this choice.

Insight into false necessity informs the practice of democratic experimentalism and helps generate the concept of **alternative pluralisms**. This concept applies the stricture against institutional fetishism to the diagnosis of our present situation. The old ideological contest between statism and privatism, command and market, is dead or dying. It is in the process of being replaced by a new conflict over the alternative institutional forms of political, economic, and social pluralism. The versions of representative democracy, of the market economy, and of free civil society now established in the North-Atlantic democracies represent a section of a broader range of institutional possibilities.

Each direction for the tapping of these opportunities would produce a different civilization, developing the powers and possibilities of humanity in a distinct way. The role of nations in a world of democracies is to represent a moral specialization within mankind. The freedom of labor to move across national frontiers is one of the practical requirements for such a recasting of the national difference. People must not be bound by the accident of birth into the society in which they happen to have been born. They must be free to find their affinities, even though few may choose to go looking for them.

The large marginalized countries of today's world – China, India, Russia, Indonesia, and Brazil – represent fertile terrain for the exploration of these possibilities, although each of them now stands inhibited in realizing the potential for divergence. The largely involuntary or half-conscious institutional experimentalism that may occur in these countries throws light upon the hidden opportunities for democratic transformation in the rich democracies.

Plan of the book

This book develops the ideas and proposals of democratic experimentalism in two settings: the circumstance of the North-

Atlantic democracies and the situation of the developing countries, especially the large marginalized societies. The whole world is now bound together by a chain of analogies: there is no fundamental difference between problems and possibilities in the richer and poorer economies.

People speak of "radical democracy" or the reivention of progressive politics, but regularly fail to give these concepts a detailed content. Here I try. I want to show that we can hope for something better than the humanization of the inevitable; in particular, for something better – better for the material and moral interests pursued by democratic experimentalism – than the reconciliation of European traditions of social protection with American-style market flexibility.

The next section of the book discusses a major problem and opportunity for democratic experimentalism: the economic and social divisions between productive vanguards and productive rearguards, and the transformation of a confederation of productive vanguards into the driving force of the world economy. I then discuss, against this background, three programs for industrial renewal in the rich industrial democracies. The democratic experimentalist cannot be satisfied with either the conservative managerial reform program or the conventional social–democratic answer to it.

The argument then turns, at greater length, to a second field in which to forge the ideas and proposals of democratic experimentalism today: the struggle over the neoliberal program – the orthodox project of institutional reform and convergence – in the developing and postcommunist countries.

The discussion of different approaches to industrial renovation in the rich economies and of alternatives to neoliberalism in the developing countries sets the stage for the elaboration of a program. This program offers an alternative to institutionally conservative social democracy as well as to neoliberalism. It interprets, for today, what it would mean to deepen or to radicalize democracy, carrying to the next step the work of democratic experimentalism.

The program is not a blueprint. It is a set of connected ideas and proposals, tentative in spirit and adaptable to circumstance. I have chosen to explore this programmatic direction at points both relatively close to present arrangements and relatively distant from them. The direction is what matters.

If I propose something distant, you may say: interesting, but utopian. If I propose something close, you may answer: feasible but trivial. In contemporary efforts to think and talk programmatically, all proposals are made to seem either utopian or trivial. We have lost confidence in our ability to imagine structural change in society, and fall back upon a surrogate standard: a proposal is realistic if it approaches what already exists. It is easy to be a realist if you accept everything.

I have tried here to solve this problem in a rough-and-ready way. The book explores, at different points of distance from present solutions, the program it offers. It also relies upon a piecemeal invocation and development of ideas enabling us better to discover hidden transformative opportunity and better to imagine alternative democratic possibility. In this way, I have tried to remain faithful in thought to the experimental practice I defend in politics.

After discussing a progressive alternative, *Democracy Realized* looks to some of the anxieties and aspirations lying beyond the horizon of institutional concerns. The politics of national differences and group identities has often seemed an overpowering threat to the progressive commitments of liberals and socialists. How should a progressive politics today understand this supposed threat, and deal with it?

A set of thirteen theses supplies a polemical summary of the progressive alternative developed and supported in the book.

VANGUARDS AND REARGUARDS

The idea of the hierarchical distribution of production

There is no privileged terrain or instrument for the institutional development of alternative pluralisms. Politics (in the narrower sense of conflict over the mastery and uses of governmental power) may matter as much as economics. Efforts to change, piece by piece, the organization of civil society outside the state may count for more than economic policy and governmental politics. Moreover, institutional changes may prove both elusive in their execution and perverse in their effects unless married to a micropolitics of the personal. Such a micropolitics reconstructs and reimagines the direct dealings among individuals. It relates to the remaking of institutions much the way that, according to classic social thinkers, religion connects with politics.

In a situation of prolonged although partial and anxious peace, however, such as the one through which we have been living since the end of the Second World War, economic opportunity and frustration come to occupy a central place in governmental politics. The relation of economic constraints to more intangible and intractable resentments and aspirations – national, racial, and religious – becomes the great axis around which much of political rivalry within and among countries revolves. One of these economic issues has now acquired paramount importance throughout the world: the relation between vanguard and rearguard.

Traditional rightwing and leftwing views of the world economy have emphasized the hierarchical distribution of production around the globe. More advanced production takes place in the rich countries; more primitive production in the poor countries. According to conservative and centrist views, long dominant in economics, this hierarchical distribution has a benign and evolutionary character. Developing economies must pass, for example, through a protracted phase of low-wage, export-oriented production. The geographical distribution of comparative advantage in factors of production and the pace of ascent up the ladder of economic evolution supposedly suffice to shape the worldwide assignment of enterprise.

These conservative views have had influential leftwing counterparts, which accept the idea of the hierarchical distribution of production while reversing its political sense. In many versions such leftist views are as fatalistic as their rightwing equivalents. They describe a process of global economic organization and transformation in which "central" economies become the staging grounds of the most capital-intensive and technologically sophisticated forms of production. Less advanced, more labor-consuming forms of production predominate in the "peripheral" economies. An interlocking system of constraints, including trade practices, military power, and cultural authority, helps keep the backward economies down. "World systems theory" and "dependency theory" have developed alternative expressions of this same idea.

What distinguishes this leftwing pessimism from its optimistic conservative cousin is the belief that the peripheral economies cannot easily escape their niches in the world economy: in a system of multiple, reinforcing constraints, one constraint will make up for the deficiencies of another. A political initiative will be defeated by an economic vulnerability, or an economic advance by a political reaction. If the leftwing version of the idea of a strongly determined and hierarchical distribution of production throughout the world differs from the rightwing version, the most important difference may lie in the differing roles that each gives to economic evolution and political resistance. For the conservatives, resistance is the problem; for the radicals, it is the solution, if any solution exists.

Disconcerting facts have now overtaken the idea of a global hierarchy of production. Vanguardist production increasingly takes place everywhere, as much in Malaysia, India, and Brazil as in Germany, Japan, and the United States. Each major national economy finds itself divided internally between a vanguard and a rearguard: an economic division entangled in a broader division of forms of life and styles of sensibility. The driving force in the world economy is fast becoming a global confederation of productive vanguards. The vanguards established in different parts of the world drive one another forward. They trade with one another. They transfer personnel, technology, and organizational practices among themselves. Above all, they emulate one another. Public and private international organizations, or regulatory agencies and business associations within countries, occasionally produce partial codifications of the standards vanguardist producers expect one another to meet.

The global mobility of capital, so often described as the central phenomenon of the contemporary world economy, remains a sideshow. For one thing, its quantitative dimensions continue to be modest: empirical study shows that national investment levels remain closely related to national savings levels; the vast preponderance of investment capital stays, to this day, at home. For another thing, hypermobile capital works largely in the service of the worldwide confederation of vanguards when it does not simply delight in short-term arbitrage opportunities for speculative gain.

Vanguardist production defined

Before turning to a simple typology of the major contemporary versions of the contrast between vanguard and rearguard, it is important to specify more clearly the character of vanguardism. By vanguardist production I mean a form of production combining

certain physical–economic and spiritual–organizational characteristics. The physical–economic attributes are often present without
the spiritual–organizational ones. The latter are more rarely
unaccompanied by the former. Vanguardism in method nevertheless may and does sometimes dispense with the capital-intensive
and skill-intensive technologies it ordinarily commands.

The physical–economic characteristics of vanguardist production are large commitments of capital per worker, technology
close to the existing frontier of technological development, and
access to large regional or global markets as well as to major
sources of capital, technology, and expertise. We must distinguish access to large scale from large scale itself, thus allowing
for the possibility – crucial to the development of advanced
production – that small, flexible firms may, through a mixture of
cooperation and competition, tap large-scale resources and
markets.

The spiritual–organizational characteristics of vanguardist production are those that approximate production to learning and
make good firms resemble good schools. Practical reason is a
dialectic between tasks and executions, between conceptions and
experiments. Production becomes vanguardist as this experimental ideal comes to inform the practices of work. Specialization in
knowledge and skill must remain fluid. It must become subordinate to the development of a pool of generic practical and
conceptual capacities. Hierarchical control must be minimized:
its disciplinary and proprietary aspects distinguished from the
real requirements of coordination. Work routines must become
provisional, and readily open to revision.

If the assimilation of teamwork to the dialectic of practical
reason is one way to define the kernel of vanguardist production,
another is the reconciliation of the requirements of cooperation
and innovation. These two imperatives and their relation to each
other stand at the heart of the material progress of society.
Together with the level of savings and the arrangements by which

savings becomes investment, they shape the context, and set the limits, of economic growth. Innovation requires cooperation: in the workplace, in the firm, within a set of firms, and within an economy and society. Yet innovation always jeopardizes cooperation by threatening to disrupt the ongoing relations, the settled expectations, and the vested rights in which any particular system of cooperation becomes embedded. For innovation will either take directly the form of a change in the character of social relations, or it will change the range of resources and opportunities available to the cooperating groups. The task is therefore to develop cooperative arrangements minimizing the constraints upon innovation. Vanguardist production is not simply production that more effectively reconciles cooperation with innovation; it is production organized around deliberative procedures that take such a reconciliation as a program.

The spiritual characteristics of vanguardist production may precede its ordinary material instruments: continuous learning and routine-revising experimentalism may help lay the basis for technological refinement and deep investment. A rearguard that has learned to behave as part of the vanguard has good claims to being considered part of the vanguard. On the other hand, brute accumulations of capital and scale, maintained in the absence of a living experimentalism, point away from vanguardism. The poor but flexible and learning firm and the rich but rigid late-fordist firm represent the two characteristic ambiguous positions complicating the contrast between vanguard and rearguard.

In some ways the distinction between vanguard and rearguard is merely relative: one form of production is more vanguardist than another. In other ways, however, the difference has an absolute character: either permanent innovation becomes a central objective by deliberative procedures designed for the purpose, or it does not. There might be a world in which the qualities of vanguard and rearguard production were arranged along a continuum. That is not, however, the world of contemporary economies.

In this world, most firms belong to either the vanguard or the rearguard.

Membership in each of these two worlds implies distinctive forms of social advantage and experience. To work in the vanguard as a vanguardist worker (given that one may physically work in the vanguard as a menial laborer) is not just to enjoy more income and consumption. It is also to benefit from greater trust and discretion at work. It is to enjoy in a major aspect of everyday life a sense of effective agency. It is to act according to a view of one's job lying somewhere between the ancient conception of the honorable calling and the modern idea of transformative power.

Four typical situations

The contrast between vanguard and rearguard presents itself now in four typical ways throughout the world. These ways differ according to two criteria: whether the division between vanguard and rearguard takes hold in the conditions of a relatively rich or a relatively poor country, and whether it is compensated by a countervailing device or allowed to operate unhindered. A particular country can exemplify each of the four typical situations, although we must always remember the difference between a real society and an ideal type.

The first situation is that of a rich country like Sweden in which an inclusive, redistributive welfare state partly compensates for the social consequences of the distinction between vanguard and rearguard. A shrinking part of the population works in industrial production and related professional and financial services. An even smaller part of the workforce holds jobs in what can properly be described as the vanguard. Those with places outside the vanguard, however, receive both direct income protection through redistributive tax-and-transfer and indirect protection through the creation of public-sector jobs. Every person has a claim to a substantial package of social safeguards and resources, insulated against the vagaries of the market. The government promotes job creation as the indirect counterpart to its direct efforts at compensatory redistribution. The typical new job is a job for a woman in provision of social services.

The crucial infirmity of such a regime is the disconnection between the mechanism of compensation and the requirements of growth. The productive capabilities of society benefit loosely from the compensatory, redistributive welfare state: first, because social peace, although expensive, is not as expensive as class warfare; second, because the universalistic welfare state helps form a laborforce schooled in generic capabilities.

However, no direct, fine-tuned connection exists between economic growth and growth in social welfare. Each develops according to a logic and a schedule of its own. The increasing number of people excluded from the productive vanguard expect the state to shield them from the consequences of their exclusion. The level of welfare entitlements, heightened at times when an economic boom coincides with a social-democratic ascendancy, comes to be viewed as a set of vested rights. It exhibits the characteristic "downward rigidity" of wages in the industrial democracies, and cannot be cut when economic trouble strikes. For these reasons, the universalistic, compensatory welfare state weighs upon the productive capabilities of society. High public debt, high interest rates, and heavy tax burdens jeopardize continued economic growth.

In a second typical situation, of a rich country like the United States, the division between vanguard and rearguard appears relatively more unqualified than in the first situation. The welfare state remains both less developed and less egalitarian than in Sweden. Programs directed to the poor are separated from those aimed at the general population, and become, for that reason, more vulnerable to resentment and reaction. The tax yield stays lower and the redistributive potential of public spending less fully realized. Paradoxically, the tax system itself may be more progressive on its face. (I discuss later the causes and consequences of this apparent paradox.)

In such a society many feel abandoned while others believe the devices of compensation to be self-defeating. A stingier welfare system may lighten the burden of compensatory redistribution upon growth but it produces burdens of its own, all the way from the educational deficiencies of the laborforce to the distractions of felt injustice, obliquely expressed in criminal violence, political disorientation, and class–racial warfare. No wonder comparative study fails to suggest that the welfare-stingy industrial democracies gain any sustained productive advantage over the welfare-generous ones.

In a third situation, of a poor country like India, the contrast between vanguard and rearguard is compensated less by a universalistic, redistributive welfare state than by the politically and socially supported diffusion of smallscale property. The prominence of agricultural smallholding is merely the most important and familiar form of this diffusion. The great majority of small rural and urban enterprises benefiting from this support do not themselves belong to the vanguard: they are capital- and technology-poor farms and shops. Nevertheless, they help sustain the material and spiritual basis of an independent life. For many millions of people, they prevent the extremes of inequality. Once established, they become the mainstay of political parties and social movements that helped develop them.

However, what helps limit inequality may not help avoid backwardness. The trouble with the diffusion of smallscale property in the traditional form it ordinarily assumes is that it relieves inequality without preventing poverty. Like the rich country's counterweight to the contrast between vanguard and rearguard – the universalistic, redistributive welfare state – it lacks an intimate connection with the conditions of economic growth and cultural innovation. The significance of this disconnection becomes clearer when related to the modern European experiences and debates about the alternative forms of industrial society.

The idea of a decentralized market economy based upon competition and cooperation among smallscale owners and entrepreneurs was the single most persistent alternative to the concentrated forms of economic power with which we have come to associate "modern capitalism" and its characteristic forms of largescale organization. Different measures of political support for smallscale agrarian property – more in France, Holland, and Denmark, for example, than in England and Germany – shaped the differing social histories of European countries.

In no country, however, did a full-fledged artisanal and cooperativist alternative succeed. It could not have succeeded without a greater distancing of government from the propertied interests than in fact took place anywhere. Had it triumphed, it could not have survived without solutions to two problems: the problem of access to capital, mass markets and advanced technology and the problem of how to contain the internal instability of a system of smallscale property owners (the successful buy out the failures) without sacrificing decentralization to the authority of a centralized redistributive agency. These two problems remain unresolved in the Indian-style support for smallscale property. The small urban and rural firms of the country remain largely cut off from the driving forces of economic growth and technological dynamism. The result is to moderate the unequalizing social effects of the division between vanguard and rearguard without overcoming the division itself.

In a fourth typical situation, of a poor country like Brazil or Mexico, the contrast between vanguard and rearguard once again appears unqualified. There is no political tradition of effective support for smallscale property. The prestigious language of social compensation and social-safety nets exercises little practical effect in a circumstance of profound dualism and extreme inequality. The compensatory redistribution of resources from the favored, organized economy to the disfavored, disorganized economy would have to be massive to address the problems of the multitude of people imprisoned in the second economy. Dominant political and economic interests would never tolerate such a redistribution. Moreover, were it ever to be attempted, it would begin to disorganize the favored economy long before it began significantly to change the lives of working people in the second economy. The redistributive intervention would threaten to kill the goose that lays the golden eggs. No wonder third-world social democracy is so easy to profess; it is often impossible to execute.

This simple, four-part classification of typical forms of the contrast between vanguard and rearguard draws attention to a troubling fact. Neither of the two established means for the moderation of the contrast – the universalistic, redistributive welfare state (for the rich countries) or the diffusion of smallscale property (for the poor countries) – has a close enough link to economic innovation and growth, close enough to make the benefit it provides overwhelm the onus it imposes. In one case, it is the burden of heavy taxation, low public savings, and high interest rates. In the other case, it is the burden of a style of economic initiative starved of the efficiencies of scale and denied the tonic of connection with the centers of economic innovation. As a result of these tensions, the material progress of society seems inevitably to take place through a vanguard that is just as inevitably separated from a rearguard. The moderating mechanisms will buy social peace at a price. For the price to be tolerable, we must show restraint in the use of such mechanisms. Thus do chastened democrats come to give up some of their first defining hope: the hope of identifying, and of realizing in institutional detail, the area of overlap between the conditions of material progress and the requirements of individual emancipation.

Compensating or overcoming the division between vanguard and rearguard

No issue has become more important in political economy than the question: Can we overcome the division between vanguard and rearguard, or must we resign ourselves to soften its effects? Both neoliberalism and institutionally conservative social democracy – the two most influential political programs worldwide – implicitly deny the possibility of overcoming the contrast between vanguard and rearguard. They differ chiefly in their relative emphasis upon equalizing redistribution. This consensus by default is neither ancient nor solid. In the United States, for example, it dates to the transformation of the "New Deal" conflicts and controversies that occurred immediately before and during the Second World War, putting a single-minded focus upon higher and more equal consumption, sustained through progressive taxation, public spending, and transfer programs, in place of more ambitious attempts to rebuild the relation between government and business. In some Western industrial democracies, the narrowing took place slowly in the aftermath of the war and was never as unequivocal in its outcome as it has been in the United States. Today, the social and economic consequences of this consensus seem clearer and more disturbing. However, because no feasible and attractive alternative presents itself, and because the collapse of state socialism seems to have deepened skepticism about the possibility of any such alternative, we are left to face these consequences as if they were an inescapable fate. A major concern of this book is to argue that they are not. Such an argument must combine the reinterpretation of a political circumstance with the development of an institutional program.

Two sets of debates and experiences, better than any others, serve today as the most significant settings in which to test the limits of the worldwide division between vanguards and rearguards. One set of debates is the contest, especially in the rich countries, among different programs for the restructuring of industry and the reorganization of the relations among firms, governments, and workers. Another set of debates is the persistent search, especially in the poor countries and, above all, in the large, continental societies of China, India, Indonesia, Russia, and Brazil, for an alternative to neoliberalism. In the first setting, the vision of the micro prevails, seeing the economy and its transformative possibilities from the perspective of the firm. In the second setting, the angle of the macro predominates, with its primary focus upon the institutional framework of the economy as a whole as well as upon the responsibilities of government. Yet the lessons to be drawn from these contrasting standpoints, of rich and poor, macro and micro, come together.

THREE PROGRAMS FOR THE REORGANIZATION OF FIRMS

The managerial program of industrial renovation

In the rich industrial democracies two major programs for the reorganization of firms and of their relations to governments and workers now compete: a managerial program of conservative industrial renovation and a social-democratic program of broadened recognition of stakeholders. Neither of these programs satisfies the requirements of democratic experimentalism. An alternative, radical-democratic program would change the institutional forms of the regulated market economy. The other two programs leave them relatively untouched.

The managerial program of conservative industrial renovation identifies excessive conflict and rigidity as the twin ills of the established industrial system. These ills are most fully manifest in the traditional industrial world of fordist mass-production. However, they have also come to characterize a large part of the production system, including the nonindustrial sectors of the economy. The answer to excessive conflict is more cooperation at work: the reorganization of work as teamwork. Within the confines of the managerial program, such a reorganization is not thought to require any transfer of ownership or of the ultimate managerial authority exercised in its name. The response to excessive rigidity is more power to capital to recombine factors of production, free from the constraints imposed by the rights of workers and of other would-be stakeholders and free as well from the limits governments impose upon capital mobility. The hypermobility of capital – its freedom to roam around the world in search of opportunity – is the crowning ideal. However, as capital acquires this license to move freely, labor should remain imprisoned in the nation-state, or in blocs of relatively homogeneous nation-states like the European Union. A combination of practical imperatives, ranging from the requirements of social peace to the conditions of human capital formation, are supposed to necessitate this sharp contrast between the treatments of capital and labor.

The two planks in the platform of the managerial program – cooperation and flexibility – clash. The outright assertion of the right of capital to move as it pleases – for example, by closing plants and relocating them abroad to benefit from cheaper labor costs or from local subsidies – may provoke a resistance that its *in terrorem* effect may fail to contain. This resistance poses a problem exemplifying the general tension between cooperation and innovation so central to demands of economic growth. Thus, the champions of the managerial program seek devices designed to reconcile these commitments. One such device is the segmentation of the laborforce. A core, stable part of the laborforce becomes the beneficiary of cooperativist initiatives as subcontractors, temporary workers, or foreign workers bear the cost of empowering capital.

Every wave of industrial reconstruction is accompanied by a characteristic and characteristically ambiguous discourse of reform. Such, today, is the language of flexible specialization and worker engagement in the planning of production. This language often emphasizes the self-directing influence of technological evolution upon the arrangements of production. It also often finds in this influence a pretext for its silence about the institutional reconstruction of the market economy as well as about the corresponding need for programmatic vision. It is then ready to be captured by the managerial program, which it serves as a congratulatory rhetoric.

There are nevertheless themes in the discourse of flexible production that work against the contrasts between task-defining and task-executing activities and between cooperation and competition. These themes suggest the superiority of arrangements moderating both those contrasts. The crucial question, however, remains unanswered and even unarticulated within the discourse of flexibility. By what pathways of cumulative institutional change in the forms of the market economy, and, more broadly, of representative democracy and free civil society, can we best hope to advance practical experimentalism, better reconciling the requirements of cooperation and innovation?

The social-democratic response

The conventional social-democratic response to this managerial program of industrial renovation takes as its primary commitments the multiplication of stakes and stakeholders in firms and the defense of the present positions and rights of workers – the translation of the positions into rights. The multiplication of stakes and stakeholders means that many groups in addition to the owners should be allowed to exercise influence over firms: workers, suppliers, consumers and local communities and governments. Whether or not this influence expresses itself in the eventual acquisition of a participation in ownership, it should receive formal recognition, through, for example, membership in the supervisory board of the firm. The translation of positions into rights means that capital should be denied the power to exploit economic opportunities in ways that destroy jobs, disrupt communities and sever the sustaining link connecting a productive apparatus to a local world, with its forms of associations and practices of trust.

The multiplication of stakes and stakeholders is itself a way of imposing constraints upon hypermobile capital. It helps create the institutional machinery for ensuring as rights the positions of the constituencies it recognizes. It wants to humanize what would otherwise be the savagery of impatient money.

This conventional social-democratic response to the managerial program runs the risk of aggravating the problems of rigidity and conflict that motivated the managerial program. It imports into the production system something like the scheme of checks and balances in American presidential government. Just as that scheme was designed to slow politics down (for the sake of liberty and property), so this corporate constitutionalism would make it necessary to achieve consensus among the constituencies of the firm for every major decision. It is one thing to forge such a consensus in a circumstance in which a long habit of deference has dulled the distinction between compromise and surrender, and another to perpetuate consensus in an environment of vested rights, jealously guarded.

It may seem less credible to see in the execution of the social-democratic program a threat of increased industrial strife. After all, its ruling concern is to recognize and respect a broader diversity of stakeholders than are effectively represented under the established distribution of property rights. Nevertheless, the social-democratic program does accept and aggravate precisely the form of conflict that should be of greatest concern to a votary of democratic experimentalism: the conflict between insiders and outsiders, entrenched in the division between vanguard and rearguard. The social-democratic program for the firm represents an effort to dig workers into their present niches, the better to defend against the opportunism of capital and the volatility of markets. It does more than take the present division among sectors of the economy for granted; in the name of defending workers and communities, it makes these divisions harder to challenge. It helps freeze the inherited distribution of economic privilege into place, benefiting most of the workers who hold jobs in the richer and more productive sectors of the economy.

Viewed from this angle, the conventional social-democratic response to the managerial program of conservative industrial renovation is simply a particular expression of one horn of what has become the dilemma of the left parties in the Western industrial democracies: defend at all costs the historical constituency of organized labor, headquartered in the capital-intensive, mass-production industries, tying your political fate to a shrinking part of the laborforce, stuck in a declining sector of the economy, or cut this link, support the vanguard of business in its project of industrial renovation, and help the people excluded from the vanguard. Help them less to join the vanguard than to survive outside it. The program of democratic experimentalism rejects both horns of this dilemma. It must therefore also repudiate the contending programs for the renewal of the firm.

Just as the managerial program of conservative industrial renovation has an ambiguous but revealing connection to the discourse of productive flexibility, so the conventional social-democratic response has a special relation to the social-corporatist practices adopted in one form by European countries such as Germany and Austria and in another by Japan. In this corporatist political economy, a way of relating the firm to labor and to capital remains loosely but powerfully connected with a practice of active dealing among national government, big business, and organized labor. One trait of social corporatism at this microscopic level is the prominence given to relational investors, such as banks or other firms, rather than to the stock market, in the surveillance of management. Another feature is the maintenance of stable relations among interlocking firms and banks. Yet another is the use of retained earnings to support a stable laborforce and managerial staff, with or without enforceable job security and participation in the equity and authority structures of the firm. From these characteristics certain others are often, with little or no justification, said to follow: a higher rate of retained earnings and a willingness to invest, on the basis of these earnings, with a long-term strategic horizon. Throughout the industrial democracies, and independent of the prominence of relational investors or of stable links among firms, retained earnings remain by far the most important source of investment funds for going concerns (in the vicinity of eighty percent). The evidence for the larger strategic horizon of firms in the circumstance of social corporatism is inconclusive, if only because patient strategy may be hard to distinguish from routinized stupidity. The significance of the resemblance between patient strategy and routinized stupidity for the inbuilt limitations of the social-corporatist political economy will soon become apparent.

Practices of overt governmental coordination of the economy make up the macroscopic side of social corporatism. These practices may emphasize, as they often have in the European corporatist economies, the negotiation of wage and income deals between organized labor and big business at the prompting of national government. They may also include commitment to a package of social benefits that, translated into a set of rights, provides the stable part of the workforce with defenses against economic insecurity. Such practices may also favor, as they have in Japan, the joint development by business and government of national trade and production strategies. They may impose on large firms the responsibility to support a core, stable, and protected laborforce.

Social corporatism enjoys a close kinship to the conventional social-democratic response to the managerial program – not because social-democratic concerns have controlled its development and effects but because it describes a larger political economy within which the imperatives of production and growth seem reconciled with the social protection, economic enhancement, and managerial participation of a major part of the laborforce. Social corporatism, however, is in trouble, and its trouble casts light on the limitations of the conventional social-democratic response to the managerial program. The trouble arises from the combination of the opportunism of the insiders with the resistance of the outsiders to the favored deals and selective protections of the corporatist political economy.

At the microscopic level, the exemplary form of the trouble is the opportunism of the insiders: the most efficient firm in the Japanese *keiretsu*, for example, may find that it is able to obtain capital more cheaply or to invest it more profitably outside its group of related firms and banks. This subversive opportunism is no anomaly; it is the lifeline of ingenuity and invention. Its attractions must steadily increase as markets become both larger and more volatile, and the deals struck within a national economy compete with those that might be struck anywhere else. If the opportunism of the insiders undermines social corporatism at the level of the firm, the restlessness of the outsiders jeopardizes it at the level of the political economy as a whole. Some of the disorganized people – small business and workers in the capital-starved parts of the economy – may belong to the rearguard. Some – small, flexible firms – may belong to the vanguard. All will sooner or later seek in national and local politics relief from the condominium of organized interests. In this campaign democracy will seem the natural ally of efficiency. The opportunism of the insiders works toward more flexibility; the restlessness of the outsiders, much less certainly, toward more inclusion.

Social corporatism has two futures according to whether the first of these subversive forces operates alone or in concert with the second force: more flexibility without more inclusion, or more flexibility with more inclusion; more flexibility within the framework of the division between vanguard and rearguard or more flexibility with a bridging of the gap between vanguard and rearguard. The first path implies a slow waning of what have been many of the distinctive characteristics of German and Japanese-style market economies. The second path is impossible to travel or even to describe without institutional innovations that the would-be champions of the outsiders have so far failed to propose.

To imagine this path is to move in the direction of a third program for the reconstruction of firms. Such a program would offer an alternative to both the conservative managerial program of industrial renovation and the social-democratic program of worker defense.

The radical-democratic alternative

Let me call this third program the radical-democratic program. It represents the commitment to democratic experimentalism as we might hope to realize it in the domain of industrial organization. If democratic experimentalism for society as a whole advances by combining the generalization of experimentalist opportunities with the enhancement of individual capacities and securities, we should expect to find a similar union in a program of business reform responsive to the ambitions of the democratic experimentalist.

Two insights animate this radical–democratic alternative, connecting the practical problems it solves to the democratizing and experimentalist spirit it expresses. The first insight is that the inherited regime of property, contract, and corporate law imposes unnecessary and unwarranted restraints upon access to productive resources and opportunities. This property regime is not, as its defenders habitually insinuate, a natural language of decentralized economic initiative, allowing anything to be done for which there is good practical reason. It makes certain restrictive choices: for example, it cares more for the absoluteness of the property right than for the number of real economic agents with access to productive resources or for the range of ways in which they have access to it. More particularly, it tolerates a weak link between saving and production, finance and industry, allowing much of the productive potential of saving to be squandered in financial gambling, requiring established business to fend largely for itself (through reliance upon retained earnings), and strangling too many businesses in the crib. We can hope to expand the mechanisms and beneficiaries of the decentralized allocation of productive resources: at first, by using the legal and institutional tools already at hand; later, by forging other such tools so that alternative property regimes come to coexist within the same economy.

The second insight informing the radical–democratic alternative is that workers can best be defended by arrangements that enhance their capabilities rather than entrench their positions. The aim is to help them thrive in the midst of innovation rather than to shield them, and their customary ways of life, from the destabilizing consequences of invention. This idea exemplifies the general commitment to develop those cooperative arrangements that are friendliest to innovation. It also makes the assumption that only such a form of social defense can be inclusive, avoiding the contrasts between insiders and outsiders with which the standard social-democratic program remains complicit.

Two planks in the radical-democratic program result from each of these two guiding ideas: the multiplication of forms of access to productive resources and opportunities and the development of the capacities and the guarantees helping people respond to quickened economic innovation. In an early phase of its development, the program can work within the limits of inherited and established institutional arrangements. Later, it must push beyond the limits defined by these arrangements.

The diversification of forms of access to productive resources and opportunities has three elements: a high and sustained level of both private and public savings; a more effective realization of the investment potential of private savings, so largely diverted by present arrangements into sterile gambling; and the organization of a new set of economic agents to invest, with entrepreneurial independence and financial responsibility, both public and private saving. We may further imagine that each of these three elements develops in two stages: one, within the confines of the present property regime; the other, beyond its limits, through the creation and coexistence, within the same economy, of several property regimes, working with different instruments for the decentralization of access to capital.

The development of the radical-democratic program in this second, more inventive stage depends upon two further connected sets of institutional innovations: one set addressed to the redistribution of resources through tax-and-transfer; the other, to the acceleration of politics through the remaking of political institutions.

Imagine a tax system working with three basic taxes: a

comprehensive, flat-rate value-added tax, the mainstay of public revenues in the first stage of the program, now accompanied by direct, redistributive taxes; a progressive tax on personal consumption (Kaldor tax), taxing on a steep slope the difference between income, inclusively defined, and saving committed to investment; and a progressive tax on gifts and estates. The emphasis upon the taxation of consumption, carried over from the first stage of the program, continues to moderate the inhibiting conflict between the demands of revenue collection and the need to encourage saving and investment. We are now able to complete this emphasis by a tax system that no longer needs to give absolute priority to the level of public spending and to the redistribution public spending produces. Through this system of three taxes we hit, separately and clearly, the two major targets of taxation – the hierarchy of living standards, or the absorption by the individual of social resources, and the accumulation of wealth as economic power, especially across generations.

We may then seek to devote each of these three taxes to a primary and distinctive use. The progressive personal consumption tax would support the core operations of government, thus linking the interest of the political-bureaucratic apparatus with the advance of redistributive taxation and signifying the stake of democratic government in the avoidance of extreme inequalities of condition. The comprehensive, flat-rate value-added tax, ever the least distortionary and most reliable of taxes, would finance the social funds and support centers, thus representing a levy upon consumption for the sake of production. The gift and estate taxes would fund the social-endowment accounts, limiting family inheritance in the service of social inheritance. These connections amount to more than idle symmetries; they invoke and help sustain a changed way of understanding the proper relations between individual enrichment and social solidarity.

Institutions like these require a state that can be both more capable and more democratized than the representative democracies now in existence, a way of organizing the conflict over the mastery and uses of government that sustains over time a higher level of political mobilization than the institutions and practices of the Western industrial democracies now countenance, and an organization of civil society enabling people to organize themselves more fully and evenly than the established devices of contract and corporate law allow. The radical–democratic alternative in the shaping of the relations among firms, workers, and governments broadens out into the radical alternative to the inherited forms of political and economic pluralism. A discussion of the worldwide search for an alternative to neoliberalism will lead back to the same problems discussed in the preceding pages, and provide an opportunity to develop these institutional proposals more fully.

NEOLIBERALISM AND ITS DISCONTENTS

Neoliberalism defined

Our most important opportunity to advance the democratic project lies in the effort to overcome within each national economy the division between vanguard and rearguard, so closely connected with a broader and vaguer contrast between insiders and outsiders. The most significant setting in which to challenge the division between vanguard and rearguard is the search for an alternative to the political–economic ideas now dominant in the world.

This dominant program, often labelled neoliberalism or "the

Washington consensus," enjoys the sponsorship of the major power – the United States – as well as of the Bretton Woods organizations and of the leading academic experts. These experts press it, relentlessly, upon the developing countries. Opposition to this program has remained most prominent in the large marginalized countries – China, Russia, India, Indonesia, and Brazil. In each of these societies a major party of opinion clings to the longing for a different path and identifies in the circumstances of a continental country the means for resistance and the materials for originality. Nevertheless, even in these countries, as in much of the rest of the world, the opposition to the program has largely failed to develop a credible alternative to it. The program of the enemies of neoliberalism has often been the neoliberal program with a discount: slowed down, or hedged in by a stronger emphasis upon social assistance. As a result, the underlying contrast between vanguard and rearguard remains nearly unchallenged and the repertory of inherited institutional arrangements almost unchanged.

In its most abstract and universal form, neoliberalism is the program committed to orthodox macroeconomic stabilization, especially through fiscal balance, achieved more by containment of public spending than by increases in the tax take; to liberalization in the form of increasing integration into the world trading system and its established rules; to privatization, understood both more narrowly as the withdrawal of government from production and more generally as the adoption of standard Western private law; and to the deployment of compensatory social policies ("social-safety nets") designed to counteract the unequalizing effects of the other planks in the orthodox platform. When this program is transported to the conditions of countries like Brazil or Mexico, in which extreme inequalities remain largely unqualified by effective compensatory devices, it helps sustain a political discourse organized around two themes: the theme of adherence to the market-based arrangements that have proved so spectacularly successful in the rich economies and the theme of redistributive correction through the development of tax-and-transfer and the social activities of government. The language of market efficiency joins the language of social conscience. Thus does institutionally conservative social democracy become an integral part of the neoliberal vision.

Even though this program comes to life only when associated with a specific set of institutional arrangements, it does not live in the imagination of its adherents as simply one feasible pathway of institutional change among others. Its advocates regularly subscribe to the convergence thesis: the belief that contemporary societies gradually converge on a connected set of the best available practices and institutions worldwide. They then identify this set with the economic and political institutions of the rich industrial democracies, and dismiss variations among the institutions of these democracies, like the contrasts among American, German, and Japanese styles of control over firms, as minor and ephemeral. Like every powerful ideology, the convergence thesis becomes a self-fulfilling prophecy, discrediting the effort to explore alternative arrangements. However, the real force of the self-fulfilling prophecy remains implicit in this abstract formulation of neoliberalism: implicit in what this program wants to do to the state and with the state.

The implication and its significance become clearer when we consider what has recently been the operative form of neoliberalism in many developing countries – the way in which the poorer countries have in fact put the neoliberal message into practice. We see this operative version most clearly exemplified in policies adopted by some of the major Latin American countries, especially Mexico and Argentina in the 1990s. The Indian government of the day moved toward it. It influenced decisively the economic policies adopted, in the name of market reform, by the governments of many postcommunist economies. In fact, after the collapse of communism in the Soviet Union and central

Europe, its waning in China, and the discrediting of the protectionist and populist policies associated with "import-substituting industrialization" and high-inflation finance, only the northeast Asian economies – Japan, South Korea, and Taiwan, as organized during the two generations subsequent to the Second World War – represented a forceful if flawed alternative to this working version of neoliberalism.

Three tenets mark the operative version of neoliberalism. The first tenet is governmental acquiescence in a low level of domestic saving, private or public, and a corresponding reliance upon major, persistent inflows of foreign capital to finance national development. Not only is the savings rate low (less than 20 percent rather than the over 35 percent achieved by the East Asian "tigers," and, more recently, by China), but the government relies upon the traditional capital markets to mobilize savings for investment. Governments that have long engaged in "financial repression," to the point of making the real rate of interest negative, now find themselves required to tolerate astronomical real rates of interest and to pay such rates themselves for the acceptance of public debt if they are to attract skeptical and impatient capital from abroad. They discover belatedly that foreign capital is more useful the less a country depends upon it. On one side, the capital inflows are rarely high or sustained enough, in a world where most capital continues to stay at home, to satiate the hunger for capital in a society that is both investing and consuming beyond its means. On the other side, the inflows threaten to rekindle high inflation and diminish the government's power effectively to guide the economy, if only by prompting the central bank to "sterilize" the new resources through increments to the costly internal debt.

The second tenet of neoliberalism is the renunciation by the state of any affirmative strategy of national development other than the strategy implicit in an unresisting adherence to the world economic order. According to the conception informing this adherence, economic progress will result from the enforcement of traditional property rights, combined with the enriching and enlightening benefits of connection with the most advanced sectors of the most advanced economies. Two denials are central to the renunciation of a national development strategy. One is a denial of the power of governmental initiative to shape the influence of preexisting factor endowments upon the direction as well the pace and consequences of economic growth. Governments might exert such an influence not only by enhancing some of the factors of production – developing the capacities of the laborforce or transferring new technologies – but also by changing the institutional context in which factors combine. Governmental action might promote a convergence on certain strategies yielding cumulative economies of scale and scope. The second denial renounces the capacity effectively to differentiate among levels of protection against foreign competition (selective protectionism), exchange rates (one rate, for example, for consumption goods and another for advanced technologies), and interest rates (to socialize some of the risks and burdens of the most long-term productive investment).

It is characteristic of much contemporary argument in economic policy to suggest that selective protectionism might be better in principle than absolute free trade, and differentiated exchange and interest rates better than unified ones. According to this standard view, however, selectivity will almost certainly be worse in practice, serving both collusion ("rent-seeking") and prejudice. It is a judgement resting upon negative assumptions about government; it excludes the possibility that changes in the institutional forms of the state and of the market economy might make what is best in principle also best in practice. Thus, both the denials underlying the renunciation of a national development project draw their force from one or another aspect of institutional fetishism: the failure fully to imagine the range of feasible institutional variation.

The third tenet of this operative version of neoliberalism is a style of monetary stabilization that relies heavily upon an exchange-rate anchor and upon very high interest rates. The architects of the neoliberal stabilization program represent these devices as temporary although necessary expedients, to be followed by the achievement of fiscal balance or surplus, through tax reform, privatization, and cuts in public spending. To this plan for weakening national government, they give the exalted name "structural adjustment."

The program of structural adjustment soon confronts an intractable dilemma. Carried to the hilt, it produces massive unemployment (over twenty percent, as in the Argentina of the 1990s), and accelerates internal dualism: the division of the country between a minority of beneficiaries and a majority of victims. More generally, it leaves government without the resources and capabilities with which to invest in either people or infrastructure. As social needs go unattended, bottlenecks in the production system begin to build up. Moreover, the draconian policy may prove self-defeating by sapping the very confidence it was designed to inspire, as domestic and foreign investors begin to expect future political trouble from present social unrest. For all these reasons, unless earlier governments have successfully met the most urgent demands of social and infrastructure investment (Chile in the 1980s and 1990s), structural adjustment is unlikely to be pushed to the extreme. As a result, punishing interest rates and overvalued exchange rates (overvalued by any of the conventional standards) will have an afterlife belying their supposed use as transitory devices. Foreign capital and inflationary concessions will be needed to lessen the burdens of debt and unemployment upon the victims of "adjustment."

Operative neoliberalism, then, combines these three tenets: a low level of public and private savings and of mobilization of savings for investment; renunciation of a national development project; and stabilization through high exchange and interest rates as well as heroic restraints upon public spending. Such rates and restraints leave government unable to invest in either people or the physical tools of development such as transport and communication. The operative version enjoys a unity lacking in the more abstract and doctrinaire formulation of the neoliberal program. This unity is social and political rather than narrowly economic and technical. It is the negative unity of the disempowerment of government: it disables the state from interfering with the established order of society. It saps the ability of government to work against the seemingly irresistible fate of assimilation to the institutions of the great powers and the rich countries, institutions made to represent the necessary face of progress.

From the micro to the macro; from the rich countries to the world at large

The criticism of neoliberalism seems to bring us to a world of concerns very different from those presented when discussing the alternative programs for the reconstruction of firms. It is a debate about poor countries rather than about rich ones. Moreover, it is a debate about the social world viewed from the macro standpoint of the entire economic and political order rather than from the micro perspective of the firm and its relations to workers and governments. Each of these distinctions, however, turns out to be superficial, disguising a deeper unity.

The core structural problems and opportunities of the rich countries have converged with those of the poor countries. The convergence thesis, false as the description of a single institutional outcome to contemporary history, turns out to be true as the portrayal of a predicament and the foreshadowing of a conversation. The earlier argument about the global recurrence of the distinction between vanguard and rearguard and the commanding role of the network of vanguards has already suggested the universality of the forces driving the world economy. For it is a distinction respecting no difference between rich and poor countries. The debate about firms and their dealings with workers and governments may be more alive in the rich countries, where basic institutions go unchallenged. It must nevertheless speak as well to the poor countries: if there is to be an alternative to neoliberalism, it must show its efficacy in the ability to extend vanguardist practices into what is now the economic rearguard as well as to sustain productive vanguards where they already thrive.

It is less obvious, but no less true, that the rich countries as well as the poor ones have a stake in the development of a practical alternative to neoliberalism. Persistent anxieties about the inverse relation between welfare and employment, or about the difficulty of doing anything about problems of stagnant production, have no satisfactory solution – so I shall argue – within the limits imposed by the inherited political and economic institutions. The most important lesson of the policy discussions of recent years is that policy debates turn into inescapable conundrums when we fail to move, in practice or in imagination, from the familiar policy choices to the institutional framework defining the range of available options.

Viewed from a more inclusive standpoint, the development of an alternative to neoliberalism is today simply the most recent variation of the broader and more enduring problem of alternative pluralisms: the diversification of the institutional forms of representative democracies, regulated market economies, and free civil societies. An effective alternative to neoliberalism, so the latter parts of this book argue, requires connected and successive institutional innovations. The cumulative effect of such innovations would be to give practical content to the idea of alternative pluralisms.

The discussion of alternatives to neoliberalism differs as well from the debate about firms in addressing directly the large world of the social institutions and their connections rather than the

smaller world of private firms and their dealings with governments and workers. Here we look at the basic structure of society
rather than at the ways in which fragments of this structure shape
economic activity. It is, however, little more than a difference of
viewpoint. Many intermediate links connect the two sets of
problems.

Of these links one of the most telling and troublesome is the
connection between finance and industry, between saving and
investment. The weakness of this link is the single most striking
flaw in the established institutional forms of the market economy.
Its transformation is essential if we are to moderate divisions
between vanguards and rearguards and develop a democratic and
productivist alternative to neoliberalism and conventional social
democracy. Consider each of these propositions in turn. Taken
together, they go a long way toward showing the unity of the
macro and the micro perspectives on the problems of this essay.

The translation of savings into productive investment is supposed to be the most important social responsibility of finance. It
is a responsibility that goes largely unmet. Compare, for example,
the relative importance of finance internal and external to firms
in present-day Great Britain and Germany. These two countries
have been widely thought to present contrasting examples of
relations between firms and banks or other institutional investors.
In Germany, according to this view, the long-term commitment
of institutional investors to firms favors a high level of retained
earnings. Retained earnings in turn allegedly encourage long-term
strategic investment as well as the continuing enhancement of the
skills and technologies at the disposal of the laborforce. In Britain
(as in the United States) the disinterest of long-term institutional
investors and the dictatorship of the stock market supposedly
focus attention upon short-term results, manifest in stock prices,
and doom the needs of long-term investment. Facts fail to bear
out these stereotypes. The most important point to grasp here is
that in Britain as much as in Germany going concerns get most

of their finance from retained earnings. Retained earnings – profits undistributed as dividends to shareholders – account today for about eighty percent of investment funds in both places. The entire finance system – banks and stock markets alike – remains sidelined in the exercise of what is supposedly its main function of providing investment funds for production. That institutional investors, even in those economies where they are most prominently placed, monitor so little of what they are described as monitoring is then of merely secondary importance.

If the bankers survive in a twilight world between accounting and gambling, gambling, in the stock markets, reigns supreme, unencumbered by the responsibilities or the opportunities of productive investment. The stock markets are supposed to be the mainstay of the movement of savings into productive investment. They are, in fact, more like casinos than standard finance theory would have us believe. The positions traded against one another make some people richer and others poorer. However, the connection of much of this trading activity with the financial needs of production remains limited and oblique.

Stock markets do indeed perform two other important functions. They create a venue for initial public offerings of stock in companies. They also establish a market in corporate control, enhancing the liquidity of ownership and the accountability of management. Neither of these two contributions, important as they are, reverses the basic weakness of finance in the mobilization of saving for production. Not only must going concerns fend largely for themselves but new ventures must regularly find ways to draw water out of stone, making do, like unassisted peasants, with family finance and self-exploitation. For all the "moral hazard" created by public systems of deposit insurance in the banking system and for all the ephemeral glamor of a few forms of entrepreneurial adventurism, venture capital occupies a miniscule part of the attention of finance in every contemporary economy.

The dearth of financial support for productive investment and the immense squandering of the productive potential of the deferred consumption of society barely excite the interest of publicists and theorists. Where is the Chayanov of industry? Where is the Hilferding with transformative hopes but without Marxist illusions? Keynesianism – the most influential economic heresy of the twentieth century – explored one aspect of the disconnection between saving and investment, emphasizing the destructive effects of nonproductive hoarding upon the translation of one into the other. The hoarding risk, however, turns out to be a special case of a more general problem for which we continue to lack an adequate account. Marxism had represented class society as the functional instrument of coercive surplus extraction – the mobilization of social saving for productive investment – under conditions of scarcity. It had explained the rise and the fall of modes of production as the end results of a driving need to develop the productive use of social saving. With Marxism and Keynesianism discredited, we have been left unequipped to understand and criticize the waste through gambling that characterizes the established forms of the market economy.

I have already suggested how a radical-democratic alternative to both the managerial program of industrial renovation and the conventional social democratic response would require that we reorganize finance by diversifying the forms of access to productive resources and opportunities, first within and then beyond the limits of the existing property regime. As we move toward successive levels of tinkering with this regime, the distinction between the narrower issues raised in a discussion of alternative programs for firms and the broader problems presented by an effort to replace neoliberalism disappears. Conversely, no alternative to neoliberalism can succeed without supporting the economic progress of society by reorganizing saving for investment.

The false necessity of comparative advantage

Neoliberalism regularly gives rise to two sets of discontents, each of which opens up a transformative opportunity. The first discontent is the reluctance to accept for the national economy a place determined by the preexisting distribution of comparative factor endowments. Economic orthodoxy would have developing countries climb, slowly and patiently, a predetermined evolutionary ladder. The initial rungs of this ladder are formed by export-oriented, low-wage production, undertaken by semiskilled labor.

In modern history, however, there have never been examples of successful national development marked by a passive state presiding over a system of definite and transparent property rights. The typical instances of success have been those in which government not only invested in people and infrastructure but also entered into active partnership with private firms. Both the institutional instruments and the economic content of this partnership have varied widely: from centralized bureaucratic agencies to decentralized cooperatives and from technical assistance and facilitated credit to direct technological and educational support. An example from the nineteenth century is the development of American family farming with the support of the federal government. An example from today is the conduct of activist trade and industrial policy, the imposition of incentives to save and to invest, and the patient training of technical and entrepreneurial cadres by the governments of the North East Asian economies.

Orthodox economists like to contrast the undoubted importance of fundamental public investment and of equalizing reforms such as agrarian reform to the mixed record of bureaucratic interventionism in the development of trade and industry. However, no plausible explanation for the successfully developing countries of today, as of Japan and Germany before them, can fail to take into account the central role of government in reshaping the apparent dictates of Ricardian comparative advantage.

In these experiences of rewarding governmental activism the efficacy of governmental policy has often depended upon the existence of a hard state – a state able to formulate and to implement policy with a substantial measure of independence from the interests of propertied elites. Such a state can initiate some of the structural reforms, such as agrarian reform, necessary to national development. It can also give to an activist economic policy a measure of protection against the perversities of clientelistic corruption, preventing the partnership between government and private firms from degenerating into straightforward collusion between business and bureaucratic elites.

Political authoritarianism offers a shortcut to the hardness of the state. It is a costly shortcut. Not only does it suppress the collective interest in political freedom; it also limits and distorts the range of economic experimentalism. The political-bureaucratic apparatus, anxious to survive, takes only those policy initiatives that seem compatible with the maintenance of its position, and seeks to arrive at an understanding with the established economic powers in the society. Moreover, progress toward political democracy may in the short term increase the clientelistic distortion of public policy; things threaten to get worse before they get better.

Thus, the partnership between governments and private firms seems necessary to escape the evolutionary determinism in growth strategy that, although implied by the neoliberal project, has been rejected by the political and business leaders of the most successful economies. Nevertheless, the example of partnership between government and private firms presented by the East Asian tigers to the other developing countries remains a flawed model; we should correct it before imitating it.

The institutional form and the economic content of the partnership must be made more decentralized and experimentalist; less vulnerable to its characteristic defects of rent-seeking, economic dogmatism, and subordination of growth to stability. Such an opening of the partnership between governments and firms cannot stop at an insistence upon respecting the prerogatives of small business, continuing in a direction that Taiwan, for example, has taken by contrast to South Korea. Many economies, rich and poor alike, remain burdened by some form of economic dualism, separating a vanguard of capital-intensive, market-integrated firms from a rearguard of small and medium-sized enterprises with tenuous access to markets, capital, and technology. An opening of the government–business partnership exercises a full democratizing and experimentalist influence only if it also succeeds in bridging the social and economic gap of dualism. The institutional innovations required to reach this antidualist goal may include the joining of many firms into cooperative–competitive networks; the development of mixed public–private forms of financial and technological support to these networks, undertaken by organizations with considerable independence from government and intimate links to the businesses with which they deal; and, later, the invention of alternatives to traditional, full-fledged and unified property rights.

Democratizing the partnership between firms and governments is a necessary condition to make the example of the East Asian tigers usable for the developing countries of the contemporary world. It is not, however, a sufficient condition: not only does it fail to go far enough in correcting the flaws of the model, but it is itself unlikely to be achieved unless more corrective work is done. A national development strategy capable of working out the partnership between business and government requires a hard state. It is, nevertheless, incompatible with hardness in the form of authoritarianism. That the idea of a state both hard and radically democratic strikes us as verging on the paradoxical only shows how inadequate and impoverished our repertory of inherited institutional arrangements remains.

One key condition for reconciling hardness and democracy is a decisive break with constitutional styles favorable to impasse among branches of government. Another condition is a sustained and institutionalized heightening of civic engagement. The constitutional organization of government must facilitate the execution of sharply defined party programs. The continuing political involvement of the people must prevent the slide of politics into the preemptive defense of narrowly drawn factional interests.

Populism offers a shortcut to inclusive popular involvement in politics just as authoritarianism offers a shortcut to the hardness of the state. It establishes a direct link between leaders and crowds, that is to say, people who remain outside formal organizations. The congenital weakness of populism is precisely its susceptibility to being undone by the ebb and flow of the political energy of the people. The task of a democratizing movement is to develop institutions sustaining the expression of this energy. Such institutions become, as only institutionalized practices can, a second nature.

People often speak as if the level of political mobilization were a natural fact about each society, deeply rooted in unalterable traits of culture. There is, however, much evidence to support the view that the level of political mobilization in a society is highly responsive to particular rules and practices, such as those governing the electoral regime, the use of money in politics, and the access to the means of mass communication. When we grasp the produced character of political mobilization, we also free ourselves from one of the central illusions of conservative political science: the idea of a simple inverse relation between institutionalization and mobilization, as if political institutions were by nature demobilizing and as if mobilization were by nature extra- and anti-institutional.

The coexistence of a constitutional style congenial to the quickening of structural reform, through the accelerated resolution of impasse, with an institutionalized heightening of political mobilization, enables people to use the indispensable tool of transformative politics: the alliance of change sponsored from above with change undertaken from below.

So it is that the practical tasks of development, and the pressure to emulate and to improve the available examples of developmental success, create an opportunity for innovation in the institutional forms of the state and of the economy. This practical imperative to recombine and renew for the sake of worldly success is the great force refocusing ideological conflict in the world today upon the alternative institutional forms of economic and political pluralism.

The unstable relation between neoliberal economics and neoliberal politics

There is no politics capable of sustaining a neoliberal political economy, not at least if we interpret the prescriptions of this political economy literally and therefore radically. To find the politics that corresponds to the neoliberal project in economics, either we must resign ourselves to a highly selective and restrictive implementation of the neoliberal program, or we must redesign the program and turn it in the direction of structural reforms that its traditional adepts prefer to avoid.

Consider what happens when we attempt to enforce the neoliberal project to the hilt in the conditions of a very hierarchical and divided society, with strong concentration of wealth, power, and income, and a business class accustomed to thrive on collusive arrangements with politicians and bureaucrats. The literal and unqualified execution of neoliberal ideas in such a circumstance would carry neoliberalism beyond the limits of the compromises defining its actual operation. It would threaten vital interests of the propertied classes and the business elites, through the systematic withdrawal of covert subsidies, the quantum leap in foreign competition, the vigorous implementation of antitrust norms, the evening of the scales between big and small business, or, even more dramatically, the redistribution of educational opportunity and political voice. The business elites can be counted on fiercely to resist so patent an assault upon their privileges even as they reaffirm their devotion to liberal principles.

The foreseeable effect of this resistance is the selective interpretation and implementation of the neoliberal project. The consequence of selectivity is to turn the program into a device for the realignment and renovation of elites. To sacrifices of elite interests there correspond, under the regime of selectivity, adequate compensations. For example, a willingness to tolerate more foreign competition in domestic markets may be compensated by opportunities to profit from the subsidized privatization of state enterprises: private interests may be allowed to buy them for a song, or with governmental paper valued at nominal rather than real, secondary-market prices, or even with funds lent, on sweetheart terms, by the government itself.

The form of politics preferred by this truncated neoliberalism is relative democracy: democracy but not too much. An authoritarian hard state, in the fashion set up by the Asian tigers, not only presents opportunities for more collusive favoritism than selective neoliberalism needs or wants; it also encourages the bureaucratic apparatus to pursue an aggressive industrial and trade policy of its own devising. Such a policy may serve the interests of existing business elites in some respects, but it is also likely to offend those interests in other ways. In fact, the masters of the authoritarian hard state may even have a hand – as they often have had in the North East Asian economies – in directly reshaping the composition of the business elite.

Too much democracy, however, may also prove an embarrassment to selective neoliberalism. The energized and rebellious populace and their demagogic captains will not wait out the slow calendar of incorporation of the marginalized into the capital-intensive, modern economy upon which the neoliberal project relies. They will demand an alternative to neoliberalism, or at least an alternative way of understanding it: one that achieves more incorporation of the excluded, and achieves it more quickly. If, as has generally been the case, they fail to advance or even to envisage such an alternative, they will persist in the election of leaders and parties who cling to a self-defeating economic populism. The pendular swing between economic populism and economic orthodoxy will begin all over again.

Not too much democracy is both the antidote and the prophy-lactic that the defenders of selective neoliberalism administer against this danger. The expression of this strategy is a preference for constitutional rules, electoral arrangements, and media systems that help maintain the people at low levels of political engagement. This mob-fearing instinct may take forms as varied as the preference for a parliamentary regime (to avoid the destabilizing surprises of plebiscitarian presidential elections while internalizing political power within the political class) and tolerance for the concentration of property in the means of mass communication (to establish a class of media magnates pliant to the politically powerful). Or, in other circumstances, it may inspire a preference for a strong presidency, creating a place for a little Bonaparte into whose attentive ears the technocrats from home and abroad can whisper the prescriptions of economic science. Mass organization of any kind will be disfavored as a costly and dangerous luxury for a country trying to lift itself out of poverty and backwardness.

These calming and preventative measures can be expected to work at best indifferently. If they succeed in discouraging mass organization and collective militancy, they do so at the cost of putting the neoliberal project at odds with the collective interest in the deepening of democracy. Moreover, the antidote is likely to prove more effective at suppressing alternatives to the neoliberal program than at avoiding a recurrence of the oscillation between orthodoxy and populism. It takes social organization to generate social alternatives. Hence, measures tending to disorganize the people, or to leave them disorganized, may indeed frustrate the formation of coherent alternatives. To prevent the return to economic populism, however, it would also be necessary to deny the excluded or disfavored part of the society the political instruments of revenge against its economic circumstance and thereby to risk crossing the line between relative democracy and sham democracy.

Turn now from the hypothesis of selective neoliberalism with its accompanying politics of relative democracy to the contrasting hypothesis of neoliberalism to the hilt. For the neoliberal program to escape its selective interpretation it would need a broad popular base of support. Suppose such a base could be assembled in the conditions of a very unequal society. It would not resign itself to the slow calendar of incorporation of the backward economy into the advanced economy. Nor, therefore, would it passively accept a protracted phase of low-wage, export-oriented production as the inescapable price of economic evolution. It would insist upon policies and arrangements freeing small business from its orbit around big business. It would demand the execution of a antidualist political economy. It would call for a national rebellion against the evolutionary fatalism condemning the poorer countries to accept the styles of industrial organization that the richer economies are in the process of discarding. The radicalized neoliberalism resulting from the satisfaction of such demands would hardly be recognizable to the defenders of the Washington consensus.

The gist of the argument is that the conventional formulation of neoliberalism undergoes an internal instability, rooted in the relations between economics and politics. For a politics of conservative co-option and relative democracy the conventional formulation is too radical; to become politically realistic it must be edited and confined. However, within a social world of heightened and broadened political engagement the conventional formulation is not radical enough. It says too little or nothing at all about the most important matters.

Subject to criticism, in the light of the actual and possible forms of democratic politics, neoliberalism turns out to suffer from a defect common to the most familiar programmatic positions in contemporary politics. To work politically, it must be either retrenched or radicalized. Because it relies upon the inherited repertory of institutional arrangements for representative democracies and market economies and because it remains silent or equivocal about the complex transactions between politics and economics, the conventional formulation gives cover to the restrictive and conservative view of economic and political orthodoxy. Thus, it amounts to a de facto retrenchment of neoliberalism, just as the conventional contemporary formulations of social democracy amount to a de facto retrenchment of social-democratic commitments.

To be sure, the political paradox of internal instability in the implementation of the neoliberal program does not apply equally to all developing countries. It applies to them according to the measure in which they remain unequal. If a society has been more thoroughly equalized by a long sequence of social and ideological conflicts, the application of conventional neoliberalism will be less invidious and less ambiguous. The choice between retrenchment and radicalization in the prosecution of the program will be less pressing. However, the country will have escaped these dilemmas only through an unintended partnership between neoliberalism at the end and something very different beforehand, a brief and uneventful neoliberal epilogue to a long and painful history of conflict about inequality. I shall soon return to the significance of this ineligible escape from the political paradox of neoliberalism.

The search for alternatives to neoliberalism in the rich countries

The opportunity for institutional experimentalism is not restricted to countries that are both big and poor. The leading powers and central economies suffer today, as their predecessors suffered before them, from a series of unresolved structural problems. The skeptic about transformation may believe that all real problems in the world fall into one of two classes: either they are insoluble or they solve themselves. The routine politics of the contemporary industrial democracies takes place as if this maxim were true. However, the cost, in human suffering and national involution, continues to mount. The difficulty in managing the transition to a more learning-friendly industrial economy, and in securing its base in associational life and continuing education; the consequent failure to influence the growth of productivity; the inability successfully to base the distributivist promises of the welfare state upon a productivist program of industrial reconstruction; the reemergence in new forms of rigid hierarchical divisions among segments of the laborforce, sustained by intertwined threads of class, race, and gender; the development of a substantial underclass, of unemployed or unstably employed workers, in flight from their society or at war against it; and the general estrangement of both white- and blue-collar workers, the broad salaried middle classes, from arrangements for the collective solution of collective problems – all this amounts to a heavy burden upon the claims of the successful industrial democracies to have in fact succeeded.

When the debate is framed, as it so often continues to be, as a contest between claims for greater or less governmental interventionism in a supposedly prepolitical economic order, these structural problems remain without structural solutions. After a while, people – both educated, employed and poor, marginalized people

– abandon hope in the transformative powers of politics. The attack on government and on its welfare responsibilities becomes an ideological second-best, credited less as a legitimate and effective doctrine than as an escape route from repeated disappointments: because we can expect nothing good from politics we should at least minimize the tax take.

There can and will be no real solutions to the structural problems until national politics takes up more willingly the work of institutional innovation and recognizes the chain of analogies connecting the difficulties of the advanced and the backward economies. The rich countries must also rebel against the fatalism of inherited comparative advantage and overcome the social, cultural, and economic gap of internal dualism. To these ends, they must also develop the partnership between governments and firms while giving to this partnership decentralized and experimentalist forms that keep it from degenerating into a collusion between business and political-bureaucratic elites. The decentralized and experimentalist forms of the partnership between public authority and private enterprise may begin by requiring the development of social institutions intermediate between governments and firms and independent from both. They may end by demanding the progressive dismemberment of traditional property rights and the vesting of the component elements of these rights in different types of rightholders, each of them enjoying part of what we continue to call property.

For such economic changes to be realized and sustained, more than economic change is needed. The governments of the industrial democracies must also acquire more of the traits of state hardness so that social and economic policies can come out from under the tutelage of the great organized interests. The hardening of the state is not feasible, however, not at least on the basis of political democracy, without further institutional changes. Among such changes are reforms in the constitutional organization of government favoring the rapid resolution of impasse as well as the decisive implementation of party-political programs. The changes also include reforms in the arrangements of electoral politics heightening the level of political engagement and fostering the self-organization of civil society.

The agents of such moves are missing. So, too, are the institutional and strategic ideas that might inform and inspire them. The political nation in the advanced countries has learned a false lesson from the disasters of twentieth-century history and, most recently, from the collapse of communism: that the idea of national alternatives – that is to say, of change in the formative institutional context of society – is a romantic irrelevance. At best, such change gets in the way of practical policy-making. At worst, it opens the way to political and economic despotism. The politically aware see historical experience through the lens of a bad idea, shared by conservative liberals and orthodox Marxists alike: the idea that structural change is necessarily total change and that all politics must be either conservative reformism or revolution. Having scorned revolution as both impossible and undesirable, they then abandon, together with the idea of revolution, the practice of repeated and cumulative institutional reconstruction.

They might more reasonably infer from their contemporary experience a different lesson: that without both sustained popular political engagement and persistent institutional experimentalism practical policy problems, such as those of industrial reorganization, unemployment, education, and health care, cannot be effectively solved. The slide of politics back into the calculus of short-term group advantages, in a world of unevenly organized groups and skeptical citizens, prevents the adoption and even the formulation of realistic proposals. What the anti-ideological and antistructural temper of routine politics holds in contempt as an obstacle to practical problem-solving is in fact its essential condition. We must be visionaries to become realists.

All this may seem remote from the present discussion about politics and policy in the advanced industrial democracies. There is nevertheless a clear passage from the current conversation to the missing and indispensable debate. Consider a typical controversy of the present day. Students of policy, comparing the United States with most Western European countries, observe that in the United States, by contrast to Europe, fewer job-security and welfare benefits coexist with relatively lower unemployment. European workers enjoy more security and benefits, but unemployment remains stubbornly higher, even through the ups and downs of the business cycle.

Everyone wants to know how to moderate this seemingly inverse relation between welfare and employment. A popular approach focuses upon the competitiveness of the national economy within the world economy, and identifies the most powerful tool of competitiveness as the education of the laborforce. Then the critics begin to demonstrate that international competitiveness has only a marginal impact upon the economic prosperity of most countries. Even the famous suppression of semiskilled industrial jobs in the advanced economies by their developing-country rivals turns out to be a phenomenon of relatively modest quantitative dimensions. The critics of the popular approach go on to demonstrate that education, whether generic or specialized, is incapable of redirecting an economy unless it encounters a congenial repertory of experimental methods in the world of firms, big and small.

Through such criticisms we arrive at a deeper view. According to this view, success at raising productivity and at moderating the inverse relation between employment and welfare depends upon more than educational investment. It depends as well upon the enlargement of a set of innovative practices in firms and schools and upon the nurturing of a dense associational life behind and beyond the school and the firm. Such a texture of associations is needed to sustain a solidaristic culture friendly to public investment and shared responsibility. It is also vital to nourish the culture of trust within which experimentalist risk-taking in education and production can flourish. It brings people into a common world, where they can grasp and address their common problems.

This deeper view has an ambiguous relation to the institutional structure of society. Does it merely invite us to inhabit and to operate the present institutions in a different spirit? Or does it summon us to change the institutions? We pass from the present conversation to the missing debate when we come to understand that we must prefer the second answer to the first.

To take one example, legal rules and institutional practices may give fordist-style mass-production industry an advantage in the competition with its more flexible rivals by allowing it to gain some immunity to instability in its product and labor markets through the hiring of a two-tier laborforce: a core of stable workers and a periphery of temporary workers or subcontractors. To take another example, the deepening of investment in people and their education will remain limited so long as it must be financed out of traditional tax-and-transfer methods, which appear in the short term as a burden upon productive capital. Such a deepening can progress only through a more thorough-going equalization of background rights modifying the regimes of property and inheritance. To take yet a third example, the potential for generalized self-organization of civil society, and thus for denser practices of association, will be influenced by the public-law framework available to the organizers; the traditional devices of contract and corporate law may prove inadequate. These are a few examples taken from a thousand. The whole social order, looked at more closely, turns out to be the unimagined outcome of countless such half-conscious institutional choices. It is because of them that politics is fate.

In answering or even in posing such institutional questions we remain inhibited by a superstition. This superstition is the belief that institutional change means the bad old idea of total substitution of one institutional system by another. We have failed to bring our public institutions fully under the control of our experimentalist creed.

The progressive, labor, and social-democratic parties in the richer economies face an apparent dilemma. By the first horn of the dilemma, these parties maintain their privileged and defining connection to a key sector of the laborforce: organized industrial labor, anchored in mass-production industry. When it makes this choice, the left finds itself tied to a declining sector of the economy and to a shrinking part of the population. This minority is increasingly seen by the rest of society, and ultimately comes to see itself, as just one more faction, clamoring for the satisfaction of factional interests, rather than as the bearer of universal social interests. The programmatic content of progressive politics then tends to become the preemptive defense, through subsidies, protectionism, and directed welfare benefits, of this part of the laborforce and of the economy.

By the second horn of the dilemma, the progressive party breaks the privileged alliance with its traditional industrial working-class constituency, and becomes a generic "quality-of-life" party with an open and indistinct social base. Such a party resigns itself to the issues that have come to dominate national politics in the rich industrial democracies: the striking of a balance between the containment of governmental expense and the provision of minimal needs in social insurance, education, and health care; the symbolic recognition of different group identities and cultures, as well as the relation of these distinct varieties of group life to the national idea; and the cleansing of politics from corruption and privilege. Not even the Keynesian supersession of sound-finance doctrine and of the functional equivalents to the gold standard can be safely taken for granted in this politics. A party that has accepted such a fate can indeed aspire to majoritarian status only at the cost of having renounced the mission of radical reform through institutional reconstruction.

To break this dilemma, the progressive parties must accomplish two tasks. They are inseparable; each is the reverse side of the other. The first task is to forge a majoritarian popular alliance, overriding the segmentation of popular interests through a solidaristic political strategy. The second task is the formulation and advancement of a reconstructive program rooting distributive claims in a productivist vision and connecting the liberation of the market to the deepening of democracy.

The progressives would need to propose and enact a plan for industrial reconstruction. Such a plan would help lay the basis for a more inclusive popular alliance by lowering the barriers separating mass-production industry from the capital-intensive, flexible vanguard of production, on one side, and from the low-skill, undercapitalized rearguard, on the other side. The advancement and redefinition of the plan over time would create both the need and the opportunity for successive institutional reforms.

In the first instance these would be innovations in the institutional forms of a market economy: entities intermediate between the state and the firm to assure that the government–business partnership would assume an experimentalist and decentralized character; cooperative-competitive arrangements among businesses to reconcile scale with flexibility; and, ultimately, alternatives to traditional property rights to broaden access to productive resources. The introduction and operation of such economic institutions would, in turn, require an acceleration of experimentalism in politics, demanding alternatives to traditional constitutionalism in the resolution of political impasse; alternatives to traditional contract and corporate law in the self-organization of civil society; and alternatives to the traditional electoral practices that now favor the permanent political demobilization of the people.

Only on the basis of such a program can the progressive parties create the arrangements within which the otherwise divided interests of their intended constituency can, in some measure, converge. An inclusive popular alliance must be a political project, pursued through institutional change, before it can become a social reality. To every sequence of strategic alliances there corresponds a sequence of structural reforms that can turn transitory agreements into lasting marriages of group interests as well as group identities.

The search for alternatives to neoliberalism in the developing countries

An analogous strategic dilemma afflicts progressive liberals, social democrats, and democratic leftists in many developing countries. This dilemma calls for a similar resolution. Progressives must rely upon the organized part of civil society: unions of industrial workers and public functionaries; neighborhood associations and churches; and the apparatus of grassroots party organization itself. In the real conditions of many developing countries, however, especially those at the forward edge of the developing world, like Brazil, Mexico, and Indonesia, these available constituencies represent a relatively privileged minority within the working classes. However substantial the interests that pit them against their employers may be, these workers also share with their bosses common interests against the interests of the disorganized. In a dualistic economy, as many economies both advanced and backward are, the inhabitants of the advanced sector may share certain political attitudes as well as economic interests. These interests and attitudes separate them from the mass of people who remain imprisoned within the second, disorganized and disfavored sector, starved of capital and disconnected from power.

In such a circumstance the left and left-leaning parties will be tempted into errors that have very largely defined their political identity and their programmatic message. The first error in the standard historical sequence, and by far the most common, has been the commitment to a populist economic policy: runaway deficit finance, used to fund direct social assistance and subsidies to consumption goods as well as to the core operational activities of government.

At the center of this economic populism stands a pseudo–Keynesian political economy. Keynesianism strengthened the state. It freed national governments from the constraints of sound-finance doctrine in exchange for the abandonment by labor and the left of any claim radically to reconstruct the regime of production and property or drastically to redistribute wealth and power. By contrast, the economic populism until recently in favor with many third-world governments betrayed a weakness of the state: instead of imposing the costs of investment in people as well as in transport and communications squarely upon the propertied interests of the advanced economy, pseudo-Keynesian political economy generalized this cost to the whole society through high and chronic inflation.

Pseudo-Keynesian public finance has often accompanied a nationalist–autarkic strategy of economic growth. Economists have traditionally labelled this strategy import-substituting industrialization. Its substance, however, lay less in any technical economic orientation than in a political and economic deal. The masters of the state – often Bonapartist nationalists and populists – struck a bargain with industrialists and labor unions they helped to create and control. The industry sustained by this bargain, dependent upon subsidies and protection, was good at reproducing the consumption goods already enjoyed by the population of the rich countries. However, it could not compete effectively abroad without relying upon wage repression. Much less was it capable of producing, on a customized basis, the inputs and the machine goods needed to lift up and transform the backward economy.

The fundamental link between pseudo-Keynesian public finance and this nationalist–autarkic strategy of import-substituting industrialization is that both of them were simultaneously creators and creatures of economic and social dualism. Working in concert, both helped entrench the privileges and diminish the responsibilities of a favored, organized economy. National governments were then held hostage by the very groups whose powers and privileges they had helped establish.

Pseudo-Keynesian public finance has repeatedly run a familiar self-destructive course, beginning with the disorganization of the public sector and ending with the inhibition of the private economy. With the degeneration of money comes the triumph of speculation over production and of craftiness over diligence. The last straw may be a balance-of-payments crisis, or the approaching shadow of hyperinflation, or hyperinflation itself. In the end, the excesses of economic populism may seem the next-to-the-last gasp preceding the unavoidable return to financial orthodoxy and the providential surrender to the IMF.

For its part, the autarkic import-substituting strategy of economic growth deepens economic and social dualism while perpetuating, behind protectionist barriers, the technological and organizational infancy of infant industries. Having begun as the instrument of national rebellion against the logic of preexisting comparative advantage and having succeeded to some extent in accomplishing its objective, it outlives its capabilities and turns into a restraint upon innovation and efficiency.

Throughout the developing world there is broadening agreement on the need to overcome economic populism and nationalist–autarkic industrialization. The question is what should replace them. The Bretton Woods institutions, the leading economic powers, and the ruling currents in economics all press upon the developing countries the imitation of the arrangements now established in the North Atlantic world as the necessary sequel to the failed program of economic nationalism and populism. However, in the real circumstances in which it is applied, this neoliberalism is likely to be meant and to be executed in the selective manner earlier described.

In this mutilated version, the neoliberal program amounts to a realignment of economic practices compatible with the interests of most preexisting elites. It suffers paradoxically from the same fundamental flaws as the economic program it is intended to replace: the perpetuation of economic and social dualism and the focus upon semiskilled, low-wage, export-oriented production. The majority of the society – the workers of the second economy – are likely to remain excluded in countries like Brazil, Mexico, Indonesia, or Russia from the immediate benefits of the new orthodoxy. The defenders of that doctrine expect the excluded to wait until they are incorporated, over several generations, into the modern economy so that, at last, they may climb up the ladder of economic evolution. The excluded, however, will not wait. They will strike back through politics, especially through the election of populist leaders, threatening to recommence the destructive pendular swing between economic populism and economic orthodoxy.

With one revealing exception, the unmutilated and radicalized form of neoliberal reform is a political impossibility. The broad popular constituency necessary to sustain it would demand its transformation. The exception occurs when society has already been relatively equalized and comprehensively educated by a long history of practical and ideological struggles. Consider the placement of Latin American countries on a spectrum describing the extent to which they have escaped extreme inequalities and ensured comprehensive education. From the more remote to the more proximate, this spectrum might begin with Brazil and Mexico. It might then pass through Argentina, Bolivia, and Chile. It might then reach Costa Rica and end with Cuba. Cuba, paradoxically, is the country that might receive neoliberalism with greatest benefit and least danger. The trouble is that no one ever would or could choose such a combination of long and violent struggles with a neoliberal aftermath to them, just as no one ever would or could have chosen total war (with the United States), and subsequent defeat and occupation by the victor, as the route to national prosperity in the twentieth century. These may be proven forms of change, but they are not available examples of deliberate transformation.

Nowhere in the developing world have progressives formulated, much less executed, an alternative sequel to economic populism and autarkic industrialization. Only in the big marginalized countries is there even much conviction that they should try or might succeed. The most common response – the path of least resistance – has been simply to split the difference between neoliberalism and economic populism and to claim that the resulting compromise, manifestly unrealistic and unstable as it is, somehow represents the extension of social democracy to the conditions of relative backwardness.

Looking beyond this ad-hoc balance, some left parties (like the Workers' Party in Brazil) have proposed a two-sided program, reflecting more than challenging the persistent constraints of dualism. For the organized economy they put forward a corporatist political economy: the negotiation of agreements among the big organized interests of industry and labor. For the disorganized economy they offer compensatory welfare assistance. In the conditions of a dualistic economy, however, compensatory social democracy, realized through tax-and-transfer programs, will always prove a hopeless enterprise. It can work only as an accessory to democratizing structural change and only insofar as it respects the priorities of social spending that can make the greatest potential contribution to the future: education and child support. The volume of resources to be transferred, through taxation and welfare, from the first economy to the second would have to be enormous in order successfully to address the practical problems of the majority of people stuck in the second economy. The link between economic and political power would prevent it from reaching this necessary magnitude. If it could reach the required size, the result would be to disorganize the first, favored economy, killing the goose that lays the golden eggs. No wonder compensatory social democracy is a program almost universally espoused by all political forces in the most unequal mass democracies; it is, in such democracies, impossible to execute.

An effective program for progressives in the conditions of contemporary developing countries must satisfy three minimal conditions. First, it must present a consistently antidualist political economy, consolidating in both public and private hands an economic and technological vanguard that can reorient itself to the productive and consumption needs of the economic rearguard. Second, it must show the way to continue the national resistance to the logic of determinate comparative advantage and unilinear economic evolution. To this end, it must reject the confinement of the state to merely social and regulatory responsibilities. It must find ways to realize a less centralized and collusive version of the partnership between governments and firms than we have yet seen realized among successful late developers. Third, the program must anchor these economic solutions in political arrangements favorable to the repeated practice of structural reform and the organized heightening of civic engagement. Each of these directions requires a sequence of institutional innovations, informed by legal–institutional ideas. To have proposed so few such ideas has been the fatal weakness of contemporary progressive thinking.

The seats of resistance: the large marginalized countries

National rebellion and international organization. The large marginalized countries of the world – China, Russia, India, Brazil, and Indonesia – enjoy a special opportunity as contexts for the development of a progressive alternative. They are less dependent upon foreign trade and less vulnerable to the disfavor of the international capital markets and the Bretton Woods organizations. Spiritual advantages accompany this practical independence: each of these countries can imagine itself as something of a world unto itself rather than as a satellite to some other system. In three of the five (China, Russia, India), the political nation has long been accustomed to turn inward, resenting the constraints imposed by the external world. In two of these three (China and India), the self-reference finds support in the history of a great, ancient, and distinctive civilization, bearing spiritual ideals capable of outlasting both foreign conquest and domestic upheaval.

For the progressive alternative to have a chance, it must find a base in at least some of these countries. Their rebellion against the orthodoxy of convergence can reinforce the effort to turn the international organizations away from their single-minded service to that same orthodoxy. Central among these organizations are the Bretton Woods agencies: the International Monetary Fund, the World Bank, and their new offshoot, the World Trade Organization. They work today to advance neoliberalism. For an alternative such as the one explored here to move beyond its initial stages, this bond would need to be broken.

The sole task that the international organizations could justifiably undertake in a single voice would be the minimalist job of administering the clearing rules of the world trading system. In this role their position would be similar to that of those who, in any market, administer the machinery of settlement. They would act, for example, to prevent the consequences of currency volatility or inconvertibility from limiting worldwide movement of goods, services, and capital. However, the performance of the clearing function must remain subject to a self-restraint calculated to favor the freedom of states to pursue alternative projects of national development.

Two other responsibilities of international economic organizations – to help countries solve temporary liquidity crises and to supply long-term development assistance – should be vested in multiple and parallel organizations, at the service of multiple development strategies, rather than in unitary organizations at the behest of a single creed. If unitary organizations such as the International Monetary Fund and the World Bank are preserved, they should become confederations of technical teams that enjoy wide-ranging independence of judgement and funding. A rule-bound system of funding to the international organizations, based, for example, upon a small surcharge to the domestic value-added tax or its closest equivalent, can supply these organizations with their resources. The rules governing international flows of goods, services, and capital should respect the power of countries selectively to opt out of the general regime for the sake of a special vision without being ostracized and punished for their temerity.

To describe such a diversification of the world economy is to see why it could take place only through the pressure of rebellion by major countries against the world order. There must be the first signs of a practical alternative to the path mapped out by the convergence thesis – and power applied persistently to its pursuit – before people can hope to escape the international imposition of convergence. Pluralism in the policies of international organizations can in turn help broaden the space for national rebellion. The dissidence of large countries and the diversification of the international organizations would combine to give smaller countries the cover they need. Without such cover they may find it impossible to overthrow the alliance of ideological superstition with financial and political coercion.

In the following pages, I consider the constraints and opportunities that the situations of three of these five countries – China, Russia, and Brazil – present for the development of a program such as the one explored here. Circumstances will change, but the concerns and ideas animating the proposal will long outlast them. Each situation throws a different light upon the relation among divided societies, economic forces, and democratic commitments. However, two themes recur in all the country discussions, connecting them with one another as well as with the programmatic argument of this book.

The first theme is the need for any alternative that would be productivist as well as democratizing to innovate in the property regime, organizing a system of multiple stakes in productive resources while preserving the capacity for decisive entrepreneurial initiative. Insiders – workers and managers – must be protected, and a system devised that favors long-term investment in their capabilities. They must also, however, be shaken up from time to time through arrangements that enable outside investors to decide, through selective turnaround, which businesses in trouble are worth trying to save and which are not.

The institutional repertory of established market economies manages these tensions by devices both blunt and one-sided. Sometimes such arrangements entrench the interests of a class of favored insiders, as in the traditional forms of Japanese and German-style social corporatism. At other times, they alternate between concentrating power in a managerial elite, supported by retained earnings, and giving the decisive say to outside investors. These investors then exercise the vital responsibility of occasional disruption under the cloud of impatient short-termism. We need to expand this repertory if we are to accelerate productive innovation while moderating the costly contrast between favored insiders and disempowered outsiders. The development of decentralized strategic coordination between governments and firms, the creation of entities in between governments and firms as agents of such an association, the disaggregation of bundled property rights, the coexistence within the same economy of different property and contract regimes, and the enhancement of the powers of the individual by means such as social-endowment accounts available to everyone are all features of this needed enlargement of the institutional forms of the market economy.

A second recurrent theme in this discussion of the constraints and opportunities faced by the large marginalized countries is the connection between economic and political reform. The institutional innovations required by a program like the one presented here are less a definitive fix than an ongoing practice. This practice requires arrangements that favor the persistent expression of popular political energy, constitutions that resolve impasse while decentralizing power, and rules that promote the general, independent organization of civil society.

A single wave of institutional innovations may be the work of an enlightened and authoritarian elite. However, a continuing collective capacity for the discovery and realization of alternative social futures requires an organized society and a quickened politics. Constraints upon institutionalized political mobilization, concessions to a style of constitutionalism associating the dispersal of power with the slowing down of politics, and legal impediments to the independent organization of civil society strengthen the hand of fate. They make successful innovation depend upon crisis and catastrophe.

The representative democracies, market economies, and free civil societies established in the North Atlantic world are the only versions of political, economic, and social pluralism now in existence. For that reason, as well as because of their long association with the immense worldly success of the societies in which they have emerged, their institutional arrangements continue to enjoy unrivalled authority throughout the world. The defects of these versions of pluralism multiply, and their strengths fade, when we transport them to societies more divided, desperate, or hierarchical than the ones in which these arrangements now flourish.

These familiar political, economic, and social institutions support a real but limited measure of democracy and democratic experimentalism in places whose history is at one with the history of the North Atlantic world. They do too little for the reconciliation of prosperity and democracy in the circumstances of the large marginalized countries today. Contrary, however, to what the reforming elites of these countries often suppose, the solution is more democracy rather than less. To understand the connection between this solution and the practical problems of political economy is to reinterpret the future of these continental and confused societies.

Russia. With the collapse of communism throughout the former Soviet Union and its empire, an old idea about contemporary history gained new strength. This idea represents both the quintessential form and the most influential instance of the convergence thesis. It teaches that modern societies followed (and, in the stronger version of the idea, could only have followed) one of two paths: the road of a democratic market society and the road of an authoritarian command economy. The second route proved to be a dead end: in sacrificing freedom, it also led to an economic disaster of stagnant productivity and misdirected production.

The failure of the "second way" has been so unequivocal that it has brought with it the repudiation of all "third ways." There is nothing these "third ways" or "market socialisms" promise, according to this dominant view, that has not been been better accomplished by the first and only way: the route taken by the existing democratic market societies. Political democracy, so the story goes, supports both a decentralization of economic opportunity and a moderate degree of corrective redistribution, making it possible to diminish inequality without sacrificing either personal freedom or economic growth. This one and only way admittedly allows for variations. However, they are minor in signficance and seem to be steadily diminishing in scope. (Witness the waning of many of the supposed distinctive features of Japanese- or German-style "capitalism.")

The countries that took the road of the command economy must now return to the fork at which they took the wrong turn.

The rectification is as painful as it is unavoidable. However, if undertaken decisively, the pain will prove shorter and less burdensome than if the reformers equivocate with half-measures. Most importantly, the basic nature of the one true way is not in doubt, although the switch itself requires ingenuity as well as patience (for example, the unique strategies of mass privatization of state industry discussed below).

Two great forces drive the reforming country forward. The first force is the clarification of property rights, especially when its effect is to unite rights of control over productive resources with rights over the financial flows those resources yield. The second force is the integration of the national economy into the world economy, multiplying examples as well as opportunities for domestic firms.

This creed – now the single most influential version of the most authoritative political-economic doctrine in the world – confronts in Russia an opposition offering no real alternative. This half-hearted opposition oscillates between the backhand defense, through fiscal and financial subsidies, of the inherited industrial system and the attempt to slow down a transformation that it recognizes to be inevitable. Thus, a discourse gains currency contrasting "shock therapy" to moderation and compromise in the pursuit of the one true way. The program of this opposition is the program of its adversaries with a discount.

In Russia, as in much of the world, such an opposition invites an orthodoxy-reaffirming answer: a slow and equivocal transition is likely to prove more costly in social as well as economic terms than a quick and decisive one. Moreover, the answer continues, the clear-headed execution of the reform program both requires and makes possible the development of a "social-safety net." Social insurance eases the unavoidable pain of industrial restructuring. In so doing, it helps prevent the political interruption of reform by a backward-looking populism. It also helps form and prepare people who can eventually join the dynamic centers of the internationally oriented part of the economy. However, the development of this program of preparatory and compensatory social investment is not an alternative to the reform program. On the contrary, only a state that has rid itself of the burden of inefficient production and has begun to finance itself through the taxation of a vibrant private economy can effectively discharge its regulatory and social responsibility.

A restrictive idea of politics sustains and perpetuates the contrast between the reform program and its populist discount. According to this idea, although democracy may be both the condition and the product of successful economic reform, too much democracy threatens to overwhelm the reform process with expectations it cannot meet. Political institutions heightening the level of political mobilization, constitutional arrangements accelerating transformative politics through the rapid resolution of impasse, and the strengthening of the basis for independent organization in civil society may all appear to be unaffordable luxuries for a country that must make the switch from the bad path to the good one. Thus, the liberal-legal elites fear they may open the path to demagogic and populist authoritarianism, undermining both economic reform and political democracy. Abhorrence of Bonapartism may seem, paradoxically, to justify restraints upon the intensity and the scope of popular self-government and mass organization.

However, this deliberate restraint upon the organizational strength and the political powers of society has a twofold effect. It creates the opportunity – even the need – for the personalist authoritarianism the liberal legalists feared; they become the architects of the political fate they had plotted to escape. The little Bonapartes step into the vacuum created by the disorganization of society and the infirmities of politics. Nothing remains as a language for politics but the menacing dialectic between mythical images of the needs of the nation and shameless appeals to the resentments of the losers.

The deliberate slowing down of politics and the fatalistic acceptance of social disorganization deny the country the means with which to formulate alternative visions – and to act upon them. The result is to establish the practical and imaginative conditions within which the sole opposition is one resigned to humanize the inevitable. These two effects – the paradoxical creation of the basis for strong-man politics through the destruction of the basis for a strong politics and the denial to civil society of the means by which to formulate alternative futures and to act upon them – combine to create the conditions for a pendular swing between economic orthodoxy and economic populism. This oscillation expresses and reinforces the impotence of transformative politics. The principle exemplified by this narrowing of reconstructive capability is one that reappears in every historical situation.

Ideas exercise their decisive power upon the demarcation of the frontier between the actual and the possible when they begin to animate the available forms of social action. An institutionalized social world becomes entrenched against challenge, and ultimately wins a mendacious semblance of necessity and authority, when the everyday forms of practical and discursive action rob people of the chance to tinker with it.

The conflict over privatization and its relation to the restructuring of firms in the postcommunist economies provides a context in which to probe the limits of this orthodox view and suggest a productivist and democratizing alternative to it. To grasp the shape of the controversy it is important to remember a few elementary facts about the character of the industrial system Russia inherited from the Soviet Union. The strategy of heroic industrialization resulted in a grossly lopsided development of heavy industry, almost all of it organized in the manner of the most rigid and traditional style of fordist mass-production.

Economic growth organized around this industry advanced through forced accumulations of inputs of capital and labor but proved incapable of sustained advance in productivity. Much of this industry made shoddy or unwanted goods. Some of it consumed more value than it produced. Hoarding, shortages, and forced substitutions became rampant as consequences of the system of centralized procurement and planning. Many big firms were near-monopoly producers of their products. Nevertheless, to diminish their dependence upon necessary inputs they found themselves pushed into runaway vertical integration. Thus, the anticompetitive concentration of production coexisted with an equally costly dispersal of productive capacity. The defense industry apparatus had elements of vanguard, experimental production. Its links with the rest of the industrial system nevertheless remained tenuous; this was industrial dualism with a vengeance. Moreover, agriculture, largely collectivized and vastly inefficient, failed, after the formative period of the 1920s and 1930s, to make the spectacular contribution to the financing and manning of industry that it has made in the most successful contemporary economies.

These familiar signs of economic failure have a less familiar meaning. Every economy faces a problem of selective turnaround. There is no self-evident point at which to draw the red line between those firms that should be allowed to die and those that should be rescued through investment and reorganization. The line is no less arbitrary when drawn so as to turn every passing payment difficulty into instantaneous and definitive economic death. For the legal rules defining obligations to creditors, workers, and shareholders are themselves capable of taking many different forms; no one set of such rules expresses the unavoidable bankruptcy rules of a market economy.

To prop up every failing business is to make a promise that cannot be kept while running up a vast charge upon the future. On the other hand, to let any firm in trouble die – and in an economy like that of Russia today virtually every long-established firm is in trouble – is to invite waste and hardship on a scale that no society tolerates for long. The established market economies vest the responsibility for selective turnaround in the capital markets, moderating the impatience and short-termism of the markets with episodic governmental intervention in support of big troubled businesses. When this machinery is absent or deficient and when the problem it is supposed to solve becomes pervasive, the haphazard character of the traditional arrangements for collective turnaround shines through. These arrangements leave much of the productive potential of saving dormant, and lead companies to finance themselves out of retained earnings.

Informed decisions about selective turnaround require two kinds of insider knowledge: intimate acquaintance with markets and productive opportunities and a detailed grasp of the social world within which economic activity takes place. Arrangements for selective turnaround that rely solely upon the greed or prudence of those who hold or control large pools of capital are blunt instruments. They satisfy these requirements of insight episodically and unevenly. As always, the question becomes: What are the alternatives, and will they do even more damage than the arrangements they replace?

In a condition such as that of the post-Soviet economy, selective turnaround ceases to be the hidden task and becomes instead the overt and central problem. It is the indispensable alternative to two forms of economic disaster: the wholesale abandonment of the production system (the scorched-earth policy) and the indiscriminate distribution of favors to preserve existing production (for example, through import or export subsidies, subsidized credits, and tax favors).

Any promising path of economic growth must begin in arrangements that help prevent these two disasters. Having helped address the problem of selective turnaround they will also lay a basis for continued economic growth. We should in turn judge the property regime envisaged by an approach to privatization by its ability to promote the experimentalism of production while deepening the experimentalism of democracy.

The doctrine of the one true way has direct implications for privatization. These implications command us to build a familiar regime of private property. If we were to accept for a moment the false idea that private property has a single basic form, we would still have to decide how to connect – or to separate – rights of control over firms with claims upon the enjoyment of the cash flows those businesses generate. The narrowest version of the doctrine of the one true way suggests that these two sets of rights should be combined in the hands of the same people, the better to buttress managerial responsibility with economic reward and punishment. Corporatization – the establishment of the independent legal personality and economic initiative of the firm – could then quickly pass into privatization, understood as the marriage of power with property in the corporation.

Comparative experience with alternative forms of corporate governance fails, however, to support this dogma; only where closely held family firms remain common in big as well as in small business do we find this combination of rights to control and rights over cash flows satisfied. The dogma nevertheless expresses, in too narrow a form, an idea important to the teaching of the one true way: the belief that market-driven activity flourishes best when brightly demarcated property rights give the manager-entrepreneur a free zone of action. They then liberate the manager-entrepreneur from the constraints of community and the impositions of government, placing greed on the side of skill.

Suppose the goal, thus enlarged, were as clear as this teaching implies. The route by which to reach it, in circumstances such as those of Russia, would continue to be obscure. To use orthodox means to achieve the orthodox objective, auctioning off the state industries, would be to give public enterprise to foreign capital and to those nationals who are likely to hold large pools of cash: the new class of hustlers and the old class of self-dealing managers of public business. The outcome of such a procedure would be as unacceptable to the country as the procedure itself. The complacent doctrine according to which the market economy, once established, would eventually convey productive assets to their most efficient users can give solace only to those who are determined to find it even in the darkest recesses of self-interest. "To imitate," wrote Piaget, "is to invent." Even the most determined effort to import the economic institutions established in the leading powers forces the would-be imitators to innovate despite themselves. Involuntary institutional experimentalism becomes, among the developing countries, the great engine of innovation and the chief opportunity for rebellion. So it is with the example of privatization.

Privatization policy emerged in the Russia of the early 1990s as a compromise between what the doctrine of the one true way required and what the established interests demanded. It was also a compromise between what these interests demanded and what the country, exhausted and demoralized, seemed ready to tolerate. "Mass privatization," executed through a combination of qualified auctions and widespread distribution of vouchers to the population, provided for several paths to privatization. The favorite proved to be an option enabling managerial insiders, associated with a new national financial oligarchy and with foreign partners, to acquire controlling stakes in the biggest businesses, inheriting almost overnight much of the productive wealth of the former Soviet Union. Thus, under the shadow of ideological superstition and rampant self-dealing, an old elite struggled to turn itself into a new one, taking into itself the boldest, luckiest, and most shameless outsiders.

When judged by the most relevant standard of its usefulness to the urgent work of selective turnaround, this solution turns out to suffer from an incurable paradox. If the aim is to let state industry collapse the better to build upon its ruins another productive system, oriented to domestic and world markets, the insider-privatization procedure does too much. It perpetuates and entrenches a lobby for the ongoing subsidization of the inherited industrial system. The new state must either serve the interests of this renovated elite, or attack them in the name of the excluded and sullen majority. The incorporation of new entrepreneurs and foreign partners into this deal may change the character of this permanent charge upon the state in the long run. In that long run, however, politics will overtake economics, and the pendular swing between economic orthodoxy and economic populism will do its full damage.

If, on the other hand, the goal of this insider-favoring privatization is to set up a framework for the urgent work of selective turnaround, the program does much too little, and this little does more to frustrate that work than to carry it out. No capital market can judge and distinguish well when to turn privatized assets around if it is dominated by the same interests commanding privatization and profiting from it. No government will have the resources, the power, or the self-confidence to support the social institutions capable of formulating and implementing an innovative industrial strategy when it has conveyed its prize possessions to a group of men and women whose newfound wealth it barely manages to tax. No community of workers, social organizations, local governments, and small firms can share in the responsibilities, benefits, and burdens of selective turnaround when it has been violently rebuffed by a government under the influence of self-serving managerial elites and their new foreign and domestic partners.

There can and will be industrial restructuring in such circumstances. However, it will be predominantly restructuring that prepares the country to join the world economy on the terms of the established order. In that order a worldwide network of vanguards remains relatively isolated from the rearguards within their countries. In that order, the new hierarchical distinction among countries becomes the difference between the richer countries, in which a disfavored, albeit substantial, minority remains locked out of the vanguard, and the poorer countries, in which only a minority belongs to the vanguard. Once again, however, the critical argument leads, relentlessly, to the programmatic question: What is the alternative? The criticism carries little force unless there is an alternative that can connect productive and democratic experimentalism while appealing to an inclusive alliance of groups and forces.

The core of such an alternative lies in the relation between the arrangements for selective turnaround and the arrangements empowering the country to imagine and explore alternative futures through a quickened democratic politics. The first task looks to a reordering of production – achieving the democratized market economy; the second, to a reordering of democratic politics – creating the conditions for a high-energy democracy. The central topic of this book is the institutional repertory of democratic and productive experimentalism. The following paragraphs describe a few variations on this repertory especially suited to circumstances such as those of post-Soviet Russia. The world has been linked by a chain of analogies: analogous problems, opportunities, and solutions. The thesis of the worldwide chain of analogies fastens on the residue of truth in the illusions of the convergence thesis.

Economic activity would be largely based in regional complexes – at the republican and subrepublican level – with a mixed political and economic character. A series of overlapping and competitive holding companies, representing the interests of both insiders (workers and managers) and outsiders (local governments, social organizations, fragmented shareholders, foreign investors), would pool the equity stakes in the privatized firms. This is a familiar aspect of many proposals for alternative privatization. One of its motives is a recognition of both the

impracticality and the inequity of outright sales to the highest
bidder: industry would fall into the hands of foriegn capital or of
the people inside the country most likely to have free-floating
capital: the former nomenklatura and black-market speculators.
At times, these holding companies have been presented as
transitional privatization agencies, to be disbanded once normal
Western-style private enterprises are in place. Imagine, however,
the holding companies as neither temporary nor subsidiary. They
help supply solutions to several puzzles: how to combine not only
broadly distributed ownership rights but different kinds of
ownership rights with effective control over management; how to
make economic activity accountable to democratic authorities
without weakening initiative or competition; and how to ensure
an orderly workplace without giving managers, in the name of
property rights, an exorbitant disciplinary power over workers.

The shares in the ownership of productive enterprises would
be distributed among these holding companies to ensure that one
such company would hold an influential but not an irresistible
stake in each firm. This influential participation might be anywhere in the range of ten to thirty percent according to the
circumstances. Smaller stakes would be distributed among other
holding companies, and their minority rights would be suitably
guaranteed.

The directors of the holding companies would, at the outset,
be appointed jointly by regional authorities responsible for executing the initial plan of industrial reconstruction in consultation
with their foreign and domestic partners. These holding-company
managers would come inevitably both from the ranks of first-line
productive activities and from the more independent sectors of
the technical intelligentsia. Once the alternative market system is
in place, the directors of the holding companies would be chosen
by their shareholders, whose identities I describe below. There is
no satisfactory solution to the problem of the initial selection of
the directors. Some force within the existing society must choose

them; any such force will inevitably bear the imprint of the society's history. Once the holding companies are established, however, the choice falls to the shareholders. The management of these companies becomes a professional business responsibility like any other, and each manager's performance can be judged by its consequences.

The staffing and policies of the holding companies must be independent of governmental control once they become going concerns. Otherwise, they would soon be perverted into rent-seeking organizations. The people most likely to rise to the top of their authority structures would be those best at playing the roles of patrons and clients. Yet the existence of this intermediate level of property rights and industrial organization makes it easier for a range of governmental and social entities to participate in the ownership and control of industry without depriving productive firms of their independence and initiative. Through this and other devices, we may hope to moderate, although we cannot efface, the tension between the goals of competitive decentralization and social accountability.

Holding companies may be expected to develop over time portfolios of firms whose production lines are different but mutually supportive. Each of these portfolios turns into the setting for a little confederation of firms. The supervisory entity becomes more than an instrument of control over managers and representation of shareholders; it helps the firms pool commercial, technological, and financial resources.

The shares of the holding companies are traded on a mass, individualized market in shares. The shares of the productive firms, on the other hand, are traded on a more closed institutional market in which only the holding companies themselves, banks, and foreign investors participate. This two-tier market system allows for a closer coordination between ownership and control and establishes greater parity among the multiple institutional owners of firms.

The discussion of the relations among governments, firms, and social funds or holding companies leads into an analysis of the diversification of the property regime and of the rights that workers and governments would enjoy under such a diversified organization of property. The ownership interests vested in the holding company belong to different types of owners and, to each of these types, those rights have a different meaning and different consequences. From the beginning, such property rights are more circumscribed than the corresponding property rights in a Western-style market economy.

Traditional property confers on the managers of the firm a generic disciplinary power over workers. Thus, the power structure of the contemporary firm rests on two independent foundations: the technical imperative of supervisory coordination and the claims of property. The boss tells the worker: You must obey me because productive efficiency requires that you obey me and because, even if it did not, I am the owner, or I stand in the place of the owners. The appeal to property, although qualified by collective labor contracts and by the direct legal regulation of the employment relation, trumps experiments in alternative forms of work organization. The technical requirements of coordination are both too weak and too subject to controversial interpretation to justify a way of organizing work that is either rigid or authoritarian.

Similarly, traditional property rights establish a protective barrier between entrepreneurial initiative and political control. The property entitlement marks out an area reserved to independent managerial decision. There is no clear legal or economic logic that justifies drawing this line in one place rather than another. Nor is political control itself a self-defining and indivisible category: some forms of political intervention in economic decision-making may increase the role for entrepreneurial initiative and independence. They may do so, for example, by enlarging both the number of agents who can gain access to productive resources and the range of ways in which these resources can be made available to the agents. The disaggregation of property rights described later in this book distributes the many faculties composing the traditional property right in ways that deny any holder of a property interest an open-ended disciplinary power over workers or a blanket guarantee against responsibility to outside social interests. The property regime discussed here is a species of such a scheme. It empowers workers in three ways. Consider them in order of mounting importance.

First, as citizens, workers are themselves owners of equity in holding companies; not necessarily, but very often, holding companies with interests in the firms in which they work. Second and more importantly, the collective laborforce of each firm retains a certain portion of ownership interests – say, twenty percent – before the distribution of the major ownership rights to the holding companies and their individual shareholders. Unlike the quotas in the holding companies, these shares are held jointly and inalienably. They supply an additional basis for influence over the management of the firm without the disadvantages of outright worker ownership. Third, such a regime assigns an important role to local governments and social organizations. The qualified character of the claims firms enjoy upon productive resources rescue the workers from the dictatorship of managers and providers of capital. It does so, however, without resorting to the idea of the worker-owned firm, with its characteristic substitution of one unified "owner" by another.

Just as it weakens the link between power and property, this scheme of industrial organization and property rights diminishes the barrier between entrepreneurial initiative and social control. For one thing, the chief agent of oversight under such a regime is an organization – the social fund or holding company – prompted by interests and influences more complex than the maximization of profit. For another thing, such a regime makes it impossible to concentrate property and control in a managerial elite empowered to distinguish cleanly its responsibilties to workers and communities from the maximization of shareholder value.

These legal–institutional devices form no perpetual-motion machine, ensuring the success of selective turnaround. They merely create a setting favorable to the deployment and development of implicit knowledge about economic opportunity and social possibility. The judgement about where to put resources and energies depends upon the combination of heterogeneous insights drawn from different realms of experience: insights into the opportunities afforded by the possible future of production and insights into the desirability of the forms of social life associated with these pathways of growth. In one instance as in the other, the subtlety of the judgement arises from its pragmatic character. Those who must make such decisions are not in the position of people predicting the future course of an object over which they exercise no power. They ask themselves whether some imagined variation on present practices is close enough to be accessible (just as a naturalist might ask whether in genetic space a particular variation may be connected by intermediate links to a visible form). They also ask themselves, however, whether they and their people – the people of their firm or community – can muster the energy and ingenuity needed to make the variation happen. When all is said and done, and the arrangements most favorable to the practice of selective turnaround have been set in place, nothing guarantees that the right decisions will be made, only that there will be the greatest clarity and the most information in making them.

Economic alternatives such as these cannot be created, nor can they be preserved, by a demobilized politics, an inhibiting constitutionalism, or a disorganized society. At the same time, the desirable alternatives would never arise simply because of the service they render to selective turnaround. They must be sought also and chiefly because they enable people to come out of silence and impotence, defending and developing their interests and affirming the power of their country to build a distinctive form of life.

In post-Soviet Russia, constititutional forms helped set the stage for the very populist and personalist authoritarianism that some feared would result from arrangements favorable to the quickening of politics. The governmental control of the means of communication and the frank alliance of the newly enriched with the power-holders discouraged sustained, deliberate, and organized citizens' engagement even as it provoked sporadic and resentful agitation under the leadership of new adventurers and old bogeys. What forms of independent organization civil society found at its disposal were tainted by their association with the Soviet state and estranged from the emerging sources of wealth and power. In this inhospitable terrain, no social scheme of selective turnaround could develop, nor could people work out deviations from economic orthodoxy or alternatives to economic populism. The doctrine of the one true way gained a purchase on the reality of the country by preventing the forms of political and social action that might defy its assumptions about the possible.

Earlier sections of this book have suggested the nature of some of the arrangements that favor the repeated practice of structural reform, heighten the level of political mobilization, and strengthen the independent organization of civil society. To develop its own version of such alternatives, Russia enjoyed an immense practical advantage and an equally formidable spiritual obstacle. The advantage was the relatively high degree of equality and education that the Soviet regime, for all its brutality and incompetence, had bequeathed to the Russian people. The obstacle was the thorough demoralization not just of the alternatives of the past but of the very idea of alternatives. The cupidity of the few and the despair of the many contributed in equal measure to a renunciation of constructive ambition. Even in this paradox of objective opportunity and subjective constraint, however, post-Soviet Russia presented in exaggerated form what had become a worldwide predicament.

China. The China contemporaneous with post-Soviet Russia exemplifies similar constraints and opportunities for constructive deviation from the doctrine of the one true way, only with one fundamental difference. This difference helps place the practices of voluntary and involuntary institutionalism in a different light. The Chinese organization of the market economy exceeds, in originality and ingenuity, the reluctant Russian departures from the Western models that the renovated Russian elites are so anxious to imitate. Yet so long as the communist regime survives, these innovations have to stay within the iron framework established by the interests, ideas, and fears of the Chinese rulers. The material of institutional innovation is there lying all around, ready to be taken as a starting point for the development of an alternative. It remains, however, truncated by the consequences of a political paradox.

While the regime continues, no such development can take place; the innovations will follow the pattern – familiar in Chinese history – of peaceful coexistence between mercantile greed and political despotism, and easy transposition of public office into private privilege. If the communist regime disintegrates, however, and joins the ranks of the frankly postcommunist states, all remaining impediments to the doctrine of the one true way will break down. What seems to be promising innovation might appear in retrospect to have been merely part of the fleeting compromise between greed and despotism. The organizational innovations of the time might then seem to have only superficial significance.

The "iron law of convergence" dictates that the catch-up of backward countries, like the cognitive development of young children, will follow a predictable pace: about two percent of the gap between richer and poorer states, or among regions of a single country, can be expected to vanish each year according to familiar wisdom. Gross governmental incompetence may slow this pace down, and special favors (as in the assistance of Germany to its new eastern provinces) may speed it up. However, the average will prove remarkably constant over a broad range of circumstances. Institutional variations, when not so wild as to smother the market, will matter, when they matter at all, for their effects upon the distribution of benefits and burdens.

Consider what some of these Chinese institutional variations of the turn of the century are. The "township–village enterprise" establishes an original form of association between government and "private" initiative at the same time that it shows how quasi-public entities can compete and innovate in a market just as well as traditional Western-style firms. The "shareholder-cooperative system" combines, in the design of corporate governance, the principle of "one share, one vote," with the principle "one person (that is to say, one worker), one vote." It also demonstrates how such a combination can preserve entrepreneurial initiative while broadening the recognition of stakes and stakeholders in productive resources. The older system of rural industry, itself an innovative response to the problems of economic development in a country of hundreds of millions of peasants, has resulted in a wide range of forms of industrial deconcentration. Even the sector of state industries, caught in a wedge between employment and benefits obligations to workers and constraints upon the power to raise prices, includes whole networks of firms on their way to productive vanguardism. These firms have secured the margin of maneuver that makes possible progress toward more advanced practices of production. In many places, a measure of local democracy, of accountability of local governments to local communities, helps sustain these economic innovations, and receives support from them.

Consider two contrasting interpretations of these Chinese novelties. According to the first interpretation, they are specific and ephemeral adaptations to the joint effect of two sets of circumstances. The first circumstance is that China continues to be a nation of peasants, or at least of workers combining agriculture with other economic activities, unlike the many developing countries in Latin America and Africa where urbanization has run ahead of industrialization. The second circumstance is that an institutionalized collective dictatorship clings to power, trying, with uneven effect, to curb only the most exorbitant forms of corruption by its officials. This regime perseveres in an idea of its mission to which, however, it can no longer give any definite or shared meaning.

Some of the institutional innovations just mentioned represent ways of reconciling the turn to markets and to market-oriented industrialization with a rural population that remains enormous in relative as well as absolute terms. These ingenious arrangements turn constraint into opportunity. Other innovations ensure that economic decentralization follows a course that serves the interests of the state elite by creating new ways to turn public place into private opportunity. Such ramshackle compromises give cover to the private business of officialdom while leaving the shell of administrative domination in place. Turning public office into a chance for profiteering and celebrating the conspiracy between political despotism and private greed, the masters of the state merely spin new variations on the most persistent theme of Chinese history. This runaway patrimonialism finds its limits in the dangers of social unrest created by the division between the participants and the outsiders to the new social contract. Viewed in the light of such a social future, China's institutional heresies would turn out in retrospect to be convenient byways, often ingenious and sometimes grotesque, on the road to convergence toward the standard version of the market economy.

According to this convergence-supporting view, the relative size of the rural population will slowly diminish, and the multiplication of new groups and new interests will ultimately help bring down the communist dictatorship. Once the special circumstances have ceased to exist, the apparent organizational novelties will lose their point. China will continue to have distinctive arrangements – expressing the influences of history and circumstance – but the innovations of this time will seem in retrospect to be the cunning of history: heresy in the service of orthodoxy.

There is, however, an alternative reading. According to this contrasting interpretation, the organizational innovations of this period represent possible points of departure for the development of a political and economic order resisting institutional convergence with the leading industrial powers. By resisting it, they can better advance the cause of democratic and productive experimentalism in China. The Chinese inventions include anticipatory and fragmentary variations on many of the themes in the progressive alternatives this book explores.

The association of local governments with private entrepreneurship could sow the seed of multiple regimes for the decentralized allocation of productive resources. The regional base, public support, and flexible forms of many of the new types of initiative could turn into a version of cooperative competition sustained by a decentralized and pluralistic practice of strategic coordination. The "one person, one vote principle" in corporate governance could show the way to worker empowerment without consolidating the most valuable property rights in the hands of a self-serving or asset-wasting coterie of tenured job-holders. The old record of rural industrialization could become the prehistory of a new dispersal of economic activity, helping, in a more distant future, to soften the contrasts among work, leisure, and family life. Even the limited forms of participatory local government, hemmed in as they are by the dictatorship of the state elite, could provide some of the early materials for combining representative and direct democracy once the Chinese dictatorship has been overthrown.

Which of these two readings of the Chinese experience is true? Will the future, by leaning more in one direction or another, tell? There is a sense in which choosing between such accounts is like choosing between alternative accounts of a natural object, and there is a sense in which it is not. The sense of the similarity is that, in social understanding as in natural explanation, insight implies imagination of the possible. The sense of the difference lies in the power of belief to change constraint. Every discourse about the social future can become a self-fulfilling prophecy. It need only tell a story about the transactions between the actual and the possible that people can act upon with institutional or ideological materials lying at hand. The story cannot become reality just by being told but it can liberate or inhibit so long as people can use it to inform action or justify conformity in the here and now.

In China one such story, its authority seemingly renewed by recent experience, continues to enjoy great influence in the political nation. According to this story, China needs strong and unified authority imposed from the center and the top if it is not to lapse into violent anarchy as it did during the Cultural Revolution. The belief in an inescapable choice between repressive order and costly disorder in a country as large and as poor as China amounts to a pointed instance of "structure fetishism." Institutional fetishism, remember, is the belief that abstract institutional concepts such as the ideas of a representative democracy, a market economy, or a free civil society have a natural and necessary expression in a particular set of legally defined arrangements. Structure fetishism is the higher-order counterpart to institutional fetishism: the view that, although we may be able to revise a particular institutional order, and even occasionally to replace one institutional system by another different one, we cannot alter the character of the relation between institutional structures and the structure-defying, structure-transcending freedom of the agents who inhabit them.

Structure fetishism has had countless manifestations in the history of social thought. One example is the existentialist equation of freedom with the doomed but redemptive rebellion against institutional structures. Another example is the thesis in conservative American political science that political mobilization and political institutionalization are locked into a simple inverse relation. No version of structure fetishism, however, has commanded greater influence than the one that opposes remorseless repression to destructive chaos, social peace to political instability. In all its many faces, structure fetishism fails to acknowledge that the relation between people and the institutionalized worlds they find, remake, and colonize is itself up for grabs in history. Institutional orders differ crucially in the extent to which they are there on a take-it-or-leave-it basis, entrenched against effective challenge in the midst of people's ordinary practical and discursive opportunities.

For the second of these two Chinese futures to prevail over the first, there will have to be democratizing innovations in the institutional setting of politics as well as in the facilities for the independent organization of civil society. Some of these innovations will have to ensure a sustained heightening of the level of political mobilization in the context of political pluralism. They will nevertheless also have to preserve in central government a capacity for decisive action and repeated reform. On the basis of such changes, there will have to emerge a state at once strong and accountable, refinanced through the high tax take needed to fund investment in people, physical apparatus, and public venture capital. Only then can the national government universalize social benefits rather than allowing such benefits to be funneled through a shrinking sector of public firms. Only then can China heal the deepening division between the beneficiaries and the victims of the entrepreneurial economy.

Such changes will create the practical means with which to seize upon the democratizing potential of economic innovations that have already occurred, and prevent them from being reduced to the role of transitory adaptations. At the same time, these reforms will give the lie to the alleged dilemma of repression or anarchy that in China has so often helped disconnect experimentalism in business from experimentalism in democracy.

The point is not that politics – narrowly understood as conflict over the mastery and uses of governmental power – enjoys a causal priority over change in other dimensions. It is rather that although a country may embark on a path of institutional divergence in one domain of its life, such as the economy, it cannot persist in its divergence, or radicalize it, unless it is willing to carry the rebellion to other parts of its life. Productive experimentalism may go a long way, as it has in China, in peaceful coexistence with political despotism. However, the development of the practices of collective tinkering and learning, of cooperative competition and decentralized coordination, puts pressure upon the devices for maintaining such a coexistence. On the one hand, the disciplines of practical, productive experimentalism create a dilemma for the dictators and their underlings: with engagement in the new entrepreneurial economy come corruption and dispersal; with disengagement comes a dangerous estrangement between the interests and experiences of the state elite and those of the economic innovators. On the other hand, the innovations cannot remain quarantined within firms. The innovators seek to establish forms of education, community life, and local government congenial to themselves, initiating a contest with the central government over the order and spirit of civil society. This contest creates an opportunity for action.

To make the second of the two social futures I have described prevail over the first, the reform movements will need ideas as well arrangements. The detailed image of an alternative is an insufficient condition, but it may also be a necessary one. The builders of an alternative will need such an image both to resist the gravitational pull of the dominant conceptions and to work out the operational logic of the institutions they establish. They will also need to tilt the scales of the understanding of recognized group interests away from the institutionally conservative and socially exclusive approaches to the definition and defense of group interests toward the transformative and solidaristic approaches. The vision of larger individual and collective possibility must make up for the absence of immediacy, for the sense of heightened obscurity and risk, that any such break with inherited arrangements and familiar ideas demands.

Brazil. Like the other major Latin American countries and many other developing countries around the world, Brazil devoted the forty years after the Second World War to the practice of import-substituting industrialization. By general consent, the capabilities of this strategy of economic growth were nearly exhausted by the time of the oil shocks of the 1980s. Moreover, the state that presided over this strategy had sunk into inflationary public finance. Having disorganized the public sector, the finance of easy money began to threaten big private business by raising the specter of hyperinflation.

After the monetary stabilization of 1994, the road seemed open to abandon all pretense of heresy and conform to the doctrine of the one true way. To achieve this goal it would be necessary, according to the Brazilian votaries of the doctrine, to consolidate monetary stabilization through a "fiscal adjustment" and to redefine the role of the state through rapid and radical privatization of the large public sector. Once the national government rid itself of the state enterprises and dedicated itself to its proper mission of regulating the economy while promoting public health and education, the country could begin to moderate its extreme inequalities. The advanced sector of the private economy, already integrated into the world economy, would then begin to incorporate increasing parts of the population.

In its Brazilian setting, as everywhere in the world, the program of convergence has become a self-fulfilling prophecy. It helps shape a politics that can generate no other future. The intended effect of many of its initiatives would be to cut the state down to size, creating a government with abilities and disabilities suited to the vision of a socially concerned neoliberalism or an institutionally conservative social democracy. Such a government would at best be able to prepare the large numbers of Brazilians who remained outside the advanced, world-integrated sector to join this vanguard. It can neither replace the economic forces driving that sector nor alter, significantly, their effect. Any attempt to do so would merely slow growth down while providing, in the name of help for the excluded, subsidies for the favored.

The Brazilian situation throws light upon a recurrent theme in the programmatic arguments of this book: the key relation between the effort to supersede the division between vanguard and rearguard and the need to reorganize and refinance activist government in the context of a quickened democracy and an organized society. The relation works in both directions. Without such a government, such a politics, and such a society, there is no prospect of overcoming dualism save through a halting and limited expansion of the vanguard sector. For an indefinitely long time the country would remain divided, as the advanced part of the production system tightened its links with all the other vanguards of the world economy. The people excluded from the advanced sector would continue to seek in politics a revenge against economics, threatening the society with a new form of the old oscillation between economic orthodoxy and economic populism. This marginalized majority, not the privileged participants in an internationalized vanguard, need a capable state.

So long as dualism keeps its strength, the dominant projects in politics will continue to renew the life of dualism in the face of changing circumstance. Thus, selective neoliberalism, embraced in Brazil as in many other developing countries, amounts to an attempt to reinvent the dualist compromises of the old importsubstitituting growth strategy that neoliberalism was supposed to replace. In the social world it began to create, dominated by an economics of institutional assimilation and by a politics of class selfishness, there could be little hope of developing, on the basis of democratic experimentalism, a distinctive civilization. The attack on the endlessly varied forms of racial subjugation and gender hierarchy that help give Brazilian society its special character would follow instead the pattern established in the North Atlantic world. Many people would then turn to a nonstructural micropolitics, disconnected from any political economy, a micropolitics more interested in alternative styles of personal life than in alternative forms of social organization.

Consider first the prehistory of neoliberalism in the political economy that it claims to replace but to which it remains bound by many hidden ties of continuity. As practiced in Brazil and other large Latin American countries, import-substituting industrialization represented the economic expression of a political initiative and a social compromise. The national government helped establish, on the basis of protection and subsidy, an industrial system oriented chiefly to the domestic market. The technological core of this system was fordist mass-production industry. This industry reproduced, for the benefit of part of the society, many of the consumption goods enjoyed by the general population of the rich industrial powers. However, it was rarely efficient enough to be internationally competitive without significant wage repression. Nor could it custom-make the materials and machines goods required for the piecemeal reconstruction of the backward sector. Big public firms produced many of the inputs used by the consumer-goods industries. These industries continued largely in the hands of multinationals and, to a lesser degree, private national capital. Finance remained family business, and family business continued to define the character of big as well as small national firms.

Although the workers who held jobs in these capital-intensive industries earned much less than their counterparts in the rich industrial democracies and faced high job insecurity and turnover, they formed a relatively privileged segment of the working population of the country. Their unions, often founded in a corporatist scheme of controlled popular mobilization, represented, alongside the national industrialists and their foreign partners, one of the two great columns on which the political economy of import-substituting industrialization rested.

The North East Asian economies – first Japan, then Taiwan, Korea, and Singapore – had also passed through a period of import-substituting industrialization, but with other characteristics. These differences throw into sharp relief the limitations of the growth strategy to which, in Brazil as in much of the developing world, neoliberalism was supposed to be the inevitable alternative. In the aftermath of the Second World War, the East Asian elites, pressed by American proconsuls anxious to immunize these countries against communism, executed equalizing reforms, such as land distribution. These reforms magnified the class-moderating effect of a much older tradition of massive governmental and family support for education. As a result, dualism never reached the dimension it habitually exhibited in Latin America. Governments paid careful attention to the management of foreign capital: thus, they preferred loan capital to direct investment until national control over major industry had become secure. To the same end, they insisted from early on upon encouraging a high level of domestic saving, convinced that no country could long grow rich on the basis of foreign money.

Most importantly, they preserved and developed the rudiments of a strong state – one capable of formulating and implementing policy with a substantial measure of independence from business elites. However, they continued to make the strength of the state rest, precariously, upon the political disempowerment of society. These North East Asian countries failed to learn, then or later, the secret of disassociating the hardness of the state from its authoritarianism – a concern central to the program of democratic experimentalism. Nor did they do any better than the leading industrial powers of the day in accelerating and generalizing the practices of productive vanguardism. The firms they began to establish during their import-substituting phase, and continued to develop during the later period of export-led growth, had protections enough for insiders. However, the setting in which these businesses thrived lacked openness to newcomers and incitements to serendipity. No wonder much of the high growth these countries achieved turned out in retrospect to depend upon the one-time effects of expanded financial, physical, and human resources rather than upon sustained increases in productivity.

For all its defects, the strategy of import-substituting industrialization worked in Brazil as in many other countries. It helped sustain for a third of a century a high rate of economic growth. It established a formidable industrial system. It nevertheless suffered from two basic flaws: one economic, the other social.

By the prodigality with which it distributed favors to the import-substituting sector, it satisfied only half of the requirements of economic growth: the half that has to do with supporting the producers of wealth, not the half that has to do with shaking them up. In the new circumstances of the world economy, the vanguard can advance only by being connected with other vanguards; linkage becomes more valuable than protection.

The extremity of the resulting dualism accounts for the distinctive social consequences of this protected and belated fordism. The dualism is at once structural, social, and regional. It defines as much as anything else the situation of the country, committing its politics to an alternation between a selective economic orthodoxy favoring the insiders and a disoriented economic populism appealing to the outsiders. While the orthodoxy draws sustenance from a deep-seated sense of incapacity among the elites to fashion an original path of national development, the populism helps arrest the culture of national opposition within a set of evasive and obsessional fantasies. Yet this fateful dualism is not itself the product of any blind economic fate; it began in a political response to an historical circumstance.

We now come to the link – political rather than narrowly economic – between the dualism of this growth strategy and the inflationary bias of the public finance accompanying it. Having become hostage to the privileged interests it had helped to form, the state could no longer impose the cost of public administration and public investment upon the privileged classes of society. The central government generalized this cost to the whole society through pseudo-Keynesian inflationary finance. Having disorganized the public sector, pseudo-Keynesian public finance soon came to threaten private big business, disturbing its domestic arrangements and weakening its international connections.

For this reason, the imposition of the neoliberal program in Brazil began, as it did in many countries, with a scheme for monetary stablization. A link to the exchange rate (an "exchange-rate anchor"), a very high real rate of interest, and a determined repression of wages, counterbalanced by a postinflationary rise in the spending power of the poor, were all supposed to be temporary expedients. They would continue only until the stability of the currency could be placed on the solid footing of "fiscal adjustment." However, what had been designed as temporary turned out to be long-lasting. There was no way to pass easily from the threshold of monetary stabilization to the solid future of reorganized public finance, dispensing with the costly and fragile devices to which the reformers had first resorted.

The bane of conservative, conventional policy argument is to ignore the institutional, even the strategic, indeterminacy of its professed commitments. So it was with the desired fiscal adjustment. The problem with the fiscal adjustment is not that it was impractical but that there were too many different ways in which it could practiced. Each of them tested in a different way the limits of the ruling set of political and social forces. Policy orthodoxy proposed to bring public spending into line with public revenue by sharp cutbacks of spending rather than sustained increases of revenue. (At the same time, the comparatively small but exorbitantly expensive public debt would need to be cut down to size, chiefly through sale of public companies.) The trouble is that this government-impoverishing version of fiscal adjustment would depress even further the level of public spending on people. Although the majority of the political class might be persuaded to accept such an adjustment, the majority of the country would be sure to rebel against it.

An alternative version of the fiscal adjustment would raise the tax take. Such a government-enriching adjustment would represent a preliminary move in a larger and longer effort to refinance and reorganize the state: a state capable of leading a new project of national development while attacking dualism head on. Government would need to spend for the capacities of people as well as for the conditions of production. To this end, it would need to free itself from the burden of the wildly remunerated public debt as well as to ensure high revenues. Ready to privatize for the strategic purpose of reducing that debt, it would remain just as ready to create new public or mixed public-private enterprises and banks in the future while subjecting them to market discipline, competitive pressure, and financial accountability. It would begin to develop within itself the technical and human resources that a democratized hard state requires if it is to be more than an occasional regulator of private initiative and a marginal moderator of social inequality. Such a fiscal adjustment would require sacrifices as well as conversions. It would need to draw much of its authority from its association with an inclusive, antidualist development strategy.

If the expense-lowering version of the fiscal adjustment is difficult to maintain, the government-enriching version is hard to inaugurate. Its political logic is the logic of a new popular alliance. Such an alliance breaks the limits of a redistributivist populism the better to establish a reorganized and refinanced state at the service of an antidualist political economy. Here is a project outstripping the intentions and capabilities of the political operation that champions selective – that is to say, real rather than textbook – neoliberalism.

Both the government-impoverishing and the government-enriching versions of the fiscal adjustment pose the problem of the relation between economics and politics. No democratic politics can accommodate the pitiless economics of selective neoliberalism or its government-impoverishing fiscal adjustment. Such an economic project would be feasible for a while if the politics that imposed it were sufficiently authoritarian, or the society that suffered it, demoralized and passive enough. Only the second, state-enriching style of fiscal adjustment would meet the objectives of democratic experimentalism. Its prospects depended upon the combination of a programmatic vision with a political force.

Neoliberalism, selective or not, repudiated what had been fertile in the political economy it sought to displace: rebellion against the blind fate of comparative advantage and disadvantage in the world economy. The point is not dogmatically to choose the most promising firms or even sectors; it is to tilt the scales of comparative advantage by organizing around a strategy oriented to increasing the future national margin of internal experimentalism and external independence. Such a strategy liberates the country from dependence upon agricultural exports and industrial imports while promoting, within the country, forms of life as well as possibilities of consumption that many desire. Instead of such a rebellion, repeated in one form or another by every successful late developer since the middle of the nineteenth century, neoliberalism offered reliance upon the hope of ascent up an inalterable ladder of economic evolution. The ascent would supposedly take place if only there were self-restrained government, low taxation, clearcut property rights, and free trade.

As it repudiates what had been subversive and progressive in the older political economy, selective, real neoliberalism remains faithful to the dualist arrangements that compromised the economic power as well as the emancipatory effect of import-substituting industrialization. Entrusting the attack upon dualism to compensatory tax-and-transfer and social spending, it proposes to await the inaccessible and undefined long run in which the inhabitants of the second economy will join the first economy.

Thus, neoliberalism represents less the radical replacement of the nationalist–populist, import-substituting strategy than its adaptation to the new rules of the world economy. Everything happens as if the commanding aim has been to renovate the dualist arrangements of an older political economy with the least possible pain to the moneyed classes and their way of life. The task of a democratizing political economy is precisely the opposite: to carry on in new form the old resistance to the blind forces of comparative advantage while ridding this resistance of the taint of dualism.

However, if today's Brazilian reformers look around the world for the rudiments of an alternative development strategy they see nothing but the ambiguous and all but discredited example of the North East Asian economies: ambiguous, first, because the extent to which their undoubted success in economic and human development should be attributed to state-led strategic coordination, rather than to "getting the fundamentals rights" and caring about education, is in dispute; second, because their practices of government–business partnership remain, to one degree or another, elitist and collusive, inviting mistakes as well as producing outsiders; and, third, because their achievements have become entangled in constraints upon democratic conflict and controversy and therefore upon the pluralism needed to keep experimentalism alive. The vocation of government as an agent of economic rebellion and reconstruction, repeatedly demonstrated in the course of modern world history, lacks convincing contemporary expression.

Brazil suffers from a low domestic savings rate, a capital market that leaves corporate control largely unchallenged, a generalized dearth of private as well as public venture capital, an exclusion of small and medium-sized firms from adequate public or private credit and investment, and, for all these reasons, a deadening of the productive potential of what saving does occur. It suffers as well from the stranglehold that relatively privileged segments of the population exercise upon social spending and that big business imposes upon public investment. In all these respects, it is typical of much of the developing world.

To cut the favored links with the privileged interests is only half of the solution required by a democratizing development strategy. The other half of the solution is affirmative. One task is to organize private saving publicly, lifting the saving level while multiplying the channels between saving and investment outside the traditional circuit of banks and stock markets. Another goal is to build upon a successful tradition of development banks to establish the independent banks, funds, and support centers that can form partnerships with associations of small and medium-sized cooperative–competitive firms. Yet another job is to satisfy the practical and cultural conditions for pushing vanguardist productive practices beyond the geographic and social frontiers of the existing advanced sector. A productive vanguard, head-quartered in both public and private firms, will custom-produce the materials, machines, and services needed by the rearguard to lift itself. It will help broaden the competitive scope of export-oriented production, lessening its dependence upon wage repression.

Such a state devotes itself to social needs as a complement rather than as a substitute for its antidualist initiatives in economic policy and economic organization. It can develop a program of social spending that assigns priority to children and education, achieving maximum effect upon the future while caring for the most vulnerable. It can lead a revolution in the content of education, committing schools to the enhancement of generic conceptual and practical capabilities. It can work toward the piecemeal replacement of family inheritance by social inheritance in the form of social-endowment accounts. The overcoming of dualism must result from the character of the new productivism rather than from a half-hearted and retrospective attempt to undo the consequences of economic arrangements through tax-and-transfer programs. Such a government, championing such a project, would need to be both the author and the product of a quickened politics and an organized society. The institutional history of the country offers opportunities on which a programmatic imagination can seize in the effort to reorganize the state, politics, and civil society.

The presidential regime introduced into a political system weighed down by economic influence and local distraction a potent plebiscitarian element, with nationalizing and subversive effect. Presidentialism can be a source of unpredictability and a lever of change in a society where everything conspires to prevent surprise. However, in its traditional form, the presidential system suffers from a crucial flaw. The people may elect a captain who promises them the earth. In office, however, he soon faces the concerted opposition of the elite interests in the other branches of government as well as in the major stations of civil society. The solution is to preserve the plebiscitarian potency of the presidential system while purging that system of its bias toward politics-slowing impasse. I later describe some of these impasse-breaking arrangements.

The reforms needed to produce a sustained heightening of institutionalized political mobilization are as hard to introduce in Brazil as they would be anywhere. However, their content is clear enough, confirming our ability to institutionalize a high-energy democracy rather than merely to temper low-energy political institutions with extra-institutional populism. Thus, expanded free access to the media, multiplication of forms of media property and production, public financing of political campaigns, and strengthening of political parties (through a closed-list system) could have a mobilizing effect. They would be more likely to produce such an effect when combined with an impasse-breaking constitutionalism, a boost to the independent and generalized organization of civil society, and an increase in the resources and opportunities enabling ordinary people to know and defend their rights.

The institutional history of the country offered similar opportunities to organize civil society. The constitution of 1988 combined the corporatist principle of automatic unionization of all workers with the contractualist principle of complete independence of the unions from government. Such a regime favors, although it cannot guarantee, a more solidaristic union movement. It economizes upon union organization and renders more transparent the political making of industrial relations. It could be made more flexible by allowing for rights to opt out of the framework and establish alternative labor-law arrangements. Thus reformed, it would represent one possible model for the independent legal organization of civil society in domains far removed from union organization. Another model would be the combination of voluntary, contractualist organization (everyone organizes or not as he or she wills) with a special, independent branch of government. Such a branch would be designed, equipped, and elected to intervene in entrenched, localized citadels of privilege and exclusion, reshaping them to conform to the minimal standards of free social life established in law.

Who could be the agent of such a program? From where would the energy for its advancement come? How could it connect with the established classes, races, groups, and parties, and the interests they recognized as their own? In Brazil as elsewhere electoral allegiance follows no simple scheme of class interest. The plutocracy would hold out for the selective, dualism-preserving neoliberalism, and the state-impoverishing version of fiscal adjustment. The perimeter of its concerns would be the contest between internationalizing economic orthodoxy and the defense of the entrepreneurial classes against the rigors of unqualified internationalization. However, the educated and almost propertyless middle classes remain the center of gravity of the polity, the great source of opinion-making and authority in a country where the rich are immobilized by cupidity and the poor distracted by need. A democratizing program and a popular movement need to turn the anxieties and aspirations of these groups in a progressive direction.

That program and that movement would have to converge, at a later moment, with the work of a changed left. Such a left needs to free itself from the division that set it on the path of least resistance. In Brazil, as in many countries, an organized, European-style left spoke to the organized working class, established in the favored economy. It proposed concerted action and social contracts for the organized interests of the favored economy and social assistance for the inhabitants of the second economy. A populist left addressed the disorganized workers of the backward economy, promising to rescue them through social spending at any price. Neither presented a credible program for the supersession of the dualism that each, in its own way, reflected. Both expressed the economic and social division that it was their historical task to overcome.

The asymmetrical relation between political and social alliances and the diversity of plausible ways to define and defend group interests make the execution of this task possible. Political and social alliances are asymmetrical. Social or class alliances develop through politics, gaining life through the institutional changes political initiatives bring about. In this sense, class alliances presuppose party-political alliances or convergences of opinion (that is to say, among parties of opinion) in civil society. However, political alliances, according to this asymmetry thesis, do not rely

THE SEATS OF RESISTANCE

in the same way upon social alliances as prior conditions; they have the making of such alliances as part of their work.

In this work, the reforming movement exploits the duality of possible ways to define and defend group interests. Some such approaches are institutionally conservative and socially exclusive; others are institutionally transformative and socially solidaristic. By appealing to the latter against the former, the movement develops and speaks an alternative language for the articulation of group interests. It must speak such a language if it is to build a majoritarian popular coalition around a program for the overcoming of dualism and the quickening of democratic politics.

A democratizing movement that focused, however, only upon the remaking of political and economic institutions and the great problems of power and wealth while remaining disconnected from the sources of frustration, fear, and dependency in everyday life could never succeed. It could never elicit from the broad masses of ordinary men and women the sustained energy needed to counterbalance the narrowest view of their interests. Nor could it prevent the perversion of its accomplishments by the enduring strategies of association in the ordinary world of work and domesticity.

Every society provides the stage for certain hardened, recurrent ways of dealing among people. These enacted images of association translate the indeterminate idea of society into particular ways of living together. Each such image connects beliefs about the possible with beliefs about the desirable and both with practical arrangements. Each is at once a promise of happiness and a device of order.

Brazil resembles many societies throughout the world in its mixture of assimilation to the political and economic arrangements pioneered by the North Atlantic countries with the persistence of styles of association that long predated the modernizing thrust. A famous novel begins with the remark that happy families are all alike while every unhappy family is unhappy in its own way. The opposite could be said of nations. The valid residue in the idea of national culture is the obsessional promise of happiness that each of them enshrines: a route to the fulfillment and reconciliation of our most deeply felt desires within everyday life.

In Brazil as in the United States, we find two voices of a New World promise of happiness: a promise to raise up human life to the exuberance of nature itself while breaking down the hierarchies and privileges that keep people distant from one another. A society of originals whose enhanced powers and self-possession enable them to accept one another more fully is the aim of this American and Brazilian dream. Translated into another, more universal vocabulary, this longing represents one form of the effort to reconcile a pagan ambition of greatness with a Christian idea of tenderness, purging the former of its impulse toward masterfulness and the latter of its knack for resentment. Thus, empowerment and solidarity can come more fully together.

In every society, however, this visionary impulse within practical culture remains imprisoned within the compulsive strategies of association that weaken its power and besmirch its meaning. These strategies define the tribute that visionary aspiration must pay to humdrum reality, turning the one into a dreamlike and empty evasion of the other.

In Brazil, as in many countries, a logic of patrons and clients continued to mark much of social life. This logic combined power, exchange, and allegiance in the same dealings. The sentimentalization of unequal exchange was its most characteristic move. No democratizing program could succeed in such a circumstance unless it lifted the burden of this habit and drew upon the energy generated by its disruption.

The remaking of political and economic institutions can contribute to this result. However, it cannot guarantee its achievement. More help can come from a strengthening of people's capacity to know and to defend their rights, substituting energy-giving action for immobilizing resentment and hopelessness. Among the tools of such a strengthening would be the proliferation of legal-aid centers, the development of judicial remedies for the rapid enforcement of rights, and the formation of a special branch of government, apart from the judiciary, charged with the work of localized and reconstructive intervention. It would be the task of such a branch of government to intervene in organizations and practices corrupted by varieties of exclusion or subjugation that the victims were powerless to escape or correct by the forms of political and economic action ordinarily available to them.

Even when broadened, however, by the strengthening of rights-demanding capacity, the politics of institutional change remains incomplete. It suffices neither to generate the energy for its own movement nor to ensure the integrity of its own work. Other forms of action and vision must complement and overtake its efforts if people are to break up the hardened strategies of association in everyday life. Consider race as one vital site of conflict over the structure of social relations.

Brazil is a racially mixed society that has had trouble acknowledging its own racism. In the variety and subtlety of its forms, this racism imposes a formidable restraint upon the advance of democratic experimentalism. In so doing, it also exemplifies the sentimentalization of unequal exchange – the transposition of subjugation and exclusion into blindness and favor – recurring in everyday life throughout the country. The nature of the problem and the route to its solution stand out when contrasted with the history of racial conflict and racial redress in the United States.

In each of these two societies, history and circumstance favor a response to racial oppression that simultaneously tempers, conceals, and preserves such oppression. In each of them, a historical script gives a semblance of self-evidence and authority to a particular way of dealing with racial division and injustice. Democratic experimentalism requires us to break with the response recommended by the script.

American politics has often confronted racial prejudice and subjugation directly. Given a history that includes the Civil War and the "one-drop" rule (one drop of negro blood makes you black), there was no way to avoid it. However, ever since the abandonment of the program of the Freedmen's Bureau in the final years of the Reconstruction period, Americans have come to deal with the racial problem as if it were separable from the problems of class hierarchy and economic reconstruction. Their insight is that racial divisions are irreducible to class divisions and that democracy, however experimentalist, guarantees no relief from racial hatred and injustice. Their illusion is that they can deal with racial suffering without undertaking economic reconstruction.

So, for example, progressive orthodoxy insists upon separating the redress of racial injustice (as in "affirmative action") from any attempt to moderate the injuries of class. Progressives fear that any concession to economic or class concerns in the design of programs for the redress of racial discrimination would dilute what is already an embattled cause, exposing it to danger and destruction. As a result, the rules of racial correction benefit least those who stand in greatest need of help: less the underclass than the organized working class, less the organized working class than the professional and business class. Moreover, it aggravates within the working class the very divisions and animosities that a progressivism bent upon institutional change requires.

An alternative regime for the redress of racial injustice, set within the broader context of democratizing institutional change, distinguishes clearly between the goal of combatting racial discrimination and the commitment to rescue people from an entrenched underclass. It offers heightened scrutiny, even criminal sanctions, against racial discrimination. It backs this scrutiny up with enforced coexistence and collaboration in schools, neighborhoods, and workplaces.

A program of active preferment in employment and schooling, through preferential admissions, has been the response to the poisonous combination of racial and class injustice that comes to a head in the situation of a racially stigmatized underclass. However, such a policy should not be narrowly based. If it is, its benefits will be largely captured by those who need it least – the elites of the racially favored groups – for example, the black and latino professional and business class in the United States. The principle should be active preferment when factors of disadvantage – including class and race – combine in the situation of particular individuals, condemning them to an entrenched disadvantage from which they cannot escape, without extraordinary talent or good fortune, by the ordinary forms of economic and political action available to them. For it is the combination of sources of exclusion and disadvantage that is most likely to overwhelm individuals, cheating them out of a chance to take the gospel of equal opportunity at its word.

Institutionally conservative (American) social democrats will object to the ambition of such a program. They will protest: If even our modest objectives (such as expanded child support and full-employment economic policies) are hard to get accepted, how much more inaccessible will such a reconstructive program be. Their position, however, suffers from a paradox of technocratic minimalism. To understand this paradox is to see the limits of this criticism.

No possible politics corresponds to the program of such social democrats. For a demobilized polity – one that despairs of the powers and possibilities of politics and collective action – what they want is too much: sacrifices for other people's children and a belated Keynesianism. Such a Keynesianism tries to democratize consumption without knowing how to reorganize production. However, for a quickened politics and an organized society, what they propose is too little. Having risen up against injury, no popular majority would rest content with a little beneficence for the downtrodden; it would demand a changed life for everyone, beginning with a change in the relation of government to society. No wonder this conventional response represents the program of a socially concerned technocratic elite. It lacks a footing in any real popular political movement.

We need a plan that can harness the energy produced by conflict over racial oppression to the democratic cause rather than allowing racial conflict to remain one more impediment to the advancement of democracy. In remaking along lines such as those described here their regime of redress for racial injustice, Americans would therefore need to keep in mind two vital characteristics of a progressive alternative. It must be productivist rather than merely distributivist, extending economic vanguard-ism beyond the territory of the present economic vanguard. It must also rely upon the energizing and enabling effect of institutional innovations directed to the quickening of politics and the organization of society. A transracial popular alliance would be, in American politics, both the agent and the product of such an institutional program, with its redesigned scheme of racial correction and its larger initiatives of political and economic reconstruction.

Only politics – the politics of movements of opinion in civil society as well as the politics of parties seeking governmental power – can break the circle of lowered expectations, initiating the programs and the alliances as twin faces of the same project.

Among the habits and illusions with which Americans have to break to achieve this result are the attitudes toward racial justice their history has suggested to them. They need to resurrect and reinvent the old post-Civil War program of the Freedmen's Bureau, generalizing the institutional experimentalism it exempli-fied. Freedom from the historical script may be part of the desired outcome; it is also part of the necessary condition. It must be a mental event before it can become an institutional possession.

Brazilians also have a history-given script and continue to think and to act prompted by its cues. In some ways, their problem is the inverse of the problem of the Americans, for they fail to recognize the practical and spiritual burden racial subjugation imposes upon their national future. One of the formative experiences of millions of middle-class Brazilian men continues to be the oppression they exercise over colored female servants. Blocked and powerless in so many aspects of their lives, these men enjoy here an experience of sham power. Their immediate victims feel themselves to live in a country that does not belong to them, and they are right. The paralyzing sense of disempowerment finds expression, but not correction, in popular culture.

The generalization of intermarriage among the working classes in most regions of Brazil destroys the factual basis for anything like the American "one-drop" rule. The preservation of a self-conscious whiteness among the propertied and educated classes turns the color line into a major and distinct dimension of class hierarchy, robbing ordinary people of respect even as it denies them opportunity. However, the micro-social logic of patron–client relations, with its characteristic metamorphosis of power into favor, dims this brutal reality in people's minds, sowing confusion and deception in the midst of oppression.

For the cause of democratic experimentalism to advance in Brazil, Brazilians need to see this reality for what it is without succumbing to the American mistake of disconnecting racial redress from economic transformation. Thus, a scheme for the redress of racial injustice in Brazil also needs to put alongside a heightened vigilance against individualized discrimination an insistence upon combining rectification by class with rectification by race. Brazilians need to take membership in the downtrodden race as a central form of disadvantage, invented by society but marked upon the human body, and recalcitrant to the barrier-breaking work of democratic experimentalism. Then, they too can treat the combination of forms of class, racial, or other disadvantages as a trigger for active preferment in schooling and employment.

Such a movement in the realm of rights and arrangements would remain weak unless completed by the assertion of an idea: the idea of the development of a distinct national culture by a people of mixed race. That idea can in turn gain reality only by being enacted in distinct institutions: not as a stable customary way of life, according to the old, tangible conception of national identities, but rather as a sustained power of collective self-reinvention, in the spirit of democratic experimentalism.

The destiny of the racial difference in a democracy is irrelevance, an irrelevance qualified only by the political power of memory, just as the destiny of the national principle in a world of democracies is to become a basis for moral specialization within humankind. The work of the nations is to develop in different directions the moral powers and possibilities of humanity, realizing distinct forms of life in different institutional settings. Civilizations must live in their own institutional homes.

The differences we shall make should count for much more than the differences we have inherited or now embody. We cannot use the differences of the past to build the differences of the future – use them and outgrow them – until we have destroyed in our minds their use as denials of our power, or our need, to remake the practical arrangements of society. Nowhere is the subtle relation between institutional remaking and the reimagination of collective identities more manifest – or more important – than in the struggle over the content and consequence of racial and national differences.

A PROGRESSIVE
ALTERNATIVE

Two stages of an alternative

What are the main lines of an alternative to neoliberalism that would be faithful to the spirit of democratic experimentalism? How do we develop such an alternative out of the institutional and ideological materials already at hand? How can we move it forward in ways that increase its attractions as a means for the solution of the practical problems of working people and national economies? How can we harness the constructive force of institutional innovation while holding fast to the essential guarantee of political realism: that no matter how far its ultimate reach may extend, every cumulative sequence of reforms begins in the here and now, through steps of transition we can imagine and enact?

In outlining this alternative, I have in mind both richer and poorer countries. The United States and Brazil will be frequent points of reference, sometimes explicit, more often implicit. The argument goes forward on the assumption of the chain of analogies binding the whole world together. The differences in national circumstance justifying differences in programmatic response do not correspond in any simple way to differing levels of wealth.

Whatever the national setting in which we imagine democratizing alternatives to neoliberalism to be realized, such alternatives will require for their development the political promotion of an enlarged popular alliance. Institutional programs and social alliances are always just the reverse side of each other, each lending the other reality and supplying the conditions on which the other may advance. For a social (or, more particularly, a class) alliance to become more than a merely tactical partnership, it must build upon practices and institutions enabling more inclusive solidarities of interest and identity to develop. A logic of group interests and group identities is never more stable, or more transparent, than the institutional arrangements it presupposes. A broadened popular alliance takes for granted the cumulative institutional changes that would cement its defining solidarities, giving them the tangible basis and the staying power they would otherwise lack. The social alliance depends upon the program, the strategy, and the combination of political forces through which the strategy works. The social alliance becomes real first through the struggle over the use of power – especially governmental power – to change society. The program, however, does not presuppose the social alliance in the same way, as an indispensable tool or precondition. It takes the making of the social alliance over time to be a core part of its work.

Imagine this progressive alternative to develop in two great stages. Call these stages the early program and the later program. The later program – realizing the transformative and democratizing promise of the alternative to neoliberalism – repairs the rift between vanguard and rearguard and quickens democratic experimentalism in each major sphere of social life. To accomplish these goals, it must innovate, clearly and decisively, in the repertory of available institutional ideas and arrangements. The early program, by contrast, stays close to established institutions. It nevertheless deals with the practical problems of large numbers of ordinary people in ways strengthening the openness of society to institutional innovation. In particular, the early program satisfies three sets of conditions that we need to fulfill if we are later to overcome the division between vanguard and rearguard, between insiders and outsiders.

The first enabling condition to be satisfied during the first stage of the alternative is economic. We must raise the level of public and private saving and develop institutional arrangements that channel much of saving into productive investment and save it from being squandered in the financial casino. A high level of saving means something above thirty percent, as has been characteristic of the North East Asian economies for much of the postwar period, and, in recent years, of China, rather than below twenty percent, as has been typical of the major Latin American economies. A high level of savings counts, to begin with, as a prop to economic growth. It moderates the need to pay court to foreign capital in the hope of making up for the deficiencies of foreign saving. This moderation is important for two reasons. Powerful constraints continue to impede the worldwide mobility of capital. Moreover, foreign capital is most likely to be useful and patient when it is least anxiously needed.

The relative importance of public saving within the aggregate of national saving increases as we come to value public investment in people. Later on, it will be needed to support the public initiatives that would bring the productive vanguard and the productive rearguard together.

The raising of the saving level matters, as well, in a more subtle way. There is no simple contrast between improved productive efficiency and a one-shot increase of inputs − of capital, labor, or technology − available for investment. An increased saving rate, sustained over a long time, creates an opportunity for persistent organizational innovation: innovation in the arrangements for public and private saving as well as innovation in the arrangements channeling saving toward productive investment. As soon as we begin to address the raising of the saving level as a task rather than as the expression of economic forces and cultural habits beyond our control, we are driven to ask how saving can become productive investment.

An effective alternative to neoliberalism must prove itself by its success at preventing the massive wastage of resources, time, and energy in the trading of speculative market positions. It must turn the sacrifices of deferred consumption to practical use. It must be a productivist rather than a compensatory program. For that very reason, we cannot mistake it for the commitment to compensatory tax-and-transfer that has remained the major theme of institutionally conservative social democracy, and become a minor theme of neoliberalism itself.

The second condition to be satisfied during the first stage in the life of the alternative is political. Neoliberalism wants severely to restrict the range of governmental action. It wants a state that does a small number of things well, renouncing productive activities in favor of regulatory vigilance and redistributive concern. However, the line separating production from regulation and compensation is the wrong place at which to set the limit of governmental activity. With government under such a constraint, society will find it harder to escape the evolutionary fatalism of established comparative advantage, the social burden of entrenched dualism, and the inhibiting reduction of markets and market-driven activity to a single property regime. Decentralization and experimentalism must count for more than the rigid contrasts between public and private, regulation and production.

Government must serve the triple goal of helping to develop the vanguard, of moderating the division between vanguard and rearguard, and of sustaining the practices of collective learning that make wealth possible and freedom real. A state with such a charge should be capable of doing precisely what neoliberalism would have government forswear: association between government and business, or between public and private enterprise, in production.

The familiar models of such arrangements of strategic coordination, as we have seen them, for example, in the political economy of the North East Asian economies, have emphasized collaboration between a centralized bureaucratic apparatus and the firms representing a productive vanguard. Under the impulse of democratic experimentalism we would have to underscore the decentralized character of such a partnership. We would need to develop the entities, intermediate between government and the firm, between the public and the private, that would make such decentralization effective. We could then start to create the institutional means with which to reach the rearguard as well as the vanguard. We would have to begin this work knowing that it would come into its own in the later program, when we innovate more decisively in the institutional forms of the market and democracy, and accept, as a result, more conflict and controversy.

A state able to act in such ways must be hard: the defining mark of its hardness is that, seated in a society still marked by resilient class divisions, it can nevertheless formulate and implement policy with a large measure of independence from moneyed elites. Authoritarianism may serve as a shortcut to the hardness of the hard state. However, an authoritarian state buys its hardness at too high a cost – too high a cost in the sacrifice of experimental openness as well as of political freedom – if it rests upon the suppression of the independent self-organization of civil society. Such an authoritarian hard state will, for example, have trouble decentralizing the practice of strategic coordination between government and business in trade and industrial policy; it will be tempted to arrogate power to a centralized bureaucracy. This bureaucracy will in turn seek to reach an understanding with a favored caste of business insiders. Just as the first stage of the alternative can only begin to develop the institutionalized forms of a decentralized partnership between government and business, so too it can only begin to give institutional content to the idea of a democratized hard state. To develop both is a large part of the work of the later program in its more institutionally ambitious afterlife.

The third enabling condition the early program must try to satisfy is cultural rather than political or economic. Defined in the broadest sense, it is the development of productive capability and critical capacity in the individual. Neither that capability nor this capacity should depend upon growing up in the right family or holding a job in the productive vanguard, two elements of good luck closely linked in contemporary class societies. Both vanguardist economic practices and civic life in a deepened democracy require the diffusion of generic capacities: learning to learn on a continuing basis, to analyze and to recombine. Specialized conceptual or practical skills are secondary and relative. Under the conditions of productive and democratic experimentalism, they become, increasingly, ephemeral and circumstantial variations on more lasting and generic capabilities. The productive vanguards of the established democracies sustain these qualities within the limits of their own domains and ambitions: only so much practical experimentalism as suits their tangible interests.

A raising of the level of social investment in education – the education of children and the continuing education of adults – is the simplest and most direct expression of this commitment. The commitment, however, is merely the gateway to two other tasks the alternative must begin to carry out early in its life. The first is the creation of a school equipping the child with the instruments of resistance to social and historical circumstance. The second is the strengthening in society of an idea of possible greatness – the greatness of ordinary men and women and the greatness of humanity. To this end, the public culture should help nourish a climate of opinion and experience in which people are more readily able to reimagine their relations to one another and to act upon what they have imagined.

In its early work, the progressive alternative must try to fulfill these economic, political, and cultural conditions with a minimum of institutional innovation. Because it may require no immediate and radical redistribution of wealth and power, it can hope to command widespread support. In many countries, it can serve as the program of an inclusive social and political alliance including large parts of the propertied and educated classes and of the national entrepreneurs. Moreover, it need not necessarily result in the second, institutionally inventive and frankly antidualistic stage later described.

Like any course of connected and cumulative reforms, the early program has alternative futures. The high-energy democracy and democratized market economy I later describe represents one such future. However, there is also an institutionally conservative sequel. Such a sequel trusts to the gradual incorporation of economic insiders rather than to the deliberate subversion of dualism. It tolerates a low level of participation in politics rather than favoring the acceleration of transformative politics and the heightening of popular energy in political and associational life.

This plurality of futures may help win friends for the progressive alternative as it begins its work. The early program may gain the support of those who would turn against the more uprooting experiments of the later program. The course of political conflict and persuasion under the early program will help determine the chances for advancing its more radical sequel.

The early program: taxation, saving, and investment

Taxation redesigned. The level of national saving is not a cultural destiny. Like everything else in social life, it responds to practical arrangements. Two sets of such arrangements matter across a broad range of contemporary societies, rich and poor alike: the tax system and the pension or social-insurance scheme. Each such set of arrangements can take a form that helps sustain a high level of national saving in both governmental and private hands. Each can be designed to hold open the opportunity for the more radical redistributive and reconstructive initiatives of the later program. Government must have the resources with which to invest in people and infrastructure and to fund the decentralized productive partnerships with business to be described later. The society must have the means with which to expand its capital stock, including its stock of the technologies enabling it to escape from the dead-end of diminishing marginal returns. Both state and society must have the freedom to develop a national political economy without depending upon the whims of foreign speculative capital or the dogmas of the international economic organizations.

Consider first the tax system. An important lesson of comparative experience in taxation is that under all conditions redistribution through major institutional change trumps redistribution through public spending. Another important lesson is that under the conditions of economically unequal and politically demobilized societies redistribution through public spending trumps redistribution through progressive taxation. Among the rich industrial democracies, the one with the most progressive tax system on paper – the United States – is also the one with the lowest tax yield and the most extreme inequality. In the presence of massive inequality and scant investment in people – especially in children – the most urgent concern becomes to raise the level of public spending. To raise it in a sustainable way we must increase the tax yield. The best way to increase it is to give a central role in the early program to the taxation of consumption.

At the outset we should prefer to tax consumption by an indirect and flat tax rather than a direct and progressive levy. (Taxation is indirect when it falls on transactions and direct when it falls on the income, consumption, or asset accounts of individuals. To be progressive, taxation must ordinarily be direct, although direct taxation may be flat rather than progressive.) The direct taxation of consumption taxes the difference between what individuals earn, either as wages or as returns to capital, and what they save and invest. Unlike the indirect taxation of consumption, the direct taxation of consumption lends itself to progressivity.

Not only may we exempt people with the lowest consumption accounts; we may also impose, beyond the threshold at which the direct tax begins to apply, a steeply progressive scale. At the upper reaches of this scale, the tax rate may run, as Kaldor proposed, into multiples of one hundred percent. For example, the taxpayer may pay, as personal consumption tax, four dollars to the government for every dollar he spends.

The moral logic of the taxation of consumption lies in its ability straightforwardly to reach the individual appropriation of social resources: the extent to which individuals spend resources on themselves rather than preserving them, although under their own control, for the future. This translation of social resources into individual consumption, sustaining a hierarchy of living standards, is one of the two great and permanent objects of taxation. The other target of taxation is the accumulation of economic power. The taxation of income reaches both these aims obliquely, and unjustly equates compensation for labor with returns to capital.

There is, however, a more immediate and practical reason to give pride of place to the taxation of consumption when we are chiefly concerned to raise the tax yield and the level of public spending. In every contemporary society taxation appears as a burden upon saving and investment; hence, upon the needs of production. This practical restraint finds a voice in the prestigious discourse of the tension between equity and efficiency: compensatory redistribution exacts a cost. The reluctance to pay for it provides a built-in inhibition against the radicalization of tax-and-transfer as a means for the overcoming of the division between advanced and backward sectors of the economy. A shift to consumption-based taxation moderates the tension between taxation and growth, particularly if a substantial part of the tax yield goes into public investment in people, physical plant, and business initiatives yielding productive benefits.

Progressives all over the world resist as regressive a reliance upon consumption taxes in general, and upon the flat taxation of consumption in particular: the less people earn, the more of what they earn they consume. The resistance, however, is misguided. We may need to abandon progressivity for the sake of progressivity, the better to assert it, more effectively, later on.

There are two ways to explain, in the circumstances of relatively unequal and depoliticized societies, the revenue–generating advantage enjoyed by the indirect taxation of consumption. The first and most basic explanation is the asymmetrical effect of redistribution through progressive taxation and redistribution through public spending, funded by a comprehensive flat–rate value–added tax (the exemplary form of the indirect taxation of consumption), upon established economic incentives and arrangements. Direct and progressive taxation, particularly if it is taxation of income or wealth, squarely reaches individual behavior. Public spending, financed through the relatively neutral device of the comprehensive flat–rate value–added tax, also influences arrangements and incentives, but more obliquely (by shifting the balance between public and private resources and responsibilities). This indirect effect becomes significant only at a higher threshold. Thus, countries like France and Denmark that have relied heavily upon the indirect taxation of consumption have also been able to achieve very high tax yields, approaching fifty percent of GDP, with limited effects upon the character and motivation of ordinary economic behavior.

The second reason for the asymmetrical effect is more troubling. The indirect taxation of consumption is less transparent than the direct taxation of consumption, income, or wealth. It therefore lends itself to collective deception and self-deception. The tax may be more willingly paid when its payment is less obvious. The taxpayers may not understand it or, understanding it in principle, they may not experience it in the flesh. The benefit of tolerance is at the same time a detriment to deliberative self-consciousness. The comprehensive flat–rate value–added tax may achieve such a benefit and such a detriment. So may, even more effectively, although with greater economic cost, a "crazy quilt" of indirect taxes: each takes a little bit, and their cumulative effect remains obscure. The cost to the deliberative integrity of democratic institutions is real. However, the more unequal the society, the more modest the relative significance of this cost becomes. For with inequality of circumstance, and therefore also of information, come many burdens upon deliberative capability. We must reach as quickly as possible the position in which the conflicts among the conditions of deliberative integrity become less urgent. To that end, we need to maintain a high level of public spending and to finance over time the social and productive activities of government in a deepened, high-energy democracy. Transparency by itself is more than a luxury and less than an absolute.

The early form of the progressive alternative should therefore assign a central role to the comprehensive, flat-rate value-added tax, as the most neutral form of the indirect taxation of consumption. We should count on a high rate, in the neighborhood, for example, of thirty percent. Within the structure of a federal state, the funds produced by such a tax may be distributed among the entities composing the federation. If there are great inequalities between rich and poor states within the federal union, we may imagine this money to be distributed according to a formula generated by the combination of two countervailing criteria: distribution according to the contribution each state or municipality makes to the tax take (that is, to the value added) and distribution according to the inverse of per capita income multiplied by population.

Two sets of direct and progressive taxes would supplement, in this early system, the comprehensive flat-rate value added tax. Each would hit one of the two principal targets of progressive taxation: the hierarchy of living standards and the accumulation of economic power.

The direct and progressive taxation of personal consumption would reach the individual appropriation of social resources. Such a tax would fall upon the difference between total income (including returns to capital) and total saving for investment. There would be an exemption beneath one threshold (accompanied, if governmental resources permitted, by a negative tax, guaranteeing minimal income, normally conditioned upon demonstrated willingness to train and work) and sharply progressive rates above another threshold. Funds not demonstrably converted into legitimate saving and investment would count as if they had been spent, bearing the full burden of the tax.

The second set of taxes – taxes on wealth – would address the accumulation of economic power. In principle, the taxation of personal consumption deals more effectively and more completely with the hierarchy of living standards than the taxation of wealth deals with the build-up of economic power. Changes in the property regime and, more broadly, in the institutional context of production and exchange must achieve what fiscal redistribution alone is powerless to accomplish. There is nevertheless one form of economic inequality that is particularly susceptible to fiscal correction. It is the form most destructive of democratic experimentalism: the hereditary transmission of property, especially when combined with the differential transmission of educational advantage.

It has been calculated that in the United States close to half of all assets held by people under the age of fifty can be imputed to inheritance or, more commonly, to anticipated inheritance by gifts *inter vivos*. The families in which the transmission of property by gift and inheritance is substantial are on the whole the same families able to offer their children a real education – in the family and in the school. The combination of economic and educational advantage is overwhelming, and gives countries like the United States and Brazil their character of relatively rigid class hierarchies.

Economic circumstance, the distinctive form of power or powerlessness at work, and the special consciousness of personal and social possibility and constraint join to shape a class. There are four main social classes in the United States (and in most of the other rich industrial countries): a professional–business class, a class of smallscale independent business people and semi-independent technicians or lower-level professionals, a working class (with both a white-collar and a blue-collar component), and an underclass. The class structure of the United States has been so rigid that no massive and sustained form of class mobility has occurred there over the last hundred years save one: the children of farmhands and blue-collar workers have, in large numbers, become white-collar workers, moving from one department of the working class to another.

Other industrial democracies have from time to time seen major episodes of change in their class systems but only as a result of institutional innovations established through political action. The radical diminishment of the hereditary transmission of property will not, by itself, destroy class hierarchy; more important is the affirmative development of social inheritance, guaranteeing that each individual inherit from society the capability-forming and opportunity-creating resources the great majority of individuals are unable, in present societies, to inherit from their parents. The decisive taxation of gifts and estates is nevertheless important both because it destroys privilege and because it may help finance equality.

Two practical constraints do much to define the real nature of contemporary market societies. Yet we cannot infer either of these constraints from the abstract conception of a market economy. One is the right of inheritance, denying the principle of equal opportunity. The other is the refusal to labor (but its bestowal upon capital) of the right to cross national frontiers, denying the principle of universal free trade. Each of these denials must therefore find excuses in practical imperatives. However, the force of such practical imperatives depends upon our institutional assumptions: our assumptions about the institutions that exist and the ones we can establish.

The taxation of gifts and estates is the most important form of the taxation of wealth. Its mission is to weaken the hold that the accidents of economic inheritance have upon the life chances of individuals. It would help fund what in a more democratized society should largely replace family inheritance: the inheritance by every individual of a stock of capability-sustaining resources through the device of the social-endowment accounts described elsewhere in this book.

Beyond a certain level of progressivity, the taxation of inheritance may indeed exact a heavy cost in the weakening of the motivation to work, save, and invest. We cannot quantify this cost beforehand, for its nature and scope depend upon the combined influence of all the institutional and cultural circumstances of a society. We must find out how great the cost is, and decide, through a collective choice rather than as the consequence of an institutional fate, how much, by way of inequality through inheritance, we are willing to tolerate in order to avoid it. Moreover, any number of practical compromises can lower this price while giving some weight to the desire of parents to provide for their children. The simplest of such compromises would be an estate-tax favor given to inheritance in the first generation, with the higher tax rate applied to the second-generation inheritance of the equivalent funds. The resulting incentive to consume would find its proper correction and penalty in the steeply progressive tax on the consumption of each taxpayer.

In the first stage of the alternative to neoliberalism the two sets of direct, redistributive taxes would have a role subsidiary to the indirect taxation of consumption. In the second, more egalitarian and democratizing phase they would begin to take the center stage. The comprehensive flat-rate value-added tax or its equivalents would now become a background guarantee of adequate revenue. With the moderation of economic inequalities, the deepening of political engagement, and the broadening of access to productive resources and investment decisions, we may reasonably hope to soften the tension between the need to ensure an adequate level of redistributive public spending and the desire to respect distributive equity in taxation. Having renounced progressivity for the sake of progressivity, we could once again embrace it without fear of perverse consequence.

In the full-fledged version of a democratizing tax system, we may want to secure a set of loose connections between each of the three major types of tax and its principal social use and justification. The progressive personal consumption tax would fund the core operations of government. We would thus link the interest of the political-bureaucratic apparatus with the advance of redistributive taxation. We would also emphasize the stake of democratic government in the avoidance of extreme inequalities of condition. The comprehensive, flat-rate value-added tax, ever the least distortionary and most reliable of taxes, would finance the social funds and support centers soon to be described as agents of a decentralized partnership between business and government. In this way this tax would be understood to impose a levy on consumption for the sake of production. The forced saving it represents would turn, directly, into productive investment. The gift and estate taxes, as the most important part of wealth taxation, would finance the social inheritance (through social-endowment accounts) replacing family inheritance.

These loose connections are neither idle symmetries nor tight and inhibiting linkages. They invoke and support a changed way of understanding the proper relations among individual enrichment, governmental responsibility, and social solidarity. To develop over time, and to command voluntary compliance, a system of public finance needs to have roots in the popular imagination of the practical, the meaningful, and the just. The connections help to grow the roots.

Pension reform. If the tax system serves to heighten the level of public and private saving, generating resources that can then be mobilized for productive investment and redistributive spending, the reform of pensions and social insurance provides an opportunity to ensure an adequate level of saving – adequate for social as well as family needs – while reorganizing the relation of saving to production. To understand the problem and the possibilities, we can best begin with the familiar and falsely exhaustive contrast between defined-contribution and defined-benefit systems.

Defined-benefit systems – still the vast majority of public-pension schemes throughout the world – impose a schedule of contributions from workers and employers. Although the resulting pension may take this contribution into account, no one-to-one relation exists between what workers or their employers put in and what, at the end, workers get out. Thus, the system allows for redistribution. By the same token, however, it creates a risk of insolvency; more may be promised, and entrenched as social right, than has collectively been saved.

Defined-contribution systems give workers what they and their employers put into each worker's pension account. The case for the private administration of these pension accounts will therefore grow. A worldwide movement of ideas, closely connected with neoliberalism, wants to embrace this defined-contribution system, supporting it with fiscal favors. It wants to use the redistributive public-pension scheme as a residual device to rescue the least lucky and the most improvident from destitution.

Such a system, however, suffers from two defects. The first flaw is that it fails to require, although it may favor, a high level of private saving. A public effort to raise and organize private saving creates an opportunity to establish institutions, like those described below, easing the passage of social saving into productive investment. The second weakness is that, by separating the pension entitlements of the poor from the pension treatment of the general population, it makes it easier to abandon the poor to their fate. More generally, it fails to exploit the imaginative ambiguity of the defined-benefit systems. These systems have a hybrid character. They combine a saving and insurance contract, helping individuals provide for themselves and their families over a lifetime. As a partial recognition of social inheritance, they assure everyone a collective legacy of elementary economic safeguards and opportunities. The universalization of defined-contribution schemes resolves this ambiguity in favor of the saving-contract idea. It is possible, however, to resolve it in favor of social inheritance, taking the pension scheme as the fragmentary expression of the more general commitment to let everyone inherit from society rather than allowing a few to inherit from their parents. The device of the social-endowment accounts, coming into prominence in the later, more radical development of this progressive alternative, would make universal in scope the principle of social inheritance that a reformed pension system anticipates.

Imagine all public and private pension or social-insurance schemes unified. Middle-income pension savers and their employers pay into their funds, neither gaining nor losing. However, low-income workers receive increments to their social-assurance accounts from the accumulations of high-wage savers.

Part of the moneys from all three categories goes into social-investment funds, which enjoy a large measure of managerial independence. These funds are mandated to engage in public venture-capital operations, and to deal with the problem of heightened risk by the standard techniques of diversification. We design their arrangements to free them from short-termism and to tap more fully than present arrangements do the productive potential of saving. We nevertheless expect them to make a gain and hold them to standards of success, imposed by both the insured (who may opt out of them) and the governments (who establish and regulate them).

It is both futile and dangerous to sustain a high level of public and private saving unless the institutional means exist with which to transform saving into productive investment. If we achieve the former without the latter, we risk creating a Keynesian-style slump. The attempt to develop the institutional means for tapping the underutilized investment potential soon becomes entangled with another defining concern of the early alternative to neoliberalism: the development of decentralized and experimental forms of the partnership between government and business.

Saving and production. A high level of saving is vital to the success of a progressive alternative. In today's conditions, high saving means something above fifteen percent of GDP for a comparatively rich economy and above thirty percent for a developing country. Such a high level of saving may easily be squandered. More commonly, it may be used to finance a one-time increase in the inputs of production rather than a sustained rise in productivity. It is nevertheless hard to see how a practical alternative can dispense with such a heightened saving level.

Low saving means dependence upon foreign money. Such dependence – experience has demonstrated – comes burdened with many conditions dangerous to both democracy and prosperity. Thus, the real-world, selective brand of neoliberalism reigning in many parts of the world has been regularly accompanied by reliance upon capital inflows to sustain both current-account deficits and exchange-rate anchors of the currency. From such reliance comes a need to to reward foreign capital with high real rates of interest, depressing domestic growth and worsening the situation of public finance.

Foreign capital, however, is the more likely to be useful the less a country depends upon it. When high rewards must be paid for immediate funds, the consequence has regularly been to place a crushing burden upon the treasury; through its service of the public debt, the government becomes the first victim of high interest rates. Lasting damage may be done to the conditions of economic growth through the strangling of productive investment and the destruction of businesses unable to rely upon retained earnings.

Meanwhile, the stage is set for speculative runs on the currency. What begins as a financial commotion ends as a setback to the real economy: the level of economic activity and real incomes begins to decline. When, by contrast, hunger for foreign capital remains moderate, the beneficial effects of foreign investment more easily prevail, and its costs are kept in check. Long-term investment in productive capacity is then more likely to predominate over short-term portfolio investment.

To be sure, these paradoxical and perverse effects of dependence upon foreign capital would be less likely to take hold if capital flowed freely though the world rather than continuing, in overwhelming proportion, to stay at home. At the end of the twentieth century, capital remained in some ways less global than it had been at the end of the nineteenth century. The relatively small percentage of capital that did cross national frontiers exerted an influence out of all proportion to its size.

The raising of the level of national saving is not only a need; it is also an opportunity. Some of the devices supportive of an increase in the saving level create one more setting in which to reform the institutional arrangements of the market economy. In providing some of the resources for growth, we also establish some of the arrangements for democracy.

Moreover, it is not enough to raise the level of saving; we must also tighten the link between saving and investment. For one thing, saving and investment are not the same thing. Saving is merely the economic means; investment is the economic end. Saving will not automatically become investment, and if it fails to be invested it may become part of the problem rather than part of the solution. For another thing, investment opportunities help determine the level of saving. There is a reciprocal relation between saving for investment and investment in production; the causal arrow goes in both directions.

A flaw in the traditional form of the market economy is the weakeness of the link it establishes between saving and production. The dominant form of economic analysis today makes it hard to address this link, and to imagine it loosened or tightened by different institutional arrangements. To the extent the market allocation of resources operates, it will, according to this analysis, direct resources to whatever uses are most productive. To the extent the market allocation of resources fails to work, we must, according to this same view, either lift the restrictions inhibiting it or willingly accept these restrictions for the sake of their social uses.

The key premise of this reasoning, as of so much else in conventional economics, is the unwarranted identification of the abstract idea of a market economy with a particular, contingent set of market arrangements. A consequence of this identification is the denial of the possible existence of alternative forms of the market economy. Such differences would include, as one of their many features, different ways of organizing the relation between saving and production. Thus, what the standard view wants to discard as a matter of definition turns out, on closer inspection, to be a problem of fact. We must rescue the unsolved riddles and the suppressed possibilities of the real economy from a view that would trivialize and suppress them.

In the 1930s and 1940s a lively debate took place among some of the most distinguished economic theorists (Hayek, Keynes, and Kalečki among them) about the dissipation of the productive potential of saving. The disappearance of this debate reflects the force of two connected developments: the failure of economic theory to make room for the institutional imagination and the narrowing of institutional conflicts and experiments in the actual world of politics. We must now force theory to compensate for the defects of history rather than allowing theory to echo and magnify them.

In the generality of contemporary economies, rich and poor, businesses of all sizes finance an average of eighty percent of their operations through retained earnings. This rate remains about the same in economies, like the German, celebrated for the close relations between banks and firms as in economies, like the British, where companies are said to contend with the short-termism of distant institutional investors. Thus, the production system is largely self-financing.

The vast pool of resources assembled in the banks and stock markets has an oblique and episodic relation to the financing of production. Initial public offerings – the subscription of new stock by investors in the stock market – make up the episodic part of the relation. They represent an insubstantial part of market activity in contemporary stock markets. Venture capital – investment in start-up firms, typically with an equity stake – amounts to an even smaller fraction of total investment, and in many rich economies it barely exists in any organized form.

Outside initial public offerings and venture capital, the vast proportion of financial activity makes at best an indirect contribution to the funding of production. Finance may establish in the equity markets a valuation benchmark helping firms finance their activities through bank debt. It may also create a market in corporate control, making it easier for entrepreneurs to take over firms they hope to reorganize and run more efficiently. These indirect contributions of finance to production are real. They are also, however, limited.

Much of the activity of finance exhausts itself in an exchange of positions, with the real world of production and innovation reduced to being more the pretext than the target. To say that, short of market failure, this peculiar way of shaping the relation of saving to production represents all that one could reasonably want or expect is to put an institutional dogma in the place of an empirical conundrum. After all, the institutions that play a central role in the established approach to the linkage of saving and production – the banks and stock markets of today's economies – represent a small set of variations on a limited range of institutional solutions fashioned in the modern history of the North Atlantic democracies.

Here, as always, the real question is: What are the alternatives? How can we reform the institutional context of the connection between saving and production to raise the level of internal saving while tightening the connection? If this question has a forward-looking answer, the complaint that much of the productive potential of saving is lost in a financial casino has force. If no such answer exists, the complaint deserves to be dismissed – not because economic analysis rules it to be meaningless, but because institutional action and imagination have failed to make it meangingful.

If it were not possible to tighten or loosen, through practical arrangements, the link between saving and production, it would also not be possible forcefully to distinguish saving from hoarding, for what distinguishes the latter from the former is its orientation, through investment, to production. Consequently, saving, under conditions of less than full employment, would always appear to be a detriment rather than a benefit, and spending for consumption would seem to be as good as spending for investment. The lack of an institutionally enriched understanding of the connection between saving and production would force us to choose between a quasi-Keynesian preference for spending under less than full employment and a pre-Keynesian celebration of thrift as a good in itself. Thus, the same basic failure to grasp the institutional indeterminacy and variability of the abstract concept of a market economy prejudices our ability to reason critically about the most familiar problems of practical economics.

Coming after several generations of intense debate about the relation of saving to prosperity such a defence of saving may seem reckless. Two traditions have been most prominent in the economics of the English-speaking world during the twentieth century. They have conspired to obscure what is at stake in this defence.

One tradition – which Keynes dubbed "classical" – sees thrift as an independent constraint upon growth. The intuition lying at the core of this idea is that we can produce only with what we have rescued from present consumption.

The second tradition – associated with Keynes himself – turned this view on its head, recognizing in an excess of saving over "effective demand" an invitation to the underemployment of productive resources. Entrepreneurs will produce only as much as consumers are willing and able to buy. A penny-pinching delay of consumption may set in motion a downward spiral of restraints upon economic activity from which only a forceful, public expansion of spending power can save us.

The intuition at the center of this view is that energy and hope rather than sacrifice, frugality, and caution are the qualities by which we become collectively rich. From the vantage point of this view, economic growth is more likely to increase national saving than a rise in national saving is likley to quicken economic growth. It is a conjecture holding a large portion of truth in a broad range of circumstances, as many empirical studies have shown.

However, this anticlassical teaching suffers from three flaws, making it a dangerous guide to the political economy of democratic experimentalism and to the institutionally informed understanding of the economy. The first deficiency – and the one that has nearly monopolized debate – is its failure fully to acknowledge the political and economic consequences of spending – governmental spending or governmentally induced private spending – as a cure for slumps. The real meaning of the frustrating experience of efforts to correct slumps through cheaper money and lower taxes in the last thirty years is not – as the monetarist polemic would have it – that all governmental influence upon the inducement to invest is self-defeating. It is rather that such influence is insufficient, and will become self-defeating unless it is completed. It is not too much. It is too little.

Demand management will often prove inadequate to ensure supply expansion. One reason is that the increase of demand may appear unsustainable to those who must make the decision to produce more. This is the point the monetarist critique has so lavishly emphasized. It is, however, subsidiary to another more fundamental reason for the recurrent failure of supply to respond to a heightening of aggregate demand. This more basic consideration would be too obvious to mention, did it not play so uncomfortable a role in economic theory.

The owners and managers of productive business are not a corps of social functionaries dedicated to bringing the greatest possible satisfaction to consumers. Their aim is to make money and rise in the world, not to act at the beck and call of buyers with increased spending power. Sometimes they may think they can make more money by selling more goods and services to consumers who have more resources with which to buy them. At least as often, however, other tacks will seem more promising: for example, selling the same goods and services at higher prices, and waiting to see what the competition does, or putting their spare time and cash into financial speculation.

The contrast between the relative ease and rapidity of an increase in aggregate demand, through looser fiscal or monetary policy, and the relative difficulty and delay of an expansion of productive output, will increase the attractions of such shortcuts to gain while providing a chance for skepticism about the sustainability of expansionary policy to deepen. The decision to expand production must often be executed over a long time, committing owners and managers to risky and irreversible decisions. Moreover, there will be no guaranteed or habitual fit between the current profile of production and the profile of consumption implied by the increased spending power. The degree of misfit depends upon who gets how much of the benefit of the governmentally induced expansion. The misfit means that production must to one or another extent be redirected. The need to redirect it lengthens the time and increases the risk.

We can now see why the point about the unsustainability of increased demand remains subsidiary to the point about the unreliability of the supply response. If we could count upon the supply response, we could indeed spend our way out of every recession. We would not be beating against the outer limits of employment that are compatible with price stability. We could count on growth without inflation rather than inflation with stagnation.

However, we cannot count on such a response. Our skepticism about governments turns out to be a mere extension of our realism about owners and managers. The fewer opportunities there are to establish new businesses in response to more demand, the greater is the likelihood that approaches to full employment will fail to result in sustainable, noninflationary growth.

Keynes showed us that supply will not ensure its own demand. However, we cannot put this insight to its proper use until we add the other half: demand will not guarantee its own supply. The trouble is that the development of this second half requires practical policies and political conceptions altogether different from those suggested by the first half. For we cannot develop it without investigating the institutional arrangements through which consumption, saving, and investment decisions are made, and asking ourselves whether other arrangements might better allow new demand to generate new supply. It will not suffice to give people more money if they do not also reorganize themselves and if ideas about their reorganization are missing. It will not be enough to pay people to dig up holes and fill them up again. We must have have a practical, productivist conception of the partnership between government and business, and of the relation of finance to firms, and a willingness to practice the institutional tinkering that would develop such a partnership and such a relation.

In thinking about such institutional innovations, a major issue will be how best to make saving available for production. It is only by addressing the failure of supply to ensure demand separately from the failure of demand to guarantee supply that we begin to recognize saving as part of the solution rather than treating it as merely part of the problem.

The second defect of the antisaving thesis is its failure to give adequate weight to the economic as well as the political value of national economic independence. An economy that saves little will also have little capacity to lend enough funds at low enough interest rates. It will have to import the investment capital that it has failed adequately to husband at home.

Dependence upon the favors of the international capital market will, however, be bought dearly. The more dependent the country becomes upon such favors, the riskier it may seem to foreigners and the more voracious capital will be in demanding high and immediate reward. Depend less upon foreign capital to profit more from it is the maxim to be followed. Only the great power in the world economy – Britain in the nineteenth century and the United States today – can afford to defy this rule on the strength of having its credit accepted as a world currency. Conversely, the more a country is committed to rebel against the interests and the ideas supported by the great powers of the day, the stronger reason it will have to ensure a high level of internal saving.

The third reason to reject the antisaving thesis is the most elusive and the most important. It also shows with the greatest clarity why we must refuse the choice between the "classical" and the Keynesian approaches to the causal priority and the political–economic primacy of saving or investment. These two

approaches share a blindness to the consequences of the distinctive, contingent institutional setting in which saving can take
place and be made available to different types of firms and
different strategies of investment. To accept a low saving rate in
the hope that economic growth will create the saving needed to
sustain it is to disregard the difference between reproducing and
reforming the established arrangements that mobilize saving for
production.

The retained earnings of firms supply, in the contemporary
market economies, the chief source of investment funds. The
financial system external to the firm – including the tapping of
foreigners' savings – remains to this day a relatively modest
supplement to retained earnings. It is modest in relation to the
role performed by retained earnings in the funding of production.
The magnitude of the resources engaged in world finance merely
serves to make more striking this disproportion between the
productive potential and the productive effect of external finance.

These two machines translating growth into saving and mobilizing saving for production – retained earnings and external
finance – generally reinforce the hierarchies and divisions of the
established economy. They give to those who have and deny to
those who lack – lack not promise and future but presence and
past.

The core of the problem is the same difficulty underlying the
failure of demand to ensure its own supply. The social value of
external finance for prosperity and democracy would be to correct
the tendency of retained earnings to reproduce the existing
distribution of access to productive resources. However, just as
the aim of owners and managers is to make money (or hold on to
power) rather than to satisfy the desires of consumers, so the aim
of financiers is to make money (or hold on to power) rather than
to fund and encourage innovators.

Financiers prefer to take no risks at all, or no risks they are
able to recognize. Their often fulfilled dream is to be rentiers in

the disguise of bankers. That is why they like to lend, directly or indirectly, to governments able, when necessary, to take or to print the money with which to pay them. If they must run risks, they prefer, if they are big, market risk to credit risk. For it is in relation to general market conditions rather than to particular businesses that they are most likely to have information and ideas. Moreover, it is by trading on the basis of conjectures about such general conditions that they are most easily and economically able to assemble large pools of funds and to make decisions about their commitment.

Nothing concerns the common cause of democracy and economic growth in the contemporary economies more than the need to break the stranglehold of a relatively small number of interests and ideas upon productive resources and opportunities. The financing of going concerns of small and medium size as well as of new businesses of any size must play prominent parts in the fulfillment of this goal.

The attempt to force a more open-minded orientation upon the professionals of finance will ordinarily prove futile and self-defeating. Favored with easy money and publicly supported credit enhancements, they are more likely to make more bad loans to big and old businesses than more good loans to little and young firms.

Nor can we solve the problem by blurring the focus. Institutional vagueness and political ambivalence overwhelm good intentions when reformers speak of the effort to gain social control over investment decisions. If we knew how to achieve this objective while preserving the decentralized vitality of a real market we would have found how to give practical institutional content to the idea of a democratized market economy. No one who had the political force or the intellectual clarity to embark upon the execution of such a program would remain content with the empty hand-shaking of a call for social control of the investment decision.

If we want to finance the small and the new we shall find it easier to organize additional saving than to expropriate or redirect existing saving, or than to wait for the future saving that future growth will create. This future saving will flow back into production through the same restrictive channels we have set out to expand. The public organization of increased, even compulsory private saving – paid, for example, into the redistributive pension funds described earlier – will help create both the opportunity and the means to open additional channels between saving and production. Once opened, such channels will in turn broaden opportunities and strengthen inducements to invest. We shall cease to treat the established system of banks and stockmarkets as the natural, necessary, and only devices by which a market economy makes capital available to firms and entrepreneurs.

Once the question, Who gets it?, becomes central to our thinking about the finance of production, we are no longer justified in treating the problem of how much saving we need as cleanly separable from the problem of how to organize the relation between saving and production. An alternative, more inclusive, and experimentalist organization of the link between saving and production will both require and cause a heightening of the saving level. The public organization of more private saving will serve as the indispensable counterpart to the democratization of finance.

It is a simple and obvious idea. To work it out, however, we must seek inspiration in traditions of economic theory conscious of the specificity and significance of the institutional arrangements that organize saving and make it available for production. "Classical" and Keynesian views have joined to suppress such an understanding. Where the understanding has existed – in Marx's economics or in "Austrian" economics – it has remained burdened by a baggage, of structural and evolutionary determinism in one instance and institutional conservatism and dogmatism in the other, that damage its utility to democracy and science.

We can raise the level of internal saving both through tax reform (exempting private saving and increasing public saving) and through the public organization of compulsory private saving along the lines explored earlier. The independently administered, decentralized, and competitive provident funds set up to receive this compulsory private saving might in turn provide resources for social venture capital, using saving to help finance production.

We can tighten the link between saving and production either by reshaping the established system of banks and stock markets or by building, alongside this system, a second bridge between the organization of saving and the funding of production. These two approaches are neither incompatible nor sharply distinct, for the existing economic arrangements lack unity and indivisibility. An example straddling the divide between the two is precisely the development of social investment funds, receiving the moneys of compulsory private saving and investing them, through equity stakes as well as loans, in start-up and emerging businesses.

The question arises whether such investment amounts to a subsidy: a subsidized allocation of credit, second-guessing the judgements of the market. Such devices do indeed trump the market as it is now organized. However, they also represent an effort to reorganize the arrangements defining the market economy: to substitute one version of the market economy for another. We can only tell after the fact whether this effort succeeds.

An experiment in the institutional reshaping of the market economy amounts to a gamble. We do not need to wait until the gamble pays off to describe the new link between investment and production as a reform rather than a subsidy. We do need to know whether the gamble is a reasonable one in the light of experience and analogy. The certitudes and tautologies of an institutionally impoverished economics give way to the lessons of experience and the trials of experimentalism.

The early program: wages and welfare

Redistributive social policy and institutional innovation. Progressive programs have traditionally been identified with egalitarianism. If they have avoided commitment to a rigid equality of resources, they have nevertheless tried to give practical content to the idea of equality of opportunity. Consequently, they have placed great emphasis upon redistributive social policy. Indeed, as hope for great institutional change faded – first, with the defeat of radical movements in the early twentieth century, then with the social-democratic compromise of the mid twentieth century, and finally with the communist collapse of the late twentieth century – egalitarian redistribution through tax-and-transfer came, increasingly, to bear the weight of the progressive cause.

The renunciation of any attempt radically to reshape the organization of economic and political life had been less a conviction than a necessity. However, what began as submission ended as belief; the practical focus upon the work of compensatory redistribution through tax-and-transfer helped make egalitarianism all the more central to the progressive cause. The new egalitarianism may have been less radical in effect and intention than its historical precursors, but it was also more single-minded. The radical liberalism, socialism, and communism of the nineteenth century had never placed equality, whether of rights, resources, or opportunities, as the supreme goal to which we must sacrifice all other concerns. Those doctrines had found inspiration in a more open and pluralistic vision of how to energize human life – the life of the individual as well as the life of peoples and of all humanity. They had tried to advance through the zone in which the conditions for the emancipation of the individual from entrenched social division and hierarchy intersect the conditions for material progress.

Progressives, however, had gone forward under the cloud of

twin illusions: the illusion that the requirements of material progress are guaranteed by history to coincide with the means of individual emancipation, and the illusion that this convergence between freedom and prosperity works through a particular, uncontroversial set or sequence of institutional arrangements. The task now is to rid ourselves of these illusions while continuing the search they confounded.

In the new search, as in the old one, egalitarianism needs to be put in its place. It needs to be seen and developed as a subsidary element within a broader vision of human empowerment rather than as the commanding value trumping all other concerns. The principle of the internal relation between thinking about interests and ideals and thinking about practices and institutions applies as well at this most general level of argument. Once we have restored our faith in the possibility and importance of institutional innovation and social invention, we can also escape the narrowness of focus to which our practical defeats and crisis of faith had condemned us.

We now have the key with which to understand the paradoxical relation between egalitarian intransigence and institutional conservatism in liberal and social-democratic political philosophy. Some of the most influential political philosophers of the day professed a thoroughgoing egalitarianism. They also affected a method of argument scrupulously removed from the complications and compromises of a particular historical context. Neverthless, much of what they produced appeared in retrospect as a metaphysical gloss upon the tax-and-transfer practices of an institutionally conservative social democracy. The more this way of thinking imagined itself to rise above its historical situation, the more cravenly it reflected that situation.

Given the repudiation of broader reconstructive ambitions, the established forms of the regulated market economy and representative democracy began to seem flawed but corrigible versions of the only type of market and democracy worth considering. The

important and available work for the ideologist was to humanize
the inevitable, justifying a more egalitarian distribution of rights
and resources within an institutional framework he could no
longer hope to reimagine or reconstruct. Thus, a single-minded
egalitarianism went hand in hand with skepticism about institutional alternatives, and a view prostrate in its relation to its
historical circumstance could flatter itself with the sincerity and
exuberance of its devotion to equality. It claimed to have
exchanged utopian irresponsibility for humanitarian concern.

The broader vision of democratic commitments animating the
argument of democratic experimentalism fastens on the possibility
of overlap between the conditions of economic and technological
progress and the requirements for the liberation of the individual.
It recognizes in expanded freedom and strengthened capacity to
rearrange social life a boost to each of these major goods. It goes
in search of the practices and institutions that promise to build
on this common ground.

Democratic experimentalism sees the core of the good of
human liberation in a a softening of the tension between two
great competing demands upon our vitality and greatness: the
need to engage in group life and the need to diminish the price,
in subjugation and loss of self-identity, that we regularly pay for
such engagement. It hopes to diminish this price by lightening,
even when it cannot hope to abolish, the burden of entrenched
division and hierarchy weighing upon our relations to one
another. The point is not to affirm the ascendancy of individual
self-assertion and self-development over our practical and imaginative ties to other people. It is to weaken the forces that make
self-development impossible without a betrayal of these bonds,
and turn communal solidarity into a limit upon the intensity of
the self and the largeness of its ambitions.

The master tool of democratic experimentalism is institutional
innovation, practiced not from on high, with fanciful blueprints
and perfectionist designs, but with the materials at hand and in

the situation of the moment. Compensatory redistribution works – nowhere more dramatically than in the willingness to invest in health and education. However, even if our goals were narrowly egalitarian, we could not allow tax-and-transfer to remain our principal instrument.

Compensatory redistribution, through progressive taxation and social spending by government, is most likely to work when it builds upon inclusive, equalizing political and economic reforms: even basic, simple reforms like the extension and the protection of the suffrage, the strengthening of labor rights, and the broader distribution of land tenure and of access to agricultural technologies and markets. As inequalities become less brutal, the necessary reforms become less familiar.

Without such institutional changes in economic activity and political life, major redistributive change will not take place. When it does occur, its effects will be frustrated.

Among the features of contemporary economic life that are most likely to defeat compensatory redistribution the most important is the rigid division between vanguard and rearguard sectors of the economy worldwide. Imagine a world in which part of the population has high-paying, knowledge-based, and knowledge-giving jobs while another part of the population has no jobs at all, or unstable, ill-paying jobs, affording no discretion and requiring little knowledge or skill.

In the best case, when the society is rich and the vanguard large, compensatory redistribution will merely soften what it cannot change, producing more makework than work and more relief than enablement. It will burden public finance and economic growth, for it will seem to be a costly, although well-intentioned, attempt to undo the unequalizing logic of economic growth.

In the worst case, when the vanguard remains small and the country poor, redistribution will prove futile. The interests commanding the vanguard will not allow redistribution to reach the magnitude necessary to make a difference. If they were to allow it, the result might be disaster rather than reform. The transfers needed to make up for such formidable inequalities would be so vast that they would crush the engines of economic growth. The solution is not to suspend compensatory redistribution; it is to underpin it with structural change through institutional invention.

Within a reenergized democratic vision, egalitarianism has an important but subsidiary place. The range and the quality of the lives a society makes possible are what matter most. For the adherent to democratic experimentalism, the genius of ordinary men and women must find expression in a strengthening of their powers. We must free people from drudgery but also from the forms of dependence and domination that make self-assertion irreconcilable with community. An absolute equality of rights and resources is too rigid a straitjacket in which to place such a vision. On the other hand, mere equality of opportunity is too empty a promise by which to convey the aims of democracy. We must define the material and moral goods to which such opportunity should give access.

Everyone should inherit from society – rather than from the family – a set of basic rights and resources needed to set upon a course of life, and to sustain it against the extremes of misfortune and insecurity. Everyone should therefore have at hand the tools necessary to effective economic and civic action. The point is to give to the ideal of a moderate independence – "forty acres and a mule" – a form consistent with present-day conditions.

No one should have to live in a society in which public policy and institutional arrangements express the outlook of a particular part of the people against other parts. A strong presumption must weigh against all arrangements – such as the hereditary transmission of substantial private property, early and strong contrasts between the education of gifted and ordinary children, or the concentration and perpetuation of supreme political power in a few individuals – that prevent the many from making history and reinventing life. A set of capacity-ensuring rights and resources must find their counterpart in practices and institutions that keep society open to alternative futures and inspire in politics and culture a contest of visions. To describe such practices and institutions is a central concern of this book.

Democratic experimentalism cannot profess to neutrality among conceptions of the good. Every set of institutional arrangements encourages some forms of experience and discourages others. In place of the illusion of neutrality we should put the real goal of openness to divergent and novel varieties of experience. Moreover, the real goal of openness, unlike the illusory aim of neutrality, is causally linked to the goods that are central to democratic experimentalism. Only arrangements that open themselves to broad-based challenge and change can flourish on the ground where the conditions of material progress overlap the conditions of individual liberation.

The progressive alternative explored in this book is a species of this democratic vision: responsive to the conditions of a particular time and committed to advance in a particular direction. Because it embraces a certain sequence of institutional changes to the exclusion of others, it also favors some possibilities of experience over others. In another book, *What Should Legal Analysis Become?* (London, Verso, 1996), I have compared this development of democracy to other possible and justifiable developments, and discussed the moral preferences and exclusions implied by each of these pathways. Each imposes moral as well as practical risks. Each makes life easier for some varieties of experience than for others. Each nevertheless gives practical content to the value of experimental openness and corrigibility.

For the progressive alternative, equalizing, comepensatory redistribution remains subsidiary to structural change just as the goal of equality remains subsidiary to the aim of empowerment. A practical problem arises from this preference. People want to

solve their day-to-day problems of health care, education, security, housing, and transport. They worry about jobs and wages. A
discourse about institutional alternatives will be Greek to them
unless it can connect with this agenda of prosaic anxieties.

Progressives must find the connection and make it transparent
in deed as well as in word. They must show how a first wave of
achievements of social policy gives people the strength and
independence to consider more ambitious changes. At the same
time they have to persuade people that such achievements cannot
be extended or sustained without embarking upon the course of
reform they propose. People must find in the practical solutions
to these urgent problems opportunities to anticipate fragments
and elements of the progressive program.

The participation of wages in national income. Compensatory,
equality-enhancing redistribution plays second place to democratizing institutional innovation. In the early program – the first
wave of the progressive alternative – the chief devices of compensatory redistribution are the increased participation of wages in
national income and the use of a high tax take to sustain a high
level of social spending by government. The progressive profile
of taxation is less important than the redistributive uses of social
spending.

In the later, second wave of the progressive alternative,
investment in people by government remains a priority. However,
the main engine of greater equality becomes the development of
an antidualist political economy, bridging the gap between vanguard and rearguard sectors of production. Once we have secured
the public finance needed to sustain high social spending and
begun to attack the division between vanguards and rearguards,
we can increase within the tax system the relative importance of
directly redistributive taxes: the progressive taxation of individual
consumption, addressing the hierarchy of living standards, and
the progressive taxation of wealth, particularly when transmitted

through inheritance and gifts, thus responding, although less adequately, to the accumulation of economic power.

No dogma commands greater authority in contemporary practical economics than the idea that attempts to raise, by political decision, the share of wages in national income will prove self-defeating. Wages, according to this dogma, can rise only in proportion to productivity gains. All attempts to make them grow more quickly will undo themselves, causing an inflation that turns real gains into nominal ones. It is an idea that enjoys as much influence as sound-finance doctrine and a commitment to the gold standard enjoyed in the period from 1870 to 1914. During that period, the high levels of unemployment that sound-finance doctrine and the gold standard helped cause were generally attributed to inexorable forces and lazy workers. However, like its precursor, this idea of the futility of attempts to make the real wage overtake productivity gains is false – another piece of false necessity masquerading as science. Its falsehood remains hidden by the limited element of truth it includes.

One statistical comparison is especially revealing: a comparison of the proportion of wages to value added in the industrial sector of a national economy. It is as close a proxy for the Marxist concept of surplus value as we could hope to find, and it speaks, as the part for the whole, to the participation of wages in national income. Marxist economic theory holds that the rate of surplus value converges in "capitalist" economies just as mainstream economics clings to the equivalent belief that wage growth across an economy hits an intractable limit in the achievement of productivity gains. However, countries at comparable levels of economic and technological development show striking disparities in the wage take of value added in the industrial sector. The rate of surplus value does not converge, and neither does the relative participation of wages in national income. One reason for the divergence is politics. Economic circumstance and constraint count for much, but not for everything. Politics make the difference.

In a recent year, for example, this percentage was 71 percent for Norway, 69 percent for Italy, 51 percent for South Africa, 38 percent for India, 35 percent for the United States, and 23 percent for Brazil. It is generally higher for richer countries and lower for poorer ones (but not always, as the case of the United States shows). However, vast differences emerge among countries at similar levels of wealth. To be sure, some of these differences can be credited to different relative scarcities of land, labor, and capital, and the relative importance of natural resources and their extraction. To that extent, comparatively independent economic and demographic factors explain the disparities.

Nevertheless, the differences are so large that something significant is left over once all such explanations have done their work. How could this residue of significant difference have arisen in the first place if the wage take of national income has a natural history indifferent to political intervention? The political shaping of different relations among government, business, and labor – relations enshrined in rights – has strengthened or weakened the wage take. When the wage take has increased in this fashion, rather than through direct efforts to legislate higher nominal wage levels, the increase has often proved both enduring and compatible with high, sustained rates of economic growth.

There is truth in the dogma of the futility of raising through politics the wage take from national income. The truth is the inadequacy of attempts to achieve by fiat rises in the real wage. A legislated rise in the wage, and therefore in the proportion of national income represented by wages, can work. However, it can work only when sustained by rights and arrangements shifting power toward workers while maintaining competitive pressure among firms in product, capital, and labor markets.

Pseudo-Keynesian public finance is indeed self-defeating. Its self-defeat, however, says little about the limitations of governmental intervention in the economy. It says more about the price society must pay for a policy that attempts to achieve by compensatory redistribution and inflationary legerdemain what it despairs of accomplishing through institutional reform.

The illusion in the dogma of the futility of efforts to ensure a political heightening of the wage take from national income is the failure to acknowledge the power of institutions to change the part falling to work in the distribution of wealth. We must seek to increase this part through the cumulative effect of three types of arrangements. The first type exerts the more immediate influence; the other two help create the conditions for this effect to apply. The first set of arrangements is the strengthening of workers' rights by devices that prevent the benefit of those rights from being captured by a defined group of workers: the insiders holding stable, well paid jobs. The second set of arrangements keeps up competitive pressure against firms, inhibiting the straightforward translation of wage increases into price rises. The third set of arrangements gives firms – including firms outside the favored, advanced sectors of the economy – adequate finance. Such practices tighten the link between saving and production in either of the two ways previously discussed: the reformation of the existing system of banks and stock markets or the building, alongside this system, of a second bridge between saving and production.

Consider now more closely the content of the workers' rights. What labor rights do the most for wage participation in national income while minimizing the negative effect of wage rises on employment levels? The generic answer is that they must be rights combining two characteristics.

The first characteristic is that they must be effectively available to the laborforce as a whole rather than to a tenured group of insiders. When policies and institutions favor insiders, holding good jobs, over job seekers and workers in backward sectors of the economy, the result is to aggravate the conflict between wage enhancement and job promotion as well as to broaden the spread between high and low wages.

Thus, in contemporary industrial democracies, unemployment has been lowest either in economies, like that of the United States, where labor rights are weakest or in economies, like that of the Scandinavian social democracies, where provisions for inclusive, collective wage bargaining persist. The former must contend with inadequate investment in the on-the-job formation of skilled labor; the latter with the relative insensitivity of negotiated wage arrangements to changing market circumstance. Unemployment has been highest where, in countries like France, a class of relatively privileged, organized, and stable workers have exercised a decisive influence upon the wage and employment policies of government and private business alike. The suppression of payroll taxes that discourage employment helps. More important, however, is the avoidance of arrangements enabling a privileged segment of the workforce to gain a stranglehold over the more capital-rich sectors of production, turning temporary advantages into vested rights.

A public-law regime automatically unionizing all workers, job seekers, and smallscale business owners helps ensure the existience of a society-wide bargaining through unions representing the entire working population. Society-wide bargaining with the participation of nationally representative unions helps balance the interests of relative insiders – the people with better jobs – against the interests of outsiders – the people with worse jobs or no jobs at all. An institutional bias in favor of such a balance supplements the ephemeral or uneven force of a labor solidarity resting on nothing but the conscience of the generous and the enlightened.

The instrument of union representation is circumstantial. As we advance in the project of democratizing the market economy, unions should increasingly give way to the combination of two

other devices for the prevention of stark divisions between
insiders and outsiders: the development of social inheritance,
including claims to continuous education and reskilling, and the
multiplication of different forms of decentralized access to productive resources and opportunities. The alliance of these two
devices is central to the later progress of the progressive alternative. This alliance culminates – so I shall argue – in the creation
of alternative property regimes, coexisting experimentally in the
same economy.

The second characteristic of the labor rights we need is that
they must be growth-friendly. They must help moderate the
conflict between two great social requirements of the material
progress of society: the acceptance of innovation and the dispo-
sition to cooperate. For economic growth to occur, people must
cooperate: most notably, workers with workers, and workers with
managers, but also firms with firms and businesses with governments. People must also, however, innovate and accept innovation. The problem is that every innovation threatens to change
the relative positions and advantages of the cooperators by altering
the context of practices, expectations, and rights in which their
cooperation is embedded. We must therefore prefer those ways
of organizing cooperation that minimize the conflict between the
requirements of cooperation and innovation. The partnership
principle – arrangements for sharing of profits and ownership
with workers – have just this attribute. They too can lead toward
the more radical departures from the established institutional
arrangements of the market economy that concern the later
program of this progressive alternative.

Country-wide wage bargaining and a preference for profit and
ownership sharing by workers have different relations to the main
conditions for the sustainable enhancement of the wage take: the
avoidance of rigid divisions between insiders and outsiders in the
labor market and the care to choose growth-friendly arrangements. Inclusive bargaining may satisfy the first condition better

than the second. Profit and ownership sharing may fulfill the second requirement better than the first. No formula determines the uniquely best way to reconcile these competing goals.

The tension, and the consequent difficulty of finding an ideal solution, will persist so long as the underlying divisions between vanguards and rearguards retain their full force. For these divisions create the opportunity perenially to recreate divisions between insiders and outsiders in the labor market while turning profit sharing into a device for the favored few. Both country-wide bargaining and rights to share in profit and wealth need to be supplemented by practices favorable to the diffusion of vanguardist economic practices beyond the frontiers of the established productive vanguards. Such practices must be decentralized to be effective. Thus, they require the creation of an intermediate level of funds and support centers between government and business. At this point, the effort to increase the real wage merges into the campaign for an antidualist political economy – a concern that becomes central to this alternative as it advances.

Free capital and unfree labor: the international context of the commitment to heighten the wage take from national income. A crucial element is still missing from the analysis: the bearing of labor mobility across national frontiers upon the progressive commitment to enhance the real wage. The efficacy of such a commitment in the richer countries seems to depend upon the continuing denial to labor of the right freely to cross national frontiers. This denial represents the single most scandalous injustice of the new economic order, and the point at which social injustice most directly coincides with economic inefficiency.

The architects of the new world economic order have built a system in which capital and goods can roam the world while labor remains imprisoned in the nation-state or in blocs of relatively homogeneous nation-states. They describe as free trade this system of privileges for things and money and disabilities for workers. It is neither just nor stable, and it is certainly not free. The ban against the free movement of labor is the single greatest reason for its present injustice and future instability.

The economic zones into which the world is now being organized differ radically in their approach to this distinction between the regimes of capital and labor. A few such zones (like the European Union) give labor the same right to move they grant to capital. Other zones, however (such as the North American Free Trade Agreement), try to make money out of the difference between the immobility of labor and the mobility of capital.

The arguments in favor of the contrast between the rights of capital and labor to cross national frontiers fall into three broad categories: those resulting from a view of the favorable economic consequences of capital mobility, those implicit in a conception of the disastrous social and political effects of the free movement of labor, and those suggested by moral and political ideas about the right of inheritance and the identity of nations. The arguments, however, hold up only in so qualified a form that they end up impugning what they appeared to justify.

The neoliberal doctrine, and the economic orthodoxy supporting it, hold that capital must become free first, so that labor can become free later. The progressive alternative supports the contrasting thesis that capital and labor should become free together, by small, incremental steps. Capital should have less freedom now so that labor may also have more freedom now. We shall then be able to ensure a more secure foundation to the freedom of both capital and labor later – secure politically and socially as well as economically.

According to the orthodox view, capital should be free to move so that labor need not move. If capital can go to where its rewards are greatest, wages and working conditions will gradually converge. Workers will no longer have to leave their homelands in search of a better life.

The problem, however, is what happens in the meantime. If capital continues to stay in overwhelming proportion at home – as has in fact happened so far – the relatively small amount of capital that does cross national frontiers will exercise a disproportionate effect, holding national policy ransom without fundamentally changing the rewards and conditions of labor. The lower the level of internal saving, the greater the dependence upon the most impatient and least productive form of capital will be. Policies and arrangements intended to raise the participation of wages in national income may then be punished all the more easily by capital flight and economic instability, increasing the price of national rebellion against economic orthodoxy. There may always be a price to pay. We can, however, hope to lower it.

A second set of arguments supporting the contrast between the mobility of capital and the immobility of labor goes to the prejudicial effects of labor mobility upon social welfare and workers' rights in the richer countries as well as to the dangers of evasion of skilled labor from the poorer countries. Indeed, if there is one reform in the world today that can produce world revolution, it is the sudden grant to labor of an unconditional right to cross national frontiers. Imagine it: free movement of labor, with subsidized transport facilities, easily paid (why not?), with an international tax on cosmetics. The dictators of China, Indonesia, and Nigeria would wander through abandoned fields and factories pleading with their once sullen and now euphoric subjects to stay behind. In the rich countries, the carefully constructed pyramid of privileges and disadvantages of different segments of the workforce would begin to topple. Even in Switzerland – that inviolate haven of self-contented serenity – trouble would break out, as hordes of dark-skinned people swarmed through the sleepy streets of Basel.

We need not contemplate that terrible day. Workers may gradually win the right to move. There are solutions to the problems arising at each stage of their progress, and each of these solutions may in turn represent an opportunity for the advancement of the democratic cause.

We should distinguish three main problems. One problem is the uncompensated drain of highly educated labor from the poorer countries, discouraging investment in people. A second problem is the depressive effect on social-welfare rights in the richer countries: the countries with the most generous rights would exert the greatest attractive force. A race to the bottom in social welfare might ensue. A third problem is the destructive impact that unrestricted labor mobility might have upon the rights and wages of workers in the prosperous countries.

All these problems result from a consequence of labor mobility that ranks high among its benefits: its equalizing tendency. The task is to channel and dose the tendency so as to prevent social conflict within countries from overwhelming and undermining this benign effect. As in any programmatic argument, the direction of movement matters more than the rate.

It is easy to imagine a scheme under which poorer countries exporting skilled labor, in the development of which they have invested scarce resources, would be compensated by a surtax, administered by the receiving country, upon the earnings of the immigrant skilled worker. So too, we can grandfather established workers in ways minimizing restraints upon employment and innovation: for example, through cashable increments to their pension accounts, funded from the general tax revenues. The race to the bottom in welfare rights could be prevented by distinguishing sequences of rights immigrant workers would win: first, health and education entitlements for their children and themselves; then, more comprehensive social claims; finally, the full participatory privileges of citizenship. The race to the bottom will be prevented as well by two loose but powerful restraints upon the minimization of social rights. People care about what life in their country is like. Moreover, economic progress, like political freedom, requires investment in people.

Once we have cut down to size the practical obstacles to labor mobility, we come to objections that are more fundamental. These objections expose some of the normative assumptions underlying current arrangements. One such objection is the collective counterpart to the idea of the hereditary transmission of private property. Our fathers and mothers built our country with sacrifice. Why should you be able to come late, and sit at the same table with us? The country was theirs; it is therefore now ours.

Conventional liberal doctrine has been shaped by the complacency with it has often embraced the familiar institutional forms of representative democracy, the market economy, and free civil society. It has treated these forms as the natural and necessary face of political, economic, and social pluralism. Liberal doctrine has also been influenced by two compromises that have never sat comfortably with its animating vision: the right to inherit property through the family and the right to exclude people from one's country.

When the right to inherit property combines, as it generally does, with the transmission of unequal educational advantage through the family, the result is to produce class societies. The class character of society prevents much of the promise of democracy from being realized, and widens the gap between liberal doctrine and social reality. In the end, we justify the hereditary transmission of property by an accumulation of practical arguments about its incentive effects.

Once demoted to this level, however, the case for family inheritance becomes tentative and insecure. The incentives it is supposed to preserve may come to rest upon other bases.

Moreover, society may prefer to forgo some amount of incentive for the sake of a great deal more equality – not the absolute equality of circumstance but the relative equality of opportunity.

When we consider the alleged right of exclusion more closely, we discover that this authority to lock people out relies upon an idea of inheritance when it does not depend instead upon a particular view of nations and of the means needed to sustain their identities over time. Once again, a confused argument about rights obscures an incomplete and relative argument about incentives. The incentive arguments, however, have even less force here than they had there: no country stops working, or works less, because fewer of its future inhabitants will be the biological descendants of its present citizens. The argument 'This is ours, why should you be able to have some of it?' weakens further when we move from the tangible succession of parents and children within the family to the intangible succession of generations within a country.

The most important consideration in favor of the denial of the right freely to cross national frontiers is that such a right would threaten the national difference as we now value and understand it. If strangers could freely enter a country, the form of life in that country would be under perpetual stress. Even if the practical problems of life with strangers could be solved, the spiritual ones would remain.

The real question is: What are nations for in a world of democracies? For the progressive, the point of nations should be to develop the powers and possibilities of humanity in different directions. The national difference should work as a moral specialization within humankind. No way of life gives the best or the definitive rendition of humanity, only a particular version. Every democracy should be open and plural, but no set of institutions, however democratic, can be neutral or all-inclusive. Each democracy must subordinate some possibilities of experience – of the most valuable, the most human forms of experience – to others. In so doing, it creates a world better suited to some visions and temperaments than to others. That is why it matters so much for nations to remain different, with differences of culture rekindled by differences of practice and institution. That is also why it is vital that people be able to leave the country in which they happen to have been born, and join another country in which they see a better chance to define and develop their life projects.

The tyranny of circumstance and class within countries, as well as the gross inequalities among countries, may make elective affinities of temperament – the affinities of an individual with a nation not his or her own – seem an inconsequential force. Such affinities will, however, become ever more important as democracy deepens.

If the nations are to fulfill the mission of moral specialization, they must learn to give relatively less weight to the biological succession of families living together. They must learn to give relatively more weight to the distinct versions of humanity they develop. In the understanding of such distinctions, they must allow more authority to the future – the differences that are yet to be worked out – than to the past – the differences that are remembered and interpreted as the collective extension of family life. Democratic nations – that is to say, nations of free and equal people – should call upon prophecy more than upon memory. Consequently, they must tolerate a greater level of disruption by the entrance of strangers than they have been accustomed to do.

It may nevertheless be much less disruption than we either hope or fear. People cling to home, and fear a new life in a strange place. The practical issue is therefore not whether to incite vast masses of people to move around the world (for they will not) but whether to allow a temperamental and social minority of risk takers to change countries and situations, extending the scope of free trade, abolishing an unjust and unnecessary distinction between the privileges of capital and labor, and reforming the sense of the national difference.

Neoliberalism wants to give capital, right now, unrestricted freedom to move around the world. The progressive alternative proposes that capital and labor should win their freedom to move at the same time and by gradual steps. The first major move in the winning of labor's right to move is the international negotiation of susbtantial minimal quotas of legal immigration and temporary work permits as well as of standards for turning the work permits into permanent residency. Every country would have to allow such quotas and respect such standards. Attempts to establish sector-specific work and immigration rules, suited to the needs of the local labor market, would be prohibited.

Short-term capital movements would be taxed and regulated on a sliding scale. The fiscal and regulatory burden upon the movement of restless capital would decline as the emancipation of labor progressed. The deepening of domestic saving, through devices such as the public organization of compulsory private saving, would help avoid the need for indiscriminate dependence upon foreign capital, a dependence blind to the patience or the use of the money. The world would become safer for free labor.

Social entitlements and social action. Equalizing redistribution through tax-and-transfer techniques remains secondary in the short run (the early program) to a strengthening of the wage take from national income as well as to the enhancement of workers' rights. Tax-and-transfer-style redistribution remains subsidiary in the long run (the later program) to a weakening of the contrast between vanaguard and rearguard sectors of the economy. A characteristic mistake of institutionally conservative social democracy has been to expect from compensatory redistribution what it cannot give.

Put in its place, however, such redistribution plays a vital role in the progressive alternative. In the later program, it develops into the general principle of social inheritance. Everyone inherits from society, rather than from his or her family, a basic set of capacity-ensuring resources. This guarantee of capacity serves as the indispensable counterpart to the energizing reconstruction of political, economic, and social institutions that the progressive alternative proposes. Without the combination of capacity and security that social inheritance safeguards, we cannot realize the project of a more experimental economy, a more mobilized polity, and a more organized society. Without that combination, we can carry this project out only in ways making it susceptible to disruption and perversion.

The animating connection between the acceleration of experimentalism and the enhancement of capability must, like everything else in the progressive alternative, be foreshadowed in its earliest forms. The true work of social rights in these early arrangements is not to diminish inequalilty except as a byproduct of the execution of another task. This task is to rescue people from the extremes of inability to take care of themselves, to shape and implement their own life plans and to participate in the contest over the alternative futures of their country. It is to give them the practical means with which to change themselves and their societies. In accord with the primacy of this goal, the highest priority of social policy must be children, their safety, health, and education.

The efficacy of social-welfare policy rests upon two major conditions: a high tax take designed in ways friendly to economic growth and an involvement of local communities in the formulation and implementation of social rights. I have already dealt with the design of the tax system in the early program of the progressive alternative. That design must acknowledge that, in the short run, redistribution depends more upon the aggregate level of the take and the progressive profile of social spending than upon the progressive character of taxation.

This acknowledgement pushes us in the direction of a tax system weighted heavily toward an economically neutral consumption tax such as the comprehensive flat-rate value-added tax. We must respect the priority need to generate public revenue while minimizing the disruption to established incentives to work, save, and invest. Having achieved this objective, we can then gradually increase the role of direct redistributive taxation. We can address the two great targets of a progressive tax system: the hierarchy of living standards (through a steeply progressive tax upon the expenditure bill of each taxpayer, combined with a minimum guaranteed income) and the accumulation of wealth and economic power (especially through the taxation of gifts and estates).

Consider the problem of social engagement in social policy as the problem arises in the most extreme conditions of social inequality, exclusion, and disorganization. There are large poor countries, like Brazil, or large rich countries, like the United States, where some of the most disadvantaged groups in society suffer from both the disruption of family life and the absence of community organization. This twin deficit favors violence, damages children, and suppresses economic opportunity while undermining the requirements for effective public help to the poor. The disorganization of society brings every evil in its wake, making governmental assistance necessary while rendering it less effective.

Two paradoxes overshadow welfare policy in such conditions. Imagine a social world of single-mother families, with the men as unstable, rotating companions. When the family has weakened, the organized community must take over some of its responsibilities – for example, through community-organized daycare centers and community associations. Such associations can connect schools, families, and social workers. The trouble is that where families are disorganized so, typically, are communities.

The disorganization of the family and the community makes it necessary for government to do what family and community are insufficient to accomplish. However, if there is one thing we have learned from the comparative experience of social policy, it is that social programs established by government are most effective when they have families and community organizations as their partners. The absence of such partners creates the need for welfare bureaucracy. It nevertheless forces this bureaucracy to operate in an alien and deranged world, and reduces it to dealing more with the symptoms than with the causes of social misery.

The basic solution is to shape social rights and public assistance in ways triggering community organization rather than suppressing it. Access to some benefits or benefit levels should be made contingent upon the engagement of community groups. Such groups should participate in the formulation as well as the implementation of local policy, helping set priorities and choose methods. The narrowing of participation in a self-appointed cadre of politicking activists should find its antidote in rules of participation. Just as local communities would need to organize to receive some resources, so individuals in these communities would need to participate to receive some of the individualized benefits resulting from such allocations.

Two great problems beset these commitments and concerns: the question of how best to encourage the self-organization of civil society and the issue of the relation between the family and the state.

The density of association in civil society is much more than a requirement for the effectiveness of compensatory social policy. It is a central aim and a basic condition of democratic experimentalism. Only a society that is densely organized outside government can generate an understanding of alternative futures and act upon it.

The traditional apparatus of private law is insufficient to achieve this goal. This apparatus draws a distinction between business-oriented organizations, devoted to moneymaking and central to daily life, and civil associations, dedicated to the reformation of society or the alleviation of its evils but confined to the sidelines of practical affairs. It leaves the ability effectively to enjoy the right of self-organization hostage to all the dependencies and vulnerabilities of an unequal and divided society. In such a society isolation is often the companion of disadvantage.

The solution – I shall argue in the description of the later versions of the progressive alternative – is to give two chances to the self-organization of civil society: one through private law; the other through public law. The conditioning of social rights and benefits upon group organization and involvement is but a step in this direction.

No amount of social organization replaces the family. No promise of social happiness through the empowerment of human faculties can prove real and reliable if it is founded upon the dissolution or the weakening of family life. Even in the most energized society people will continue to want a life outside historical time as well as within it. Adventure and ambition will meet their match in closeness and love. In the early stages of the progressive alternative the alliance of school, family, and local community remains key to the success of the most important forms of social assistance.

However, as we redress the most abject forms of social disadvantage and incapacity and move toward later moments of the progressive alternative, a countervailing consideration comes into play, revealing the tragic conflict between the claims of the family and the promptings of democratic experimentalism. Democracy needs a school forming individuals able to imagine distant possibilities and to resist present opinions. Such a school must recognize and develop the child's prophetic voice, and give the child the means with which to think differently from his or her family, class, country, and time. The school depends upon the family. If the school need not make imaginative war upon the teachings of the family, the fulfillment of its liberating mission nevertheless creates some of the conditions that make such a war possible. For family and school to make peace, love and respect must become less dependent upon agreement and sameness. To diminish this dependence, through the gradual reformation of our ideas about ourselves, is an essential part of the practice and culture of democratic experimentalism.

The early program: coordination decentralized

Two tasks: the mobilization of savings for investment and the diffusion of vanguardist practices. A democratizing alternative to neo-liberalism and traditional social democracy must develop economic institutions strengthening the translation of social saving into productive investment. It will be especially interested in those ways of organizing the relation between saving and production that increase opportunities for investment in the rearguard and reach out to economic and social outsiders. Among such solutions it will in turn prefer those that favor the extension of democratic experimentalism outside the production system as well as within it. The democratizing alternative to neoliberalism must also establish the economic institutions that help promote the extension of vanguardist practices – the practices of production as learning – throughout the economy rather than leaving these practices quarantined an island of advanced insight and habit.

These two tasks – the inclusive mobilization of saving for production and the generalization of vanguardist practices – both require initiative beyond the frontiers of isolated firms: initiative among firms, acting cooperatively, as well as between firms and governments, both national and local. Thus, both tasks raise the central problem of partnership between government and business. To embrace this partnership and to remake it, in decentralized

form, is a central tenet of this progressive alternative just as
insistence upon a clear line between the regulatory and social
responsibilities of the state and its productive passivity represents
a defining claim of the neoliberal program. Such a recasting of
the government–business partnership soon turns out to require
the development of economic organizations – social funds and
support centers – intermediate between the government and the
firms. The creation of these new economic agents in turn provides
an opportunity to innovate in the form of the property regime – a
characteristic concern of the later program. At last, we shall be
led to abandon the fetishistic idea that the market economy has a
natural legal form, organized around the logic of traditional
property rights. In place of that idea we shall put a willingness to
allow different legal–institutional versions of the market economy,
and different property regimes, to coexist experimentally within
the same economy.

Antiexperimentalist illusions. In thinking about the role and form
of the government–business partnership we must first free ourselves from the inhibitions that here, as everywhere, conventional
economic thinking imposes upon the institutional imagination.
The most significant such inhibitions result from two connected
sets of assumptions. Each set plays a prominent role in establishing the intellectual climate within which neoliberal ideas command authority. One such group of assumptions takes the form
of a recurrent argumentative pattern in policy discussions. The
repeated theme is that some practice of economic selection or
coordination, acknowledged as attractive or even superior in
principle, is dismissed as inferior in practice. It is inferior in
practice because it would multiply the opportunities for the twin
evils of economic favoritism and bureaucratic dogmatism. Stupidity and collusion would unite to bring out the worst in such
apparently attractive arrangements. For example, differential
exchange rates (one rate for consumption goods, another for

capital goods), differential tariffs and import controls (higher for consumption goods, lower for capital goods and capability-creating services), and differential interest rates (lower for innovation than for reproducing established products, and lower for investment in the human and physical resources of production than for consumer spending) may often seem the best solution in principle. In practice, however, such theoretically best approaches will, according to this view, almost always prove to be inferior to what may have seemed the second-best solution of uniform rates, differentiated, if differentiated at all, by freely operating market forces. The theoretical second-best is in practice the best solution. It wrests power away from a bureaucracy deluded by dogma when not corrupted by interests and self-interest. It disperses initiative among decentralized economic agents.

We soon see that such beliefs about the reason why the second-best solutions become the preferred ones depend upon yet another set of assumptions: assumptions about the range of institutional solutions open to us in connecting government with business. According to these assumptions, sanctioned by economic analysis and prominent in neoliberal ideology, a clearcut contrast opposes governmental activism to private initiative. We hold in our minds a tangible picture of the practices and institutions defining each. In this picture, governmental activism in strategic coordination is represented by the national government and, within the national government, by centralized bureaucratic staffs, specialized in trade and industrial policy. These staffs deal with associations of firms: especially the biggest and best organized companies. Such is the model of strategic coordination made familiar by the experience of the North East Asian economies.

As soon as we start to tinker with the institutional assumptions of this picture, we begin to shake as well the premises leading us to abandon, as impractical and dangerous, policies such as differentiated exchange and interest rates. A large potential space separates the extremes of isolated private initiative and one-way bureaucratic imposition. It is a potential space because it is not just there like a natural object. We can make it exist by acts of institutional invention. By decentralizing the forms and practices of strategic coordination we can change the ratio, not just shift the distribution, of benefit and burden. We can have more independent initiative and more public accountability at the same time.

The fundamental reason why the policy discussions of the last generation in the rich industrial democracies have proved so fruitless is that they leave unexplored the institutional issues on which their fate depends. The closing of the agenda of structural debates in the postwar period and the anti-institutionalism of conventional economics combined to blind the policy mandarins. In practical politics hopes of institutional restructuring before and during the war gave way to a single-minded focus upon redistributive tax-and-transfer policies. As the economic limits of these policies became apparent, no richer set of structural alternatives existed to which besieged social democrats could turn. In economics there emerged, to confirm the blindness, a brand of anti-institutional institutionalism. Its point was to show how institutional arrangements were either largely irrelevant or capable of being explained as the cumulative and convergent discovery by rational economic actors of the institutional requirements of their own rationality.

Examples and warnings: national governments and family farms. We can strengthen ourselves for the work of reimagining the government–business relation and escaping the dogmas and superstitions I have just described through reflection on three sets of contemporary experiences: the alliance between national governments and family farmers, the varieties of strategic coordination between government and business pioneered by the northeast Asian economies, and the practices of vanguardist production developed in the most advanced regions of the Western industrial democracies. Each of these experiences offers an instructive although flawed starting point. Each provides inspiration and demands correction when turned into material for a democratizing alternative to neoliberalism.

Consider first the collaborative and transformative effort in the partnership between business and government on which the success of modern family farming has so heavily depended. Under many circumstances farming of family dimensions can prove incomparably efficient. It is nevertheless vulnerable to a combination of economic and climatic risks. In the absence of countervailing support, these risks will produce bouts of bankruptcy and land concentration. Once a structure of support is put in place, it can gradually acquire additional functions, giving the family farm access to economies of scale and assisting its technical and technological improvement. Very often this alliance between the state and the farmer has thrived against a background of cooperative competition among farmers. American agriculture – for much of the history of the United States the star performer in the economy – benefited from such arrangements, from the early land distribution of the nineteenth-century Homestead Acts to the technical work of the Agricultural Extension Services. We lack, however, save for the relatively centralized, collusive, and exclusive trade and industrial policies used by the North East Asian economies, a developed institutional example of the generalization of these agrarian innovations to the economy as a whole.

Examples and warnings: strategic coordination and hard states in North East Asia. The practice of strategic coordination in the North East Asian economies (first Japan and then South Korea, Taiwan, and Singapore) is a second contemporary experience we can use in imagining an alternative construction of the government–business relationship. A conventional explanation of their past economic success concedes that something must be credited to the success of governmental activism in specific areas: for example, in the performance-based and subsidized allocation of credit to innovative, export-oriented firms, or in the orchestrated transfer of technologies, skills, and talent to an up-and-coming branch of industry. However, the conventional analysis immediately surrounds this concession with two qualifications. The first qualification is that other, orthodox economic policies, such as sound public finance (balanced budgets), and sensible social commitments, such as sustained and large-scale investment in public education, counted for more than efforts at governmental guidance of the market. Although these efforts sometimes succeeded, they just as often failed, producing costly mistakes that a greater self-restraint would have avoided. The second qualification is that whatever efficacy these interventions may have possessed depended upon the special histories and circumstances resulting in the formation of strong, capable, and independent bureaucracies. To emulate these interventionist practices in conditions where such bureaucracies do not exist is to court the disasters of runaway clientelism.

This reassuring account combines a series of half-truths: what cuts the insight in half, and ruins its value as guidance, is precisely the poverty of the institutional imagination informing it – imagination about the institutional inventions of the past and the institutional possibilities of the future. Once we add this missing element, we discover that the accomplishments and the limits of these North East Asian economies were bound together, and rested on a distinctive range of institutional compromises. These compromises imposed and impose constraints upon democratic experimentalism. Our task is not to imitate such examples but to reimagine and reconstruct them so that they come to serve the larger purpose of advancing democratic experimentalism.

The most important point to understand is that both the orthodox accomplishments of the North East Asian economies and their heterodox inventions depended upon the special character of the authoritarian or semi-democratic hard state. The forms of strategic coordination in these societies were more inclusive in some countries than in others: for example, they were more inclusive in Taiwan, where many medium-sized firms became, through their associations, beneficiaries of governmental support. Nevertheless, in every North East Asian economy, including the prototype, Japan, the formulation of trade and industrial policy remained largely centralized in a national bureaucratic staff. In every such economy, a distinction persisted between those who sat at the table of the dealmakers and those who did not, although the list of participants was more inclusive in some countries than in others. The content of the deal consisted in a set of selective favors. In designing these favors, bureaucracies were checked only by the broad consensus of interest and outlook within the ruling political and entrepreneurial elites.

Such a form of the government–business partnership may resist the most brazen forms of collusion between bureaucrats and entrepreneurs by the professionalism and independence of the bureaucratic staff. Ultimately, it must find protection in the measured autonomy of government from subservience to particular business interests. On the other hand, however, it remains a selective bargain, authored and imposed from above. When it escapes collusion, it does so by drawing upon the political arsenal of authoritarianism.

Now consider those respects in which the North East Asian economies are said to have walked on the straight and narrow path of economic orthodoxy, not so far, after all, from what neoliberalism recommends. Investment in education like agrarian reform was no technical policy decision. It was the expression of a capacity for equalizing structural reform, sustained by cultural traditions (the reverence for learning) and inspired by historical emergencies (the rescue of Japan during the nineteenth century from the danger of subjugation, the shared stake of American proconsuls and national elites after the Second World War in immunizing their societies against communism and in preparing them for a new life). Even the simple accomplishment of paying for the government by taxes rather than by inflation requires a capacity for independent public action, undertaken by a state capable of resisting, as well as of accommodating, the propertied and the privileged. The North East Asian economies did not have to accept liberal or neoliberal economic orthodoxy wholesale. They could, for example, operate according to sound-finance doctrine while rejecting doctrinaire free trade. They could welcome foreign loan capital while maintaining an intransigent hostility to speculative finance capital. They could dose and channel foreign direct investment to suit the learning capabilities and the market needs of national industry. They could pick and choose because, unlike their Latin American counterparts, they had a state that was capable of doing so.

Thus, we see that both the relative success of the North East Asian economies at orthodoxy – as in their capacity to finance government adequately and transparently – and their relative success at heterodoxy – as in their sustained experiments with directed trade and industrial policy – had their basis in the same condition: the existence of an authoritarian (or semi-democratic) hard state. In its relation to the entrepreneurial elites and the moneyed interests, such a state was in a position analogous to that of the most serious reformers of the agrarian-bureaucratic empires of the past in their dealings with the landed magnates: independent but not too independent; anxious to preserve a class of free smallholders as a counterweight to the magnates and a requirement of prosperity and strength; but equally determined not to turn restraint upon the magnates into an antiaristocratic revolutionary despotism. Such a state is powerful enough to demand payment, up front, for its operations, to impose effective limits upon extreme inequality, and to enter into active partnership with (some) businesses. However, it cannot make its deals more inclusive in their participants, nor more decentralized and experimentalist in their forms, without changing its own character and its relation to the people. So long as government-led strategic coordination operated under such constraints, it remained, for all its professionalism, vulnerable to the twin evils of dogmatism and collusion. It diminished opportunities for one only by increasing occasions for the other.

The earlier remark that authoritarianism is a shortcut to the hardness of the hard state can now take on its full meaning. An authoritarian government can more easily resist influence and impose decisions. It can do so, however, only within the narrow framework of the social compromise that allows it to subsist. It dare not defy the interests paramount in that compromise. In every initiative, including its trade and industrial policy, it looks, with a second eye, to the convenience of its own power. Moreover, as it begins to democratize, it becomes more porous and pliant. As a result, its hardness and its authoritarianism begin to seem inseparable. Things will get worse before they get better: a relative or partial democracy, in an unequal and unequally organized society, will be one in which the perversion of strategic coordination into prejudice and favoritism becomes most likely. A deepening of democracy, achieved through cumulative institutional change, will broaden the range of expansion of the organizations and organized interests that can act as agents and beneficiaries of economic policy. It will also cause a change in the nature and method of policy, allowing for more experimental decentralization in the making and implementation of policy.

A progressive alternative can gain help and inspiration from attempting to reconstruct the government–business partnership as practiced by the North East Asian economies. Rather than being attributed to a centralized bureaucratic staff – ministries of trade and industry – such a partnership should be progressively decentralized to the point that alternative entities, within and outside government, become its authors and agents. Rather than being unitary, it should be pluralistic: the responsible agencies should be able to try out different strategies. Rather than remaining bureaucratic in style, under a mixed regime of administrative law and administrative discretion, it should be discursive and open-ended in character, taking as its content the step-by-step fulfillment of the conditions of productive vanguardism. Rather than being selective in its range of agents and beneficiaries, it should be inclusive, touching the rearguard as well as the vanguard.

Such a reconstruction of the government–business partnership might start, in a country with the institutional traditions of the Asian tiger economies, with the fragmentation of trade and industrial policy within the state apparatus: different bureaucratic teams and public banks might be encouraged to try out alternative strategies, working together with different groups of firms. It might continue with the creation of entities – financial and technical support centers – standing between the government and the firms, with considerable independence from both, and the mandate to extend vanguardist practices to the rearguard economy. It might lead to cumulative experiments with the property regime, as such entities begin to develop alternative rules and practices in dealing with their client firms. Little by little, we would come to fill the empty space between arm's-length regulation and spontaneous market initiative.

To describe this change in the nature of strategic coordination is to see that it embodies a political vision rather than a technical solution. In many contemporary circumstances it could begin with little institutional innovation. However, it could not progress without a sustained series of reforms and inventions in the organization of government and politics. Neither an authoritarian hard state nor a democratic soft state would do. We would need a democratized hard state. The idea of a democratized hard state converges with the conception of the deepened democracy I later describe.

Examples and warnings: industrial reorganization in the rich countries. A third usable contemporary experience is the recent history of industrial reform in the most advanced regions and sectors of the most advanced economies: that is to say, those parts of the production system most proficient in vanguardist method. The famous example of the "third Italy" – the pioneering firms of Emilia Romagna and other areas of northern Italy – has been repeated, with variations, in many places, both in Europe and in the United States. Consider the elements of what has been repeated.

First, there are the surface phenomena of vanguardism: the destandardization of production, the high-technology, capital-intensive work environment, the dependence upon highly skilled labor, and the orientation to world markets and to the standards of other advanced competitors, suppliers, and customers around the world. These are the distinguishing traits of the actual vanguards, contrasted to the actual rearguard, that make up the advanced economies of the contemporary world. They are not always present when poorer, more technologically primitive firms achieve the vanguardism of method described next. However, in a world where vanguards and rearguards remain separated and opposed, they are usually at hand.

Second, there are the deeper and more intangible character-istics of a practical experimentalism: the softening of the contrast between task-defining and task-executing jobs and activities, the erosion of barriers among task-executing jobs, as the horizontal division of labor weakens together with the vertical division of labor; the mixture of competition and cooperation in regimes of cooperative competition among firms as well as within them; and the practice of permanent trial and error with organizations, deals and tools that both cooperative competition and a flexible division of labor encourage. Such a vanguardism can also flourish in what is, financially and technologically, the economic rearguard. How-ever, in the world as now organized, it rarely does. When it does prosper in the rearguard, persistently and on a broader scale, we invariably find the hand of local or national government pushing it forward.

Third, there are the familiar social and cultural conditions of practical experimentalism in the conventional vanguard, where it normally lives. One of these conditions is the existence of a preexisting pool of high knowledge and high skill, provided either by a tradition of artisanal work, or by the university-based training of a technical elite, or, most often, by some combination of the two. Another condition is a high level of voluntary association and community life. Such social organization supports effective local government. It both provides on its own account, and demands from government, investment in people. It nourishes the climate of trust and trustworthiness upon which both cooperative competition and flexible specialization depend.

Fourth, there is a typical path of development. Firms begin their apprenticeship by trying out in their internal affairs both the deeper and the surface aspects of productive vanguardism. Then they develop among themselves practices of cooperative competition, forming associations and tightening their links with local communities and governments. Finally, they learn to use their association with both national and local governments more effectively. They use it, for example, to help supply those same more-than-private and less-than-public goods on which their progress so heavily depends: access, for example, to the right kind of educated worker or to up-to-date information and advice about standards and methods of production. In the United States, state governments of both major political parties have disregarded neoliberal dogma enough to promote just such a form of the government–business partnership. Together, local governments and business associations have secured the support of federal departments and agencies.

It is this package of four sets of characteristics that has been repeated worldwide through the establishment of productive vanguards in poorer as well as in richer countries. When we say that a network of vanguards has become a driving force in the world economy we mean a network of firms with these attributes. Prominent vanguardist producers often become more linked to one another around the world than to the rest of the national economies in which they are located.

Economic vanguardism reoriented. To advance a democratizing alternative to the neoliberal program that refuses to take compensatory social transfer as the limit of its transformative ambition, we must pull this package apart. We must disentangle, step by step, the second set of traits in this list – the deeper, more intangible features of practical experimentalism – from the other three sets of features. For these other attributes are all more circumstantial. In particular, they express the circumstance in which vanguards and rearguards remain divided. A fuller disentanglement must await the realization of the later, antidualistic stage of this progressive alternative.

Even in its earliest moments, however, the program should seek the diffusion of vanguardist practices. It must do so the better to serve the goal of promoting economic growth while overcoming the separation between vanguards and rearguards. Only a difference of degree separates such an encouragement to the diffusion of better practice from a more militant antidualism.

Decentralized association between business and government and cooperative competition among firms can support each other. Both have as their chief aim the promotion of vanguardist practices: the weakening of the contrasts among task-executing jobs as well as between task-executing and task-defining positions. Both favor an overcoming of obsessional contrasts between the domains of cooperation and competition in work. Both foster ongoing revisionism about plans, procedures, and bargains, a revisionism sustained by trust, given and shared. These fundamental characteristics can dispense with major concentrations of capital, technology, and technical assistance, but not for long nor without active support from the government or from the decentralized public–private entities that would take over governmental responsibilities. Even a samba school in Rio de Janeiro can exemplify in its organization and methods many of the features of practical experimentalism. However, no set of knowledge-poor firms can begin moving in the direction of the worldwide network of vanguards without a route of access to the missing resources of capital and technology. That is why some public scheme for the broadened supply of these resources becomes necessary.

So, too, once we imagine such experimentalist practices carried beyond the frontiers of the most advanced sectors of the richest economies we can no longer take the existence of the usual supporting conditions for granted – a high level of trust-creating civic and community organization and a rich legacy of practical knowledge, jointly produced by artisans and universities. Instead, we must create these conditions, or their functional equivalents, as we go along. Deliberate public action must achieve what spontaneous economic evolution proves insufficient to ensure.

Finally, in this transportation of vanguardism beyond its habitual terrain, the different stages of the typical developmental sequence – first reform within the firm, then association among firms, and only later alliance with government – may need to be jumbled up. In fact, the work of the different stages may have to be executed simultaneously, although piece by piece.

Who should do the job? In the early stages we can imagine the work to be undertaken by decentralized governmental bodies joining with groups of firms. The earlier discussion of the reform of the style of strategic coordination pioneered by the North East Asian economies suggests how such collaboration might go forward. Instead of centralized ministries of trade and industry, a diversity of teams might try out alternative policies. Significant freedom of initiative would combine with ultimate supervision by elected governments, local communities, and associations of firms.

Later, this collaboration between decentralized public entities and groups of firms might begin to turn into a cast of social funds or support centers, operating in between the government and the firms. Imagine these funds to have a mixed public–private character, to be accountable to both the governments that established them and the firms they assisted, to enjoy nevertheless a wide-ranging measure of decision-making authority, and to specialize in a diversified range of different types of investment in different sectors of the economy. Some of these funds or centers would be charged with investment in the rearguard as well as with the work of leading the transformation of rearguard firms. Part of public savings and of private pension savings would be mandatorily committed to the funds, and a proportion of this part would go to those funds responsible for the enhancement of the rearguard.

It is impossible to say beforehand or in formulaic terms whether this engagement in the rearguard represents an outright subsidy or simply an institutionally favored stretching of the time horizon of investment. There is no such clearcut distinction; the success of the funds depends both on their ability to provoke a sequence of innovation and growth in the marginalized, capital-poor part of the real economy and upon the existence of legal–institutional arrangements allowing this productive contribution to generate a financial gain. Contrary to the suppositions of much conventional economics, these are distinct conditions. A great deal more than transactions costs and asymmetries of information separate the second from the first.

The further away such funds and centers move from the world of the economic vanguard, the more their responsibilities go beyond arm's-length investment to collaborative engagement in the reorganization of firms. A vast intermediate space of joint productive activities stands between the familiar extremes of passive provision of capital and one-way imposition of policy. We already know from the development of vanguardist production in the most thriving industrial regions of the rich countries that the experimentalist practices of vanguardism depend upon the provision of certain goods. Neither the isolated firms nor agencies external to them can by themselves supply such goods. They require joint definition, creation, and provision, arranged among firms as well as between firms and local or national governments, against a supporting background of associational life in the local society. Moreover, they call for ongoing reformulation in markets that are simultaneously volatile, global, and destandardized.

Such goods, escaping the traditional division between public and private goods, may include pooled technological and financial resources, the sharing of information, the joint development of production and trade strategies, the reskilling of workers, and the improvement of social conditions in the local communities within which production takes place. What is required is more than an organizational technique or an institutional fix: a set of conversational practices and habits of discovery, supported by arrangements, in the firm, in the sector, and in the economy as a whole. The point of these habits and practices is to moderate the conflict between cooperation and innovation.

The great variety of circumstances in the relations between funds and firms in different areas of production and at different levels of vanguardist sophistication suggests a further reconstructive move. This move would have its day in the later, antidualistic stage of the alternative. It may, however, find early encouragement in the effort to establish institutional arrangements congenial to productive vanguardism, and deeper inspiration in the commitment to prefer those forms of economic organization that enjoy a democratizing potential.

As we pass from the early to the later program, innovating in the institutional forms of property and democracy, the relations between funds and firms would begin to differ in the property regime they presupposed as well as in the sectors and strategies they preferred. Some funds would keep an arm's-length relation to the firms with which they dealt, maintaining something close to the conventional form of the property right, with its clearly demarcated zones of entitlement, risk, and responsibility. Other funds would develop an intimate relation to a cluster of firms, as part of a system of more inclusive pooling of financial, commercial, and technological resources. From these practices many fragmentary, conditional, and temporary forms of property would emerge. In the end alternative systems of property and contract rights would mark different parts of the economy.

Such a reshaping of property need not mimic the paralyzing multiplication of vetoes upon entrepreneurial decisions favored by the conventional social-democratic response to the managerial program of industrial innovation. The key point in the firm, as in government, is that there exist a design for resolving impasse quickly, either by discriminating areas of decisional authority or by providing a procedure for decision in the face of disagreement among stakeholders. In the end, multiple systems of private law give alternative content to the idea of decentralized economic opportunity and initiative. We can then hope to assess their costs and benefits experimentally. Thus, the idea of the institutional indeterminacy of the market ceases to be a speculative hypothesis and gains practical weight.

The institutional arrangements for production and exchange should be as open to experimental variation as all other parts of social life. The assumptions about property underlying this turn contrast with the view, still characteristic of much of economics, that the market economy has a single natural and necessary basic form, expressed in the classical, nineteenth-century legal system of unified, sharply demarcated property rights. The formative episode in the development of twentieth-century legal thought was the redefinition of property as a bundle of legal relations and the simultaneous development of the awareness that property rights inevitably conflict. No single logic of the property regime can settle such conflicts; decisions of policy are required to resolve them. This legal thesis, however, has failed to develop into the conception, central to this argument for reconstruction, that market economies, like representative democracies and free civil societies, can take radically different institutional forms. Legal thought has yet to complete its rebellion against institutional fetishism. The partisans of democratic experimentalism should not wait for it to do so.

The early program: from democratic education to social inheritance

The progressive alternative to neoliberalism is the counterpart writ large to what I earlier described as the radical-democratic alternative to conventional social democracy in the redesign of relations among firms, workers, and governments. Remember that if the first plank in that radical-democratic platform was the broadening of access, and of types of access, to productive resources, the second plank was the enhancement of individual capability. The point there was to establish security through increased power to prosper and change in the midst of innovation. The implication is to reject job tenure imposed as a constraint upon innovation. An enhancement of capability requires a great expansion of rights to both original and continuing education – to a permanent reskilling. Such a program must include the ongoing development of generic conceptual and practical capacities as well as the cultivation of specialized skills. As one of the most important areas of overlap and convergence between the requirements of productive vanguardism and the needs of democratic experimentalism, education should be considered under two different aspects: first, as an area in which a tension central to democratic practices and ideals becomes most clearly manifest;

second, as the field in which we can most easily begin to develop the institutional and ideological structure of a principle vital to democratic experimentalism, the principle of social inheritance.

The family transmission of property and the family transmission of differential educational opportunity are the two great mechanisms sustaining the class structure of contemporary societies. The strengthening of rights to education should be seen as the germ of a more ambitious idea: the idea of social inheritance, according to which people inherit primarily from society rather than from their parents. The primary tool of social inheritance is the social-endowment account.

Rights to original and continuing education would gradually turn into a generalized form of social inheritance. Each individual would have a social-endowment account consisting in funds freely cashable at certain life turning points, other funds whose use would be conditioned upon the agreement of family or community trustees, and claims for the provision of public services. The account would vary upward according to the two countervailing criteria of compensation for a special vulnerability or disability and reward for competitively demonstrated capacity.

The impulse animating social-endowment accounts in particular and social inheritance in general is the mutual relation that exists between accelerated institutional experimentalism and enhanced individual capacity. For the institutions of democratic experimentalism to be secure, the individual must both be and feel safe and empowered. Experimentalism must be qualified out of respect for concerns that may go beyond it. We must rethink each part of the program of democratic experimentalism in the light of this demand for individual security and capacity. We must also rethink the language of rights in which this demand is ordinarily expressed in the light of the ideas and ideals informing that program. People learn to disengage not only their sense of self and of personal capacity but also their experience of solidarity and community from ways of life that depend for their survival upon exclusion of outsiders and resistance to challenge. This is a move in the construction of personality as much as it is a move in the reconstruction of society. The development of social endowment and of the link it exemplifies between experimentalism and capability brings us to the threshold of a second more institutionally innovative stage in the development of a progressive alternative.

The later program: redistribution and antidualism

Early and later programs redefined. The arrangements and policies described in the preceding pages offer a clear alternative to neoliberalism. Their combined and cumulative effect is far-reaching. Considered individually, they nevertheless remain close to the established and inherited institutional structure. For that very reason, the early program can serve as the proposal for an inclusive alliance. It can hope to earn the support of groups that lack an historical connection with the left.

In the antinecessitarian spirit informing these ideas, we should recognize that the early program has more than one future. It can become a resting point in a path of institutional change. The focus of experimental innovation will then pass from the larges-cale institutions of society to the activities of individuals and small groups. (The result would be similar to what I call in *What Should Legal Analysis Become?* extended social democracy, presented there as one of several alternative futures of a free society.) The practical and spiritual problems characteristic of this relatively conservative sequel to the early program would resemble in many ways the problems of the contemporary industrial democracies.

Any interruption in the effort to deepen democratic experimentalism may make possible the emergence of new social and economic divisions. An elite of skilled conceptual operators may concentrate in its own hands the effective work of governance and production while the mass of ordinary people find themselves confined to a decent and secure insignificance. The family will continue to serve as a vehicle for transmitting from one generation to the next many of the cultural and some of the material privileges of this elite. Vivid impulses and desires, necessary to strong individuals, will find little room for public expression. They will lose themselves in the labyrinth of subjectivity, amid the excitements and disappointments of private gratification.

The later program described in the following pages represents a different sequel: one that keeps up the pressure of institutional innovation and draws more closely together the conditions of material progress and individual emancipation. The result is a proposal more controversial and divisive than its forerunner. Everything in this later program is nevertheless foreshadowed in the early one. The basic method is still the analogical extension and reinterpretation of what came before. The condition of its feasibility remains the same: that it propose arrangements responsive to the interests and aspirations of all but the most privileged beneficiaries of the established order. An inclusive popular alliance, built by a convergence of leftist and centrist political parties and forces, must continue to be its primary agent.

The redistributive side. Under democratic experimentalism, we do not entrust to compensatory tax-and-transfer the cause of a more egalitarian distribution of rights, resources, and opportunities. We challenge the institutional arrangements locking us into a rigid tension between the requirements of efficiency and the demands of equity. The method is to shape economic and political institutions that both independently and by their combined effect produce more equality. Redistribution through compensatory tax-and-transfer nevertheless must continue to play an important subsidiary role, a role in which it extends, rather than seeking to reverse, the redistributive work of the institutions. Part of this

role lies, in the later program as in the earlier one, in the funding
of a strong and capable government rather than in direct charges
upon individuals (through progressive taxation) or direct transfers
to them (through social welfare).

In the tax system the two major sets of direct and progressive
taxes – the progressive taxation of personal consumption and the
progressive taxation of wealth, especially wealth in the form of
gifts and estates – must now gain the upper hand. Thus, the
tax system comes to hit, straightforwardly and transparently,
each of the two major targets of direct taxation. By preferring
this combination of taxes, we hit both targets in a manner
lightening the burden taxation imposes upon saving and investment. The guarantee of a minimum income to everyone, conditioned upon the willingness of the capable to learn and to work,
can begin to develop into the establishment of social-endowment
accounts.

The indirect taxation of consumption, most often in the form
of a comprehensive flat-rate value-added tax, can continue to
perform its residual role as a guarantee of adequate funding for
government. In this role, however, it may slowly be supplanted
by a basic underlying rate of interest charged by the government
to the independent funds that administer and lend out capital
under a variety of alternative property regimes. (The multiplication of property regimes, and its consequences for governmental
finance, are discussed further below.) There may, in fact, be a
loose functional equivalence between these two devices. The
difference is that the underlying interest charge allows for a more
direct social guarantee of saving and investment, and does so
without sacrificing the decentralization of economic initiative that
represents the heart of a market economy. Moreover, because
the interest is charged to the funds rather than to the ultimate
capital-takers, and because the different funds can serve as
protagonists of different sets of property rules coexisting within
the same economy, we have here part of the means with which to

increase experimental diversity in the legal–institutional forms of the market economy. We give practical effect to the idea of the relativity of the distinction between public and private law.

The full-fledged development of social endowment accounts completes the redistributive strategy of the later program. The financial basis for a richer social endowment will have increased through the more aggressive taxation of family inheritance. The diversification of arrangements for the decentralized allocation of capital will have made entrepreneurial initiative and personal development less dependent upon family support. A style of constitutionalism friendly to the repeated practice of structural reform, a way of organizing politics encouraging of civic engagement, and a deepening of associational life will have helped form and energize individuals who can put their social endowment to use.

Just as the tax system under the later program should give more room than does the early program to redistributive taxation, so the social-endowment account in this second phase can move beyond the guarantee of a minimum of rights and resources to each individual. It can assign greater weight to the countervailing device of increments to the endowment according to special need as well as to special capability. Increments will be paid to the endowment of those who suffer a physical or mental handicap. Increments will be won by those who are able to demonstrate competitively special abilities.

The single most important object of social endowment under democratic experimentalism is education, begun in childhood and continued throughout a working life. The political and social institutions of democratic experimentalism must, I shall soon argue, find an independent and trouble-making ally in the emancipatory school. Such a school must do more than teach experimentalism. It must nourish the prophetic powers of ordinary humanity.

The antidualist side. The core of this progressive alternative lies in the combination of a deepened, high-energy democracy with a political economy committed to overcome stark divisions between productive vanguards and productive rearguards. This combination promises to make good on the zone of potential overlap between the conditions of practical, productive progress and the conditions for the cumulative emancipation of individuals from entrenched social divisions and hierarchies.

The early stages of the alternative prepare an antidualist political economy by beginning to forge the institutional tools for a decentralized, participatory style of strategic coordination between government and private enterprise. The later stages of the alternative continue this work. By continuing it, they give institutional content to the idea of democratizing the market economy rather than merely regulating it.

In the early stages the emphasis falls upon the development of a level of independent economic agents – funds and support centers – standing in between government and private producers. Among the resources they would tap would be the mandatory private saving held in the pension system. These intermediate organizations would support the development and diffusion of better work and production practices. They would often help bring groups of firms into a setting of cooperative competition, enabling them to cooperate and compete at the same time. They would sometimes undertake a more general form of venture-capital finance – investment in start-up businesses – than now exists outside a few regions of the world.

It would be their central mission to make productive resources and opportunities more widely available. They would extend vanguardist practices of continuous learning and innovation beyond the frontiers of well established economic vanguards. Together with the strengthened social endowment of the individual worker–citizen such initiatives would help create the functional equivalent to the prefordist conditions that so often favor postfordist forms of production. These conditions include a well established tradition of craft labor and a dense community life, encouraging mutual help and nourishing trust.

We can expect many regimes of private and social property to develop over time from the different styles of association that the intermediate organizations would establish with the firms with which they dealt. Thus, at one extreme, we can imagine funds that would maintain an arm's-length relation with the firms, auctioning off resources to the businesses able to ensure the best risk-adjusted returns. At another extreme would be funds participating actively in the ownership and management of their associated firms, and serving as the financial, technical, and strategic centers of little confederations of cooperative-competitive businesses.*

The disaggregation and recombination of the constituent elements of the conventional property right would allow such alternative property regimes to emerge and coexist experimentally within the same economy. Some of these alternatives would qualify the absoluteness of the discretion the traditional property owner enjoys over the resources at his command. In so doing, however, they would also broaden the range of people with access to productive resources and opportunities.

The "stakeholding" solution imposes social constraints upon the market by giving organized constituencies – workers, consumer groups, and local communities – voices and vetoes in the management decisions of established firms. The result risks paralysis while also threatening to reinforce existing divisions between economic insiders and outsiders. The alternative seeks to make the market economy more pluralistic in its institutional forms and more inclusive in its social beneficiaries. It tries to

---

* For an analysis of some of these forms of private or social property, see Roberto Mangabeira Unger, *Politics: The Central Texts*, edited and introduced by Zhiyuan Cui, Verso, London, 1997, pp. 340–66.

achieve this goal, however, without imposing on the market the straitjacket of a single institutional form or suppressing the opportunity for decisive action and contrarian risk-taking. No form of the market economy will do any good – for growth or democracy – if it denies space to the individual or collective entrepreneur who says: To hell with you, I'll do it my way.

Why enforce, under the dogmatic label of private property, a single legal–institutional species of economic decentralization? Why not give practical consequence to the institutional indeterminacy of the market idea? Why not try out some of the more promising alternatives simultaneously and see what works? The kernel of productive vanguardism is spiritual before it is material: a practice of redefining tasks in the course of executing them. A more experimental market economy must apply the same principle to its own arrangements. So, too, deepened democracy multiplies opportunities for people to challenge and change features of their institutional context in the course of going about their daily lives. The project of an antidualist political economy brings economic arms and gives wings to this idea.

The later program: a deepened democracy and an emancipatory school

The economic institutions described in the preceding pages require a government that is both activist and accountable, a sustained heightening of the level of popular political engagement, a more even and general organization of civil society, and a strengthening of individual capacities. Deepened democracy and the emancipatory school are two major agents of such a society; their relation to each other presents some of the most delicate problems of a democratizing alternative to neoliberalism.

It would, however, be a mistake to treat such changes in politics and society as mere means to economic reconstruction.

The pressure of practical problems in peacetime, and the links connecting structural change to redistribution and economic redistribution to economic growth, make the reshaping of production and of its relation to politics a natural point of departure. However, we could just as well see economic reforms as an opportunity to advance the political and social program of democratic experimentalism. Nor is there any reason to view the economic reforms as prior in time to the changes leading up to deepened democracy and the emancipatory school. There is no natural beginning or sequence. Movement must take place simultaneously and on many fronts. Advances on one front – economic, political, social, or educational – may occur before advances in others. There will then be thresholds at which the next step on one front becomes impossible without reinforcing changes in others. The idea of combined and uneven development takes on its realistic social meaning.

The constitutionalism of accelerated politics. Two features have dominated the modern Western constitutional tradition: a style of constitutional organization of government slowing politics down, for the sake of freedom connected with private property, and a set of practices and institutions helping to keep society at a relatively low level of political mobilization. Democratic experimentalism demands that we replace both these sets of political and constitutional conventions.

Traditional constitutionalism attributes an effective veto power over any major reform proposal to many independent powers within government. The requirement of consensus within the state apparatus slows politics down, and gives the social forces hostile to the reform project time and occasion to organize themselves in opposition. The social vetoes are thus superimposed on the political vetoes. The overall result is to encourage a style of politics in which transformative projects must run so many hurdles before they can succeed that they will gain acceptance, in normal times, only in diluted form. Politics will then take place as a succession of each party's second-best solutions. Only in the presence of extreme economic or military crisis will major institutional innovation appear feasible. The role of disaster as midwife of innovation will begin to seem a law of history, when it in fact results from institutional facts and omissions.

The American system of checks and balances, and the Madisonian constitutionalism upon which it draws, may be the purest examples of this tendency, but they are not the only ones. A parliamentary system operating in a context of low political engagement may produce a similar effect thanks to the interaction between the need to sustain fragile electoral majorities during protracted periods of transition and the need to uphold party-political union.

The major consequence of low civic engagement and slow-motion politics is to leave the established logic of group interests and identities unshaken. For the solidity and transparency of a system of group interests and identities depend upon the entrenchment of the background institutions and practices of society. When this institutional template is left unchallenged, each group or class interest takes on a semblance of naturalness: it is the interest that consists in the defense of a well-defined place within the social division of labor and within the established system of relations between government and society. The exclusive ways of defining and defending group interests – those that, taking established arrangements for granted, define each group as the rival of its immediate neighbors in the social division of labor – will, in such circumstances, prevail over the solidaristic ways – those that seek convergences of interest on the basis of cumulative institutional changes. Politics will become a matter of negotiation among the organized interests – a practice of harmonization in which each interest counts according to the measure of its present power. Because there are not only many interests, but also more than one measure of effective power (for example, power to elect politicians as contrasted with power to disrupt production and investment), all but the most narrowly focused deals will seem too hard to strike and, once struck, too hard to keep. As a result, institutional innovation and structural change will begin to seem all but impossible. Once again, crisis will appear to be the indispensable cradle of invention. In such a setting, the parliamentary demand for a government with broad party-political support, which might otherwise serve decisive experiments, may be converted into a tool for slowing politics down.

Two great impulses motivate a democratizing constitutional alternative. The first such impulse is the commitment to introduce into the practice of representative democracy some of the elements of direct democracy. The conflict over the control and uses of governmental power should be shaped so as to help loosen the hold of narrow sectional concerns over the imaginative life of the political nation. The task is to accomplish this objective in a way that, unlike traditional forms of populist plebiscitarianism, encourages the independent self-organization of civil society.

The second animating impulse is the effort to accelerate politics – favoring decisive programs over each party's second-best solutions – by providing for the rapid resolution of inhibiting impasse. The inhibiting impasse may arise from the formal vetoes that independent branches of government are able to impose upon one another or from the informal vetoes that the independent powers of society may force upon transformative ambition in politics. Moreover, we should seek to resolve the impasse through the engagement of the general electorate, thus joining the commitment to combine direct and representative democracy with the effort to quicken politics. We need to achieve this goal in a way upholding and deepening party-political pluralism and political freedom.

There are different combinations of constitutional arrangements by which, according to circumstance, we may be able to further these objectives. Where social inequalities have already been moderated, strong political parties exist, and a vigorous parliamentary democracy lives, it may be enough to energize the parliamentary regime with practices conducive to a sustained heightening of political mobilization. When these conditions remain unfulfilled, however, we may have reason to prefer a certain combination of characteristics of the presidential and parliamentary regimes. The direct election of a strong president may, in such circumstances, provide a route to power less susceptible to plutocratic management and more open to national and structural concerns than are decentralized parliamentary contests. In office, such a president may discover a stake in the development of a direct, plebiscitarian channel to popular support. Thus, the presidential election and presidential power may excite the resistance of political power to the organized and privileged interests of society, and serve as levers of destabilization in an otherwise closely guarded political society.

The precise character of the combination of constitutional arrangements is what matters, for, like all institutional conceptions, the ideas of the presidential and the parliamentary regimes are institutionally indeterminate. They have no inherent institutional logic, only a makeshift collection of organizational characteristics history has thrown together. The constitution of the French Fifth Republic, for example, joins aspects of conventional presidentialism and parliamentarianism in ways providing for both a political fast time (when the president and the parliamentary majority converge) and a political slow time (when they diverge). However, you can readily envisage such system without the slow time. So revised, the constitutional design encourages the rapid resolution of impasse. It also brings elements of direct democracy into representative democracy. Under such a regime, a strong, directly elected presidency would coexist with a parliament equipped both to collaborate with the president and to resist him.

Three constitutional mechanisms, arranged in sequence, would ensure the prevalence of the fast time. The first such mechanism is the priority that the acceptance, rejection, or renegotiation of the electoral program should enjoy over episodic legislation in the dealings between president and parliament. The parliament must confirm, reject, or renegotiate the program. If there is a divergence over the program, the second mechanism begins to operate. President and parliament may agree to the realization and the terms of a plebiscite or referendum about the program or its disputed parts. The need for agreement prevents the plebiscitarian option from becoming, as it sometimes has, a caesaristic device by which to turn the political nation against the parliamentary institutions. The broad programmatic scope of the popular consultation prevents it from being used, as it has been in other circumstances, to dissolve broad alternatives into narrow issues. If the president and parliament fail to agree to the realization and the terms of the plebiscite or if the result is inconclusive, the hybrid regime appeals to a third impasse-resolving and politics-accelerating mechanism. Each of the two branches – president or parliament – may call for anticipated elections independently of agreement by the other. Both branches must then stand again for office. The need to face this electoral risk should normally prevent the reckless abuse of the right to provoke early elections.

The heightening of political participation. In the history of the dominant constitutional tradition, half-designed devices for the discouragement of political mobilization succeeded the earlier filtering mechanisms of proto-democratic liberalism. These mechanisms, such as the proliferation of intermediate levels of representation and the property qualification on the suffrage, helped filter out demagogic influence and dampen down popular enthusiasm. In the mid nineteenth century, conservatives and radicals alike expected universal suffrage to have subversive consequences. They were mistaken. The combination of effective social compromise and relentless economic pressure, together with the demobilizing consequences of the new way of organizing mass party politics, usually proved sufficient to tame the suffrage.

Two general ideas help explain the institutional conditions and the social consequences of political mobilization. The first idea is that political institutions differ significantly in their hospitality to political mobilization. A conservative political science claims there to be an unyielding inverse relation between institutions and mobilization: mobilization is, according to this view, inherently anti-institutional. It is a special, rightwing version of the structure fetishism recurring in the history of philosophy and social thought. According to this social counterpart to the theological *via negativa*, institutional arrangements, like cultural conventions, have a rigid, hostile relation to the structure-transcending freedom that helps create them. The structures may be the necessary form of ordinary social and cultural life but they are also the unmistakable enemies of individual or collective creativity or authenticity. The moments of refoundation are the interludes in which, for a while, we loosen the hold of such institutions. However, although we may temporarily overthrow them, and replace some by others, we are powerless to change the character of the structures and of their relation to freedom.

The truth, however, is that institutional and discursive structures vary in their quality as well as in their content; they differ in the extent to which they are just there, on a take-it-or-leave-it basis, rather than accessible to challenge and reconstruction. We should value this disentrenchment of the structures not just for its own sake, as an aspect of freedom, but also and chiefly as a condition for the achievement of other substantive goals of insight, liberation, equality, and material progress.

This possibility of variation in the entrenchment of institutional arrangements brings us to a second idea important to an understanding of political energy. There is a causal connection between the energy level in politics – the level of popular political engagement – and the structural content of politics. A politics capable of producing frequent structural reform in the direction of democratic experimentalism is necessarily a high-energy politics. A single program may be imposed from above in the face of popular indifference thanks to the victory of one part of a ruling circle over another. However, a capacity for repeated reform, without the incitement of crisis, requires sustained popular political involvement. Such involvement cannot be sustained unless it is also institutionalized.

The level of popular participation in politics is not an elusive and unyielding cultural fate, summarily reflecting the history of a people. Like everything else in society, it remains, to a significant extent, the product of particular arrangements on which, once established, it continues to depend. The failure to press, or even to imagine, alternative arrangements makes the resulting approach to politics seem natural. However, a few relatively modest institutional changes would be likely to heighten popular engagement in democracies that now seem deenergized. Each of these changes alone would prove ineffective, but not all of them would have to operate at once for the result to be achieved. Among such changes are: rules of mandatory voting; expanded free access to the means of mass communication in favor of social movements as well as political parties; regimes strengthening political parties, such as "closed-list" systems (the voter must choose among parties rather than among individual candidates); and public financing of political campaigns.

Electoral regimes may be only circumstantially related to these concerns. Thus, for example, proportional representation, when combined with rules limiting the number of parties as well as with the other mobilization-favoring arrangements just enumerated, may often help intensify politics. There will nevertheless be situations in which a winner-take-all, majority-oriented electoral regime will prove more mobilizing because it will help disrupt a rigidified party system, revealing and empowering large coalitions of opinion that this system helps suppress. Machiavelli remarked upon the difficulty of changing a character that no longer suits a situation. So, too, a polity may prove unable readily to discard the character an electoral regime imposed upon it. It must learn how to do so, and establish the arrangements that help it learn more quickly.

The capacity to sustain a high measure of political involvement rests upon more than the narrow organization of partisan electoral conflict. It relies as well upon many other resources of democratic experimentalism: the democratic school as a maker of rebellious minds and the widespread practice of productive vanguardism in the economy as an experience of empowerment in everyday life. The promises of political mobilization will soon be disbelieved if they are not confirmed by the lessons of the school and the workplace.

The independent organization of civil society. A disorganized society can neither generate nor implement alternative futures. It can at best have alternatives imposed upon it, or produce them in a haze of misunderstood options and unintended consequences. An unequally organized society finds that every attempt at decentralization and devolution threatens to relinquish power to the privileged, with the result that people must choose between public and private authoritarianism.

An influential strand of contemporary politics and political thought emphasizes the enabling role of the spontaneous self-organization of civil society. Thus, on one side, we find the idea that a politics of grassroots social organization, changing civil society, department by department, can make it unnecessary to win and use governmental power. Left to its own devices, however, the state strikes back, driving toward a future that organized civil society may despise, and narrowing the terrain on which the work of organization can advance. Every transformative politics must therefore seek to combine movement from the top down with movement from the bottom up.

A familiar tradition in the history of modern social thought has emphasized the role of voluntary association as "social capital": a machine for creating trust, which in turn makes possible the development of styles of cooperation in learning, production, and government that are hospitable to innovation. Every version of cooperation, embedded in a set of real social relations, gives rise to expectations and rights hostile to innovation. A trust-consuming and trust-producing practice such as voluntary association has the power to diminish such impediments. For trust implies a greater willingness to accept the incompleteness of incomplete contracts, to forswear short-term reciprocity in the distribution of benefits and burdens, and to run risks in the conviction that our co-workers will willingly share their outcomes.

The conventional advocacy of social capital, accumulated through voluntary association, suffers, however, from two points of blindness. They are connected, and neither can be cured without a change in the political practices and institutional arrangements of civil society.

For one thing, although voluntary association may produce trust and, through trust, capacity for action, it also depends upon trust and upon belief in the feasibility and efficacy of action. That is why an extreme inequality of power and advantage is inimical to the spread of voluntary association except when transformative hope compensates for an unequal reality. To be effective, such a plan requires institutional change. As a result, voluntary association remains impotent to create its own conditions unless it gains institutional vision and joins forces with a different style of politics. Its temporary accomplishments will soon be reversed, for although hope results from action it cannot survive without achievement.

For another thing, like market-driven exchange or democratic politics, voluntary association lacks a natural institutional setting. Its actual setting will influence not only how much voluntary association takes place but also what kind. The discussion of social capital in contemporary political economy and political science has a paradoxical character. Sometimes – in political economy – association has been demonized as "common-interest organization," a tool in the quest for economic rents from a weakened state and a source of rigidity in economic life. Thus, for example, some have seen the destruction of such common-interest organizations in Germany and Japan in the aftermath of the mid-century war as a contributing cause of those countries' later successes as economies and democracies. At other times – in political science, sociology, and comparative history – association has been hailed as a major condition of economic development and good government. Thus, the success of the north-central Italian economy and local government, and of any number of its counterparts elsewhere in Europe, has been credited to dense norms and networks of community organization: the history-shaped ascendancy of horizontal over vertical organization.

How can each of these seemingly contrasting approaches enjoy, as each evidently does, an element of truth? The answer lies in a feature of social life closely related to the duality of ways to define and defend group interests: the exclusive and conservative, contrasted to the solidaristic and transformative. If the organization represents the exclusive defense of a group interest, in a larger setting in which the opportunities and resources for effective association remain very unevenly distributed, it is likely to go in search of rents and privileges, to define the organizations socially contiguous to it as its main enemies, and to wage war against innovation. The result will be "bad" association. If, however, the organization has a more inclusive, solidaristic, and transformative perspective, and puts the definition of the group interest and identity of its members on the line in the course of seeking to advance them, it will be more likely to represent the "good," enabling type of association. If such an organization does not already exist in a setting where the capacity to associate is evenly and widely distributed, it will treat the diffusion of this capacity as part of its work. The institutional context of associa-tion eases the way of one of these approaches and makes the other harder to adopt and sustain.

Suppose that in an effort to cure the double blindness of the conventional focus upon trust and social capital we address the institutional setting of association. Suppose, further, that we define the problem of association broadly to cover the entire structure of civil society, rather than narrowly, as it ordinarily is in the liberal tradition, to include only those aspects of associa-tional life that are dissociated from the responsibilities of produc-tion. We then face a conundrum. Reliance upon the voluntarist private-law devices of contract and corporate law is too little. The appeal to a public-law framework for the self-organization of civil society is too much.

The sense of the too little and the too much can best be illustrated through the example of alternative labor-law regimes. One regime is contractualist. It seeks to reestablish amid the inequalities of the employment relation the reality of contract. Its preferred tool is the practice of collective contracts, arranged freely between workers and employers, who are in turn free to unionize or not. The law of collective bargaining polices the practice of voluntary unionization, seeking to ensure that the arrangements of collective bargaining will fairly embody its defining goal: to reestablish amid the stark inequalities of the employment relation the reality of contract. The "countervailing power" of the unions gives workers the measure of equality enabling them to bargain with their employers; it saves the wage contract from being so unequal as to conceal, under the appear-ance of contract, the reality of one-sided power. Two institutional mechanisms define such a labor-law regime. First, unions are completely independent of government. Second, they are crea-tures of the independent initiatives of different groups of workers; they fit into no overall design.

Such a regime has regularly exacted a price – from democracy as well as from workers. Each component of this price represents a special case of a class of effects of the private-law approach to association.

First, the initial effort to unionize, and to maintain the union, consumes much of the energy of the labor movement. It must act like Sisyphus and wait like Penelope. The corresponding general problem is that the willing and effective use of the devices of association presupposes practical conditions many groups are likely to lack. Consequently, the politics of the organization of civil society threatens to become a politics about how to organize rather than about what to do with organization.

Second, episodic unionization is likely to reinforce the preexisting segmentation of the laborforce when it takes place, as it usually does, in the setting of a starkly hierarchical social division of labor. Skilled workers in the capital-intensive sectors of industry will ordinarily have greater bargaining power. They will find it easier to unionize and to keep their unions. Paradoxically, however, they will be the workers who need their unions least and who stand most likely to benefit from schemes for the active engagement of workers in the governance of the firm and the planning of production. At the end of this road lies "business unionism": unions become instruments for cooperative relations with employers. The difference between having and not having a union may then begin to seem unimportant.

The corresponding general problem is that the private-law approach to association is likely to reinforce rather than to undermine the divisions and hierarchies of civil society. Voluntary association, practiced under conditions of dualism, will be most likely to flourish in the favored, capital-intensive sector and least likely to nurture a solidaristic orientation. A political project in the rearguard may keep organizational work alive. A solidaristic orientation in the vanguard may diminish the force of fragmentation. However, both the solidaristic orientation and the political project will have to work against the tilt of the institutional arrangements. The spirit will tire because the institutions fail to sustain it.

Third, the contractualist labor-law regime favors a middle-level, economistic style of labor militancy. Such a style of militancy focuses upon wages, benefits, and job security rather than upon the organization of the firm and the economy. The need constantly to make the case for unionization keeps economistic concerns at the center of attention. The assimilation of labor relations to private contract conceals the political constitution of labor relations, helping to push the political economy of work just beyond the reach of active and conscious response by workers.

The corresponding general problem shows up in a characteristic feature of associational life in the existing representative democracies and market economies. The associations with a message for society at large – clubs and churches as well as political parties – remain detached from the everyday world of work and production. The organizations involved in this everyday world – firms and unions – lack such a message; their job is to make money and defend the interests of their members. If, according to a metaphor preferred by the champions of the private-law regime of associations, contract and corporate law are like a natural language, capable of expressing any thought, then the problem is that those who are able to speak this language may have little to say while those who have something to say are unable to speak it.

This contrast of attitudes may seem too natural to question. It is, however, partly the product of arrangements disconnecting the internal problems of the production system from the larger conflict and controversy over society. The proof that this contrast is less natural than it seems is that it has in fact been qualified by successful contemporary experiences of industrial innovation. Such are the experiences in which groups of cooperative–competitive firms work together with local governments to spread the practices of economic vanguardism and to secure the social and educational requirements of such vanguard-ist practices.

The alternative to the private-law approach to voluntary association is the establishment of a public-law framework for the organization of civil society. To call it a public-law framework is not to say that it amounts to a corporatist regime of controlled popular mobilization: the organization of civil society under governmental tutelage. The framework can establish provisions for the comprehensive self-organization of civil society, according to residence, work, and shared concern. The resulting associations can nevertheless be completely independent from government. Despite this independence, the public-law alternative turns out to impose too much of a structure, just as the private-law tradition offers too little of one, for the good of democratic experimental-ism. Once again, the labor-law example makes both the alternative and its limits clear.

Consider a labor-law regime combining the contractualist principle of complete independence of the unions from govern-ment with the corporatist principle of automatic unionization of all workers according to the industry in which they work. The courts – including specialized labor courts – supervise the integrity of the legal framework but the government enjoys no tutelary power. Elections at each level determine the allocation of place within this comprehensive but extra-governmental union system. Different labor movements, affiliated or not with political parties, compete for position in this system, just as political parties compete for position in democratic government. In at least one country – Brazil – such a hybrid regime is no longer a mere hypothesis; it has become law.

The advantages of such an approach are the reverse side of the disadvantages of the contractualist collective-bargaining regime. Because everyone who has a job is automatically unionized, the energy of the labor movement can be devoted to the use and development of union power rather than to its elementary requirements of survival. Because all segments of the laborforce meet within the same structure, and all factions of the labor movement compete for position within it, there is, if not a tilt toward inclusive and solidaristic definitions and defenses of labor interests, at least no tilt in the opposite direction. Because the achievements and failures of this national union system so directly influence the status of workers throughout the economy, and because the system becomes a major locus of power, the shaping of industrial relations by politics – not blind economic fate – becomes more manifest. This greater transparency of the political constitution of labor relations, together with the openness toward solidaristic strategies, help move the agenda of the labor movement beyond economism to a broader range of concerns with the organization of society.

Nevertheless, such a hybrid regime depends, for its utility, upon circumstances in which social inequalities remain prominent in society at large, and workers strongly separated from co-workers as well as from managers. It may help encourage the early stages of a democratizing style of economic vanguardism – the radical-democratic alternative to the conservative managerial program of industrial renovation. However, it loses much of its point once this program begins to be realized.

The limits of the hybrid labor-law regime as a model for the general organization of civil society are even more evident, no matter how halting progress in the direction of democratic experimentalism may remain. Imagine multiple frameworks for the public-law organization of civil society: according to job, as in the hybrid labor-law regime; according to residency, as in a scheme of neighborhood associations running parallel to local government; according to shared concern, as in the comprehensive organization of the parents of schoolchildren or the users of health and social services at different stages of the life cycle. Such a scheme is simply too rigid to do justice to the self-reconstructive force of civil society. Moreover, it can easily fall under the control of a small, officious, and self-promoting cadre of busy-bodies, who bore and repel their fellow citizens.

A solution to the conundrum of the excesses of the public-law solution and the frailities of the private-law one should remain faithful to democratic experimentalism. Such a solution would enable the private-law and the public-law approaches to coexist, thus giving practical effect to the idea that a free civil society lacks a "natural" legal form, while combining each approach with a corrective mechanism suited to its special defects.

The corrective mechanism for the public-law arrangements should be the private-law arrangements, available as means by which to opt out of the arrangements established by public law. The exercise of this right to opt out and redesign a piece of civil society should remain subject to two conditions. The first condition is that those who opt out find themselves, vis-à-vis one another, in a circumstance of relative equality rather than in a relation of dependency and domination. The second condition is that the right to opt out not be exercised to entrench a little citadel of despotism, recalcitrant to effective challenge and revision.

The corrective mechanism for the private-law regime of contract and corporate law is the foundation of a branch of government – different from the branches we know – that would be charged with the task of localized and reconstructive intervention in particular organizations and areas of social practice. Generalizing and extending the American judicial practice of "complex enforcement" through structural injunctions, it would intervene in particular social organizations and areas of social life in which the normal forms of economic and political action and defense have ceased to be effective, leaving unchallenged microworlds of subjugation and exclusion. Its work would be both remedial and reconstructive, both structural and episodic. Among its responsibilities would be to act directly against the practices that help prevent the disorganized from using the legal devices of organization. It would need resources, capabilities, and powers the traditional judiciary lacks.

The school. No organization is more important to the progress of democratic experimentalism than the school. But a school is no more the tool of a particular institutional program, however experimentalist the temper of such a program may be, than a mind is the faithful expression of a social and cultural system, however inclusive and tolerant such a system may become. The school exists at the same level as the institutions of politics and production. The school and the political and economic order set constraints upon each other. Our thinking about both the school and the order can draw upon the same body of ideas about personality and society. What type of education responds to the concerns about self and society motivating the program of democratic experimentalism? A good place to start in answering this question is the revision of the conventional idea of "progressive education," as it stands today, after repeated dilutions.

First, there can be no progressive education without a significant measure of social endowment. It is not enough for the school to be available to children; children must also be available to the school. Children must enjoy the economic and medical support enabling them, whenever possible, to remain in their families. Often, such support will prove most effective, and most likely to bind school and family together, when it is administered through the school over the entire, extended working day. This child support will in turn work best when community organizations help formulate and administer it, from the bottom up as well as from the top down. In the sustaining climate of this associational life, families, too, can organize to work with schools. The complication comes later, when we consider the third element in progressive education and the pressure it brings to bear against the other two elements.

Second, the school, like its successors in the education of the adult, should concern itself primarily with the development of generic capacities by contrast to both training in specialized skills and the passive transmittal of information. Such capacities may be practical as well as conceptual, and they will include the core substantive tools of learning. The heart of this education in capacities is the transfiguration of the actual by the imagination of the possible. In natural science and social and historical study we come to understand how and why things work by discovering the conditions under which each thing can become something else. We rob the existent of naturalness the better to make it intelligible. In art we make another world, freeing the social regime we are in from some of its dumb facticity and somber authority. In manual labor and technology we establish a living, fluid correspondence, of method and intention, between practical reason and cooperative work until we render insubstantial the differences between the conception and the execution of practical tasks. In all these ways, we make the world – the practical world of society as well as the imaginative world of culture – safer not just for experimentalism and democracy – but for the type of context-transcending being who should become the agent of democracy and experimentalism alike. Thus, by placing the development of practical capacities at the center of education, we also give tangible expression to the idea, fundamental to any experimentalism, in science or in knowledge, that there is more in us – more in our capacities of insight, invention, and association – than there is in any list of the social and cultural orders, the sciences and the arts, that we have established.

Thus deepened and generalized, the experimentalist commitment produces a moral and psychological complication. The problem lies in the implications that detachment from context has for wholehearted engagement and action. If the price of freedom from context is an increased division of the heart in each of our undertakings, then the price is too high. I later discuss this problem as part of the gamble required by a commitment to democratic experimentalism.

If progressive education were limited to these two commitments – the commitment to make the child available to the school and the commitment to place capacity above memory – it would suffer no internal conflict. It would imply an unqualified acceptance of family and community control of the schools and an equally unqualified rejection of the ideal of a "classical canon." However, there is a third, regularly suppressed element in the idea of progressive education. This third element dramatically complicates the character and position of the other two and changes their implications for communities and canons.

The third element in the program of progressive education is the commitment to rescue the child from its family, its class, its country, and its historical epoch. It is to give children the powers of insight and action and the access to alien experience enabling them to become little prophets. The remaking of our understanding of the actual by the imagination of the possible requires a large measure of detachment from the now dominant culture.

As they grow, the little prophets may turn against the democratic experimentalism that redoubled their powers of apostasy. As democrats and experimentalists, however, we trust that more little prophets will reinvent, reform, and deepen democratic experimentalism, connecting it with concerns it seems to exclude, than will repudiate it. It is a gamble no different in character from the one made by the entire institutional program developed in this book. What makes this gamble reasonable, in one instance as in the other, is a view of the psychological force, the spiritual authority, and the practical benefits of a loosening of the stranglehold of circumstance over self. This turning of the tables in our relation to the institutional and discursive contexts of our lives is bound up in science with the correction of our mistakes; in production, with our relative success at reconciling the requirements of cooperation and innovation; in politics, with the lifting of the grid of entrenched division and hierarchy weighing upon our relations to one another; and in moral experience, with the development of some check upon the destiny of character (for a person's character is a rigidified version of his or her self as an institutional order is the rigidified version of a society). We value the powers of the little prophet for these causal connections as well as for the direct witness they bear to our nature, as spirit situated in context, the infinite caught within the finite.

The prophetic element in the idea of progressive education modifies the unreserved commitment to community or family control as well as the straightforward rejection of a "classical" education. If it is part of the task of the school to rescue children from their communities and families, we cannot deliver the school to families and communities. But what is the alternative? A traditional European model of elite education entrusted the leading role to a centralized educational bureaucracy. It expected this bureaucracy to serve as a counterweight to the local milieu of the child and the school and to do so in the interest of elite capability rather than of social diversity. A Prussian Minister of Education and his professorial staff claimed to have established an educational system that would enable a gifted Pomeranian child to see beyond the horizons of his village and prepare him for service to the state. In the program of progressive education, there can be no such authoritarian solution. A central, reforming educational bureaucracy must become, at best, one of a number of counterweights to the family and community control of the school. The most important agent should be the movement of teachers themselves. The teachers must act against a background in which families, local powers, and central authorities create, through their parallel and conflicting involvements, a space for the educators, and in which society, through the transforming work of democratic experimentalism, becomes less anxious to reproduce itself. Imaginative empathy for a possible humanity must gain the ascendancy in many minds.

Similarly, once we reintroduce into the idea of progressive education the suppressed element of the cultivation of critical and prophetic powers, we must begin to take a more qualified attitude to the discarded ideal of classical education. This ideal is defined by the combination of two ambitions: (a) an intense study of a culture standing at some distance from the now dominant beliefs but one that (b) enjoys a genealogical relation to the present culture and a canonical status within it. In European civilization, there was always a double basis for such a program: the study of Graeco-Roman antiquity but also the study of Christian doctrine. The doubleness of the canon turns out to be of more than accidental interest; it is a principle we must radicalize if we are to reinvent the idea of classical education in a progressive spirit.

The benefit of an education satisfying the classical requirements is to give mastery in a mode of a judgement placed at a subversive, suggestive middle distance from the present and its faith. Max Weber remarked that inspiration for many of the greatest cultural accomplishments has often come from being placed at the periphery of a civilization. At its best, a classical education enables us to hold such a place with respect to the culture into which we were born. In the circumstance of self-appointed exile and proud authority in which it puts us, it equips us to see the familiar as strange. It strengthens us in the capacity and the willingness to pass judgement upon modes of conduct and sensibility that seem at first unassailable. It gives us the imaginative nourishment that can come from being simultaneously insiders and outsiders.

However, a twin taint burdens the traditional form of classical education, preventing it from fulfilling this role more powerfully. One taint is social: the use of the education as an ornament of elite status and a marker of social distinction. The other taint is cultural: the weakening of reconstructive power and faith that may result from devotion to a closed, rather than a living, canon. What limited both these burdens in the Western practice and understanding of classical education was the duality of the pagan and Christian genealogies. Despite all efforts at reconciliation, their continuing coexistence produced imaginative trouble and opportunity. Moreover, the content of Christian faith made the trouble hard to contain, for it inspired an incurable ambivalence about worldly wisdom and power, a belief in the centrality of personal love and personal transcendence as well as of the inevitability of their conflict with society and its arrangements, and an insight into the decisive, dramatic, non-cyclical character of historical experience. We have only to read the nineteenth- and early twentieth-century European novel, a typical example of a genre deriving much of its force from its place in the imaginative afterlife of Christianity, to recognize the persistently explosive potential of the second of our two canons.

For all its usefulness, the double canon – classical and Christian – cannot provide an acceptable solution to the problem of education under democratic experimentalism: first, because it is a local solution, unavailable, as a matter of belief, to the majority of humanity, including the majority of what have historically been Christian societies; second, because the secular character of public education is an intrinsic rather than an accidental feature of the school system in a democracy; third, because the development of the suppressed prophetic element in the idea of progressive education requires an imaginative enlargement of the number of our canons and change in the character of their relation to our creative freedom.

A democracy needs to educate the young in varieties of vision and judgement at some critical distance from the here and now. It cannot remain content with an outward celebration of cultural diversity or a pretense of the equality of cultures. We must indeed find power of insight and inspiration where they in fact reside. However, there is no reason to suppose that they reside only in those traditions toward which, as individuals, societies, or cultures, we acknowledge a genealogical relation. Just as the diversity we can construct in the future matters more to the democratic experimentalist than the diversity we have inherited from the past, so we are capable of finding genealogies rather than of merely inheriting them. We can redefine the idea of the classical canon as a special case of a larger family of ways of gaining distance from the established culture just as we redefine the centralized educational bureaucracy as a special case of a larger set of ways to limit community influence over the school.

The triple gamble of democratic experimentalism

Program and risk. The democratizing alternative to neoliberalism described here is far from being the only plausible way in which to advance democratic and experimentalist ideals. It is simply one of several directions of departure from present institutional arrangements. (In another book, *What Should Legal Analysis Become?*, I have explored this larger family of alternatives.) We can develop and reshape each such alternative in the particular circumstances of a broad range of contemporary countries, rich or poor; differences of material circumstance or historical experience fail to predetermine the direction in which a society must go. The greater the progress toward democratic experimentalism, the weaker this or any other form of social predetermination becomes. Each pathway for the development of democracy may begin as a set of modest innovations embraced in the hope of realizing more fully recognized group interests and professed social ideals. Each, however, when pushed far enough, begins to reshape established definitions of group interest and identity by changing the social stations on which the existing logic of group interests and identities depends. Each, therefore, ends up implying over time a preference for certain types of personal and social experience.

Although it is a virtue of an institutional order to be open to many types of people and of life, no order can be neutral among varieties of experience. It will encourage some and discourage others. The pretense of neutrality gets in the way of the realistic objective of openness by favoring the illusion of a definitive institutional fix by which to distinguish the impersonal right from the factional good. Each trajectory connects back to present arrangements by countless steps of transition. Each comes with an agenda of distinctive problems, defining and developing its character by the way it manages these problems. Each requires us to take certain risks with ourselves and with society. Each amounts to a calculated risk to be run with open eyes.

The following pages discuss three risks that beset the democratizing alternative explored in this book. The first risk has to do with the ability of this proposal to satisfy the requirements of political and social stability once it succeeds in the objective of further weakening the fixed social hierarchies and roles. Divisions of opinion and temperament may occupy some of the space left vacant by the diminishing force of rigid classes and communities. Can they be enough to organize the public conversation and render stable the public institutions? The second risk concerns the existence of agents capable of engaging in the political practices on which a developed version of this democratic experimentalism must depend. What are the consequences for democratic experimentalism of the absence of agents capable of coordinating the macropolitics of institutions with the micropolitics of personal relations and of doing for politics writ large what political parties have done for the traditional politics of governmental power? The third risk arises from the implications of the program for the ideal of personality. Democratic experimentalism should not be a repeat version of "classical republicanism," with its narrow-minded and unrealistic attempt to suppress private concerns for the sake of public commitments. It wants to enlarge the range of those concerns rather than to displace them. Does it nevertheless fail adequately to economize upon political virtue, and give too much room to a cadre of officious and self-promoting activists while intimidating other people into resentful withdrawal? More generally, does it undermine the opportunity for wholeheartedness by denying us a relation to groups and cultures we can embrace without irony and reservation? Does it therefore sap the very vitality it wants to promote?

These perils amount to calculated risks. The risks, however, are also hopes. The hopes become reasonable in the light of an understanding of personality and society as well as of a conception of what matters most to us in the ideals we profess and the interests we acknowledge. We are used to thinking of programmatic ideas as presupposing beliefs about social reality and possibility. The reverse relation, however, is just as important: a programmatic effort stretches the limit of our understanding. Our programmatic ideas have a pragmatic residue: an element of self-fulfilling prophecy. We act as if a certain conception were possible in the hope of making it possible. However, such hopes are justified only so long as the self-fulfilling prophecy they embody tells a story that we can begin to live out in the here and now.

We lack the metric with which to measure the proximity of our programs to our circumstances. We must walk, in relative darkness, the narrow path between wishful thinking and the denial of the pragmatic, prophetic residue in our understanding of transformative possibility. We lack the metric, and always will. However, we can do better than we have done if we continue to develop a style of thought that exploits the internal relation between interests or ideals and institutions or practices, and imagines as projects what crisis and drift would produce as fate.

The risk of instability: strong politics, weak groups. Democratic experimentalism weakens the hold of group fate over individual experience. In so doing, it also makes democratic politics unstable, denying the individual a strongly marked group home, denying civil society the instruments for the organization of collective choice, and denying deepened democracy the social partners and interlocutors it needs. The arrangements of a deepened democracy weaken the role of rigid hierarchies of class and work. Thus, they help overcome the divisions between the small business class and skilled industrial workers, or between skilled industrial workers and underclass laborers, or, at a more minute level, between high-skilled machine technicians and ordinary assembly-line workers, or even between the children of the aspiring professional–business classes and the trust-fund beneficiaries of the inheritance right.

The weakening of groups based upon the inheritance of race, religion, and community culture may be more oblique. It is nevertheless powerful. Democratic experimentalism loosens the hold of such groups through several influences. It multiplies opportunities to challenge the practical arrangements with which we associate the realization of our interests and ideals. It uses the school to rescue the child from the family. It encourages practices and conversations in which the group identities and distinctions we make weigh more than the ones we inherit and the differences of the future count right now for more than the differences of the past. The problem of political stability is only one aspect of a larger worry about the relation of strong people to strong politics.

Contrast two societies. In one – a society of castes, classes, and birth-determined groupings sanctioned by religious authority and reinforced by economic constraint – most individuals feel secure in a place. Worldly failure and success may give them more or less but it cannot ordinarily make them more or less. They are what they are in the eyes of society as they were what they were in the eyes of their parents. They can be expressive to the point of being boisterous; in such circumstances ordinary men and women at every level of the social hierarchy often display a natural dignity that may strike us, in our half-democratized societies, as aristocratic.

In the other society – in which the hold of class has been weakened but not broken – distinctions of inherited economic and educational advantage are as powerful in effect as they are uncertain in authority, and self-promoting individualism is worshipped while association is preferred to be voluntary. Many are anxious about their dealings to one another. Their relations and conversations lack a script, and the lack of a script both silences people and gives them room to speak. In the first of these two societies, expressiveness remains hostage to subjugation and superstition. In the second society, we hope that more equality, and more association on the basis of equality, will cure the defects of partial equality. However, this hope rests as much upon moral vision as upon historical inference.

Together with the gamble about the effects of the weakening of inherited collective self-identities upon self-possession goes a wager about its effects upon social and political stability. We need groups with a continuing life to organize public conversation and collective choice: to "articulate and aggregate interests," in the language of political science. Democratic mass politics has had in the political party a group agent relatively unmoored from inherited hierarchies and divisions, classes and communities. Political parties may claim to represent particular classes and communities. However, one of the most common findings of electoral research is that votes for parties regularly fail to track a simple scheme of class interest or community affinity. With surprising frequency, individual opinion overcomes group origin. Nevertheless, political parties have operated in a social world where such groupings continue to flourish. Indeed, part of their work has been to connect such groups and group interests to a more general debate about what to do with government and how to change society.

Something important has changed if we imagine that the

principle embodied in the political party – union according to shared opinion, commitment, and temperament – has been generalized as a commanding form of group life. Can such groupings, with no more ascriptive basis than may result from the inheritance of our traits and the influence of our families, sustain strong personalities and a vibrant civic life?

We have two reasons to hope they can. The first and fundamental reason is that the half-chosen destinies of character and conversion may be as tenacious as the unchosen tyrannies of class and race. The second and subsidiary reason is that, in loosening the grip of ascriptive groups upon individual experience, democratic experimentalism does not abolish the subtle transactions between group differences and individual habits. It is only by the greatest energy that we resist the gravitational pull of the distinct forms of group life into which our families have introduced us and our careers have confirmed us. Each such distinct form of life draws force from its contrast with other forms of life and supports a repertory of practical and psychological routines. They survive entrenched class and ethnic divisions, giving society a shape that opinion and temperament would be insufficient to produce.

Such expectations of stability highlight the moral consequences of democratic experimentalism. These consequences are hardly neutral among religions and ideals. Many religious traditions, such as Hinduism in one way and Judaism in another, have given special moral weight to the bonds of blood. The desire for unchosen connections remains deeply set in the human heart; the force with which we experience commitments that no inheritance has imposed upon us may not be enough to counterbalance this desire. The problem that remains then is not political and social instability but a stubborn conflict in our desires.

The risk of failure in agency: the missing agent of inclusive politics. The advancement of democratic experimentalism requires an inclusive political practice capable of spanning the gap between the macropolitics of institutional change and the micropolitics of personal relations. This requirement results in a conundrum about agency. It is unthinkable that there could be a coordinating agent for such a politics and troubling that there is none. Facing this trouble requires another calculated risk.

The alternative to neoliberalism and traditional social democracy explored in this book describes one among several possible directions for the deepening of democracy. Any transformative and democratic politics – that is to say, any politics that moves in one of these directions – must possess the following characteristics.

First, such a political practice must take advantage of the duality of attitudes to the definition and defense of group interests, preferring institutionally transformative and socially solidaristic to conservative and exclusive approaches. We can often translate this imperative into the demand for a broadened popular alliance. Such an alliance should typically include: the worker-technicians of the vanguard; the people who, often in insecure jobs, labor in the capital- and technology-poor sectors of the economy, both as blue-collar and white-collar workers; and the workers of mass-production industry. This third group – the mainstay of traditional social democracy – often finds itself in industries that, straddling the division between vanguard and rearguard, are in the process of being lifted up into the one or pushed down into the other. A program beginning with a decentralized partnership between private firms and a refinanced government and ending with the adoption of a frankly antidualist political economy can help strengthen the basis for such an enlarged popular alliance.

The second feature of this political practice is the counterpart to the first in the realm of discourse and imagination. Each of the major programmatic positions in contemporary politics suffers from a characteristic internal instability. Each defines itself at the same time by its devotion to certain interests and ideals – such as the ideals of economic decentralization or egalitarian redistribution or the interests of small business or industrial workers – and by its acquiescence in political and economic arrangements that frustrate the realization of those interests and eviscerate the meaning of those ideals. We can resolve the instability by diminishing our conceptions of the interests and ideals – cutting them down to the size of the inherited and established institutional horizon – or by radicalizing the conceptions – pushing them beyond the boundaries of the inherited and established institutional settlement. If we do the latter, what began as a redesign of the institutions will end, given the internal relation between thinking about institutions and thinking about interests and ideals, as a redefinition of these goals. Most often, we neither radicalize the conceptions nor overtly diminish them. We simply leave the internal instability as it is, which amounts to a de facto retrenchment. In the political practice of democratic experimentalism we must radicalize the conceptions, exposing the hidden internal instability. In the debates of contemporary politics, the best places to begin may be the radicalization of the social-democratic vocabulary of equality, security, inclusion, and participation, and the radicalization of the liberal language of flexibility and decentralization.

Such a political practice cannot think and talk in pure strategy. It must have a vision, however fragmentary and tentative, of a changed social world and of the changed group interests and identities this new world would support. It must represent this vision in ways that connect it with pressing and tangible concerns. The choice of transformative and solidaristic approaches to the definition and defense of group interests will always seem too risky from the vantage point of cold instrumental calculation. The shrinking benefits of the conservative and exclusive approaches may enjoy underserved authority just because they are palpable and familiar. A temporal bias may increase this advantage. We live in biographical, not historical time. The costs of the transformative approaches may be most evident during our time; their benefits may survive us.

A third trait of transformative political practice is therefore its capacity to speak in two tongues, appealing, at the same time, to interest and vision, strategy and prophecy. Its visionary or prophetic language must learn to tell stories about the larger meaning of partial experiments, and draw energy and authority from the resonance of its proposals in intimate aspects of personal experience. Parables must give sense to events.

A fourth attribute of transformative political practice is to unite action from the bottom up with action from the top down. State-promoted reform suffers perversion when government lacks organized partners in civil society. As the dumb resistance of a sullen, amorphous populace stands against the centralist blueprint, the reformers must choose between imposition and retreat. If they choose imposition, they soon find that the methods and apparatus needed to sustain it overshadow their intentions and redirect their plans. At the same time, however, no "politics of civil society" can render superfluous the exercise of state power. For those who control that power can influence not only the opportunities for independent group organization but also the range of living alternatives presented to a civil society that has organized. Moreover, the cause of group organization in civil society can never hope to command for long more than an ambivalent allegiance. Even under the best of circumstances, a voluntary association will always be on the verge of falling under the sway of a cadre of self-promoting activists. It will always want more attention from its members than they want to give it, or should. Thus, a democratic society needs two tracks to politics: one passing through the organizations of civil society; the other circumventing them.

These four requirements of democratic politics are ambitious. They are, however, at least thinkable and feasible in one form or another. A fifth characteristic of transformative politics, however, presents a deeper and more intractable problem about transformative agency. In the view of politics informing the arguments of this book, two assumptions coexist. There is an antinecessitarian assumption. According to this assumption there is no foreordained script of structural change, no closed list of possible institutional orders, no indivisible institutional systems presenting themselves on a take-it-or-leave-it basis. There is also an assumption of the incompleteness of a state-oriented politics: politics understood in the narrow sense of conflict over the mastery and uses of governmental power. Politics in this sense must connect with politics in the broader sense of conflict over the shape of social relations, the terms of people's relations to one another. The macropolitics of institutional change must find its complement and completion in the micropolitics of personal relations, and embrace the vast space lying between these two: for example, the politics of the professions and professional expertise, or the politics of the power structure of large-scale organizations.

If we had an inclusive conception of politics but necessitarian ideas about institutional change, the problem of agency would solve itself: we would always count (although mistakenly) on an agent at hand to do the work of the historical dialectic. If, however, we hold antinecessitarian beliefs about institutional change but subscribe, at the same time, to an inclusive view of politics, we face a problem of agency that is novel in the history of politics and political thought.

Consider the consequences of the absence of such an agent. The practical effects of institutional change depend upon the context in which such change takes place. Part of this context consists of recurrent styles of association that, in each domain of social life, mark the relations among individuals. It is one thing for an institutional alternative like the one outlined in these pages to be realized in a society in which individual roles remain subject to discussion and tinkering, and community and contract must meet a test of relative equality among their participants. It is another thing for such an alternative to be realized in a society in which patron–client relations prevail, and power regularly combines with exchange and allegiance in many of the ordinary events of daily life.

The promises of a democratizing program may, in this second situation, soon be perverted or circumvented. It is as if the shape of social relations were the resultant of many vectors: the directional significance of each of the vectors remains uncertain until we know how it will interact with the others. If no agent coordinates the macropolitics of institutions and the micropolitics of personal relations, this resultant will be unchosen and even unimagined. It may also be uninviting and unwanted. The implication of the absence of a coordinating agent with a dimension and a capability proportional to the setting of action – the setting of an inclusive conception of politics – is to disempower the individual and collective will, strengthening the hand of fate.

Thus, we must fall back upon a weaker and more general form of coordination between micropolitics and macropolitics: one that results from the only partly expressed collaboration between political parties and movements of opinion in civil society. Some of these movements may be relatively organized and ideologically articulate, as feminism became in many countries by the end of the twentieth century. Whether organized and articulate or not, their vitality depends upon the depth and density of association in civil society. This associational intensity rests in turn upon our relative success at solving the conundrum that makes a private-law solution to the problem of the legal framework of civil society too little and a public-law one too much.

However, even if we succeed, and sustain over time a vigorous associational life, the reciprocal influences between political parties and movements of opinions may fail to make up for the missing agent of an inclusive politics. Such influences may be too weak to generate a real conversation between reconstruction in the large and in the small, leaving a broader politics without agents proportional to its scope. The political transformation of society will then continue to be the sum of these two types of politics, but it will not then become a sum anyone thought out or intended.

The risk of conflict between personal need and the demands of democracy: the ideal of personality. Social institutions shape moral experience. They encourage some forms of life and discourage others. We may value the openness of institutional arrangements to novel forms of experience and their tolerance for diverse forms of life. However, no set of arrangements can be neutral. The mirage of neutrality gets in the way of the realistic objective of relative openness. It invites the sanctification of a particular institutional order as the expression of a system of right supposedly neutral among clashing interests and conflicting visions of the good. We lack a basis for distinguishing within human nature attributes that are permanent and universal from others that vary with circumstance, including institutional circumstance. Even the most intimate aspects of experience remain hostage to their historical context: the arrangements of society and the dogmas of culture.

We are nevertheless not readily redesigned under the influence of the latest institutional blueprint. The dialectic between self and context moves slowly and works at the margin of what we are like now. What we are like now is the only safe definition of "human nature," and it is reckless to assume that any institutional rearrangement can change it suddenly or radically.

From these general concerns two practical precautions result. The first precaution is that in choosing a pathway of cumulative institutional change, we should be attentive to the effects of such change upon personal experience. One reason why an institutional program is fateful is that it represents, no matter how strong its commitment to openness and toleration, a preference for a certain range of moral experience over others. The second precaution is that we not make the introduction or persistence of the program depend upon the hope of some great regeneration of our present nature. We are hostage to our politics, but we are not there for the taking. We need to worry about the dependence of an institutional program upon assumptions about personality and personal need that are unrealistic and narrow-minded, sacrificing humanity to ideology.

The progressive alternative presented in this book requires more than a transitory period of more intense political engagement. It demands as well a persistent heightening of popular political action. In the absence of such a heightening, the very potency of politics can present a risk of new rigidities. Those in possession of governmental power may be tempted to turn the temporary advantages of the groups that support them into vested rights. The weakening of the idea of a prepolitical, naturalized system of private property rights would make their work all the easier.

There are three great safeguards in the institutional arrangements of this democratizing program against such a perversion. The first safeguard is the multiplicity of spheres of social and political power. The goal is to ensure such a pluralism without the deliberate inhibition upon transformative politics imposed by devices such as the American system of "checks and balances." The second safeguard is the existence of a set of fundamental rights – including rights to political participation, defiance, and dissent – that we withdraw from the agenda of short-term politics. It is true that we forswear under democratic experimentalism the pretense that this package of immunities, although protected against constant reordering, has a definitive shape and a sustaining link to a particular property regime. However, if such a renunciation weakens these liberties in some ways, it strengthens them in others. It helps disentangle them from restraints upon practical innovation as well as from tools of economic subjugation. The third safeguard is the institutionally supported engagement of the citizenry. This engagement represents a condition of vigilance against the turning of temporary advantage into vested right. It helps ensure that when the constitutional regime calls the spirits they will come.

The practical question is whether such a regime fails properly to economize on political virtue. It should form no part of the program of a democratic experimentalist to replace the real interest-bearing, interest-pursuing individual with the mythical selfless citizen of classical republicanism. The aim is rather to broaden the scope of our ordinary interests, weakening the contrast between the private and the public by strengthening the intermediate category of the social. If the regime imposes too high a tax upon individual energy and attention – if, as in Oscar Wilde's complaint about socialism, it requires too many meetings – the lack of psychological realism will result in a political perversion. The suppression of private concern will not occur, nor should it. The majority of people will be alternately bored and repelled by the meeting-mania and by the self-promoting activitists who thrive on it. They will withdraw all the more into their own lives. Their withdrawal will enable those who govern to act with fewer restraints. It is therefore crucial to develop the economic and political institutions of democratic experimentalism in ways limiting their hunger for human energy and respecting the force and authority of private concerns. The assurance of social endowment, the empowering mission of the school, the survival of forms of property giving broad discretion to the individual, should all contribute to this end. So should the multiplication of political and economic fora in which people can address the ordinary problems of daily life.

These precautions should not, however, disguise the temperamental *parti pris* of democratic experimentalism. Our temperaments may divide us as much as class, race, or religion. Any set of institutions has temperamental biases. We should be conscious of them the better to contain them. The institutions I have described may give too many chances to the talkers and seducers. We must counteract this bias. We run the risk, under democratic experimentalism, that we shall be unable to do so.

The relation of politics to personality in this deepening of democracy has a scope broader than the need to economize on political virtue. One way to explore this relation is to consider the bearing of a program like the one outlined here upon two great sources of human sadness: the loss of vitality and the disproportion between such vitality as we keep and the activities normally available for its expression.

We lose our intensity as we mature, most of us, and this loss, accumulating through setback and compromise, represents a death in life. The institutions of society cannot solve this problem, but they can aggravate or moderate it. Every aspect of our experience remains susceptible to influence by the institutional experience in which we undergo it. The partnership between the progressive school and the deepened democracy may help to nourish the ordinary childlike intensity of ordinary people as they grow older. The school accomplishes this goal by giving the child the intellectual instruments with which to combine the experimental and the prophetic. Democratic experimentalism does it through the cumulative and combined effect of three circumstances it seeks to produce.

The first circumstance is the loosening of the bonds of social division and hierarchy. (Remember the conjecture of a causal connection between the relative openness of a set of arrangements to challenge and revision and the likelihood that they will weaken the hold of rigid place and rank.) Thanks to this weakening we become more fully available to one another as the originals we all know ourselves to be rather than as performers of a social role handed down to us.

The second circumstance is the encouragement to a high level of independent organization in civil society as well as to an organized invitation to stronger civic engagement. Only an organized and engaged political society is capable of generating alternatives and acting upon them. This social fact connects to a psychological reality. Vitality depends upon hope. Hope is more the consequence of action than its cause. Action, however, whether practical or imaginative, requires opportunities. The opportunities most important to the efficacy as well as the intensity of action are those that connect us with others as we pursue our goals. In this way, we not only renew vitality but also prevent it from turning inward toward self-destructive subjectivity and narcissism.

The third circumstance is the achievement of a dialectic between capability and safeguard, between what we withdraw from the scope of short-term experimentalism and what we put into it. The progressive school, the social endowment, and the system of political guarantees work together to equip the individual with the means for effective action. They push back the wall that society ordinarily builds around our desires.

If the waning of our life-force is one great source of human sadness, another is the contrast between the intensity of the desires we nevertheless continue to experience and the smallness of the objects and tasks in which we are ordinarily compelled to express them. Any casual observer of humankind will have been struck by the incongruity with which we may lavish great passion upon the trivial, the frivolous, and the ephemeral or upon collective crusades to which, suddenly and with little reason or reflection, we sacrifice everything. When ordinary men and women, living in the ordinary situations society offers them, move beyond the domain of their most intimate personal relations, they often find little to deserve their surviving intensity – little other than great historical storms that occasionally sweep them up or fanciful individual escapes that remain disconnected from their daily lives.

For the vast majority of people, work cannot perform this role. The idea of an "honorable calling" – a respectable craft, carrying prestige, demanding devotion, shaping experience – has become archaic and impractical. The commitment to a "transformative vocation" – linking work with the reimagination and remaking of a shared context of action and insight – remains the preserve of a lucky and gifted elite. For most people, work amounts to little more than a necessary instrument for the satisfaction of practical need and a means by which to discharge responsibility to those closest to us.

The progress of the democratic cause has an indirect but nonetheless significant bearing upon this second great source of human sadness. A program like the one outlined here remains united to the cause of progressive thought by its emphasis upon the liberation of ordinary people from drudgery and humiliation. It holds fast to belief in the potential overlap between the conditions of economic progress and the conditions of individual emancipation. It values material progress for its promise to liberate mind and body from deadening repetition as well as to enhance our powers and redress our infirmities. The progressive program sustains this commitment by bringing the exceptional work of the transformative vocation – the reimagination and the remaking of the context – closer to the tenor of ordinary experience. It moderates the duality of consciousness, the division between what we know ourselves to be within the established structure and what we may seek to become beyond its constraints and supports. We need democratic politics, not just self-criticism and self-reconstruction, so that we can become wholehearted and free at the same time.

BEYOND INSTITUTIONS

Nationalism and institutional change

According to a commonly voiced thesis, resurgent nationalism has replaced the ideological politics and class warfare of the earlier twentieth century. Liberal and leftist doctrines are faulted for having drastically underestimated the virulence of nationalist sentiment. There is, however, a paradox. Understanding it enables us to see from a different and ultimately more hopeful perspective the relation between nationalist struggle and institutional reconstruction.

A traditional form of collective identity throughout world history has been the attachment to a distinct form of life, defined in the detail of practices and institutions. For the Roman, to be a Roman was to live according to Roman custom: a dense texture of social life informed by ideas and ideals of human association – enacted images of the possible and desirable relations among people in different domains of experience. These were concrete, collective identities. Because these group identities were visible, they were also porous, recombinable, and negotiable. Real social practices, and the beliefs informing them, remain loosely connected. They are not the plausible beneficiaries of an absolutist faith.

By contrast, the most distinctive trait of many contemporary assertions of group identity is their abstract quality. They express a will to difference in the face of the waning of actual difference more often and more strongly than they reflect the possession and defense of a unique form of life. One people hates its neighbor and struggles against it less because they are so different than because they are becoming the same. The remaining differences of religion and language, or the economic rivalries among nations or groups, may further excite the will to difference, giving it something tangible although limited upon which to seize. It is a process recalling Tocqueville's idea of how intolerable remaining inequalities become as privileges diminish without vanishing.

Thus, the defense of actual difference combines with the rage of impotence in the expression and enjoyment of actual difference. The emptier collective identities produced by this process – less rooted than their predecessors in stable custom and belief – invite intransigence precisely because they remain more elusive. They must draw more and more of their life from a belief rather than from an experience. They lack practical detail to serve as material for experiment and compromise.

A great practical force empties out collective identities embodied in customary ways of life. Success at national development requires practical experimentalism, and practical experimentalism demands ceaseless recombination. The most successful countries have been those like Japan that have proved to be the most assiduous imitators and recombiners. For generations now they have roamed the world pillaging and mixing institutions, practices, and ideas. When, content with success, they stop this pillaging and mixing they begin to fail. The self-appointed custodians and propagandists of the national identity may still claim that the national spirit reveals its unmistakable hand by the singular way it recombines this world-historical booty. As the recombination advances, however, the spirit they invoke becomes increasingly hard to define.

Innovation in the institutional forms of political and economic pluralism changes the predicament to which nationalism responds. In so doing, it can channel nationalist sentiment in a more productive direction. The excited antagonism of evanescent group identities need not amount to a diversion from the work of institutional reform. Rather, it is a problem that the political work of reconstruction can hope to moderate. The will to difference becomes less dangerous as it becomes less frustrated and more capable of producing actual difference. In the making of forms of social life, actual difference must gain institutional and ideological content. The need to deliver the goods and the creation of a world civilization have joined, fatally wounding cultures that put their faith in an autarky of experience and belief. Neither, however, as this book has argued, do practical imperatives and world culture compel convergence upon a single institutional and ideological order.

The way to make differences less dangerous is, paradoxically, to make them more real. The way to make them more real is to develop practices and institutions, and ways of thinking and talking, that can both generate and express them.

The political and the personal

This book has explored the institutions a deepened democracy needs. However, institutional change is not enough to advance democratic experimentalism. It is incomplete for two different reasons: first, because there is more in social life, more of concern to democratic experimentalism, than what institutions can shape and, second, because some of what they cannot shape nevertheless strikes back, influencing their significance and effect.

Politics, in the broadest sense, is the contest over the full, dense texture of social relations: all the terms of people's practical, cognitive, and emotional access to one another. The macropolitics of conflict over the control and use of government to maintain or reform the institutional arrangements of society is one species of politics. Another species is what Fourier first called the micropolitics of personal relations.

In between the macropolitics of institutional change and the micropolitics of personal relations stand other large regions of social experience that an inclusive view of politics must acknowledge. Part of this middle space is the power structure of large-scale organizations: the extent, for example, to which unyielding imperatives of coordination justify hierarchies in the workplace and the extent to which such hierarchies exceed what the needs of effective collaboration can justify. Another part of the middle space is the nature and content of professional practice. For in the relatively deenergized democracies of today much of the controversy over the basic structure of social life, driven out from the arena of government-centered politics, passes into the hands of the professions and lives under the disguise of technical expertise. It matters how the professions relate to the citizenry and how the discourse and practice of each profession suppresses or exhibits transformative opportunity in social life.

What is the micropolitics of personal relations about? In every society there are hardened, recurrent styles of personal dealing: between bosses and underlings, men and women, parents and children, workers and their fellows, or strangers on the street. These stereotyped forms of association may be sustained by institutional arrangements, especially the arrangements that distribute power and police trust. However, they also have a life of their own, rooted in the most intimate experiences of childhood and family, robbed of their strangeness by repetition in daily life, and given sense and authority by the stories we tell ourselves in high and popular culture.

Together with these enacted images of what relations among people can and should be like in different regions of social experience go images of exemplary social danger: lived beliefs about the most pervasive threats to a life together. In their public culture, Americans, for example, have traditionally worried about the horror of personal dependence. They often think that the most pressing task in every well-ordered community is to factor out the element of power and then clamp down on it. They want to withdraw from the reformed but continuing reality of power the sting of individual subjugation. They resort to two main solutions. One response is to appeal to impersonal rules, impersonally applied. The other method is to bathe social life in pseudointimacy, a cheerful impersonal friendliness.

Such habits of association and images of social danger put people under a spell. The half-forgotten terrors of a compelling collective history live on all the more stubbornly in a diffuse atmosphere of routine and preconception. Self-fulfilling prophecies, as are all our powerful beliefs, they give rise to a second-order reality, threatening to confuse and demoralize us even in our moments of insight and invention.

Today, all over the world, the educated population repeats that the personal is political. Nevertheless, progressives have often made the mistake of focusing their attention upon political and economic proposals while leaving the fine texture of social life to take care of itself. Democratizing reforms in government and the economy, however, will be frustrated or perverted if established within a society that continues, in the little, to operate on principles antagonistic to them. The quality of personal life and personal encounter remains the ultimate prize in politics. If it fails to change, nothing important has really happened despite all the bustle and drama at the commanding heights of political action.

What can we say in general about the content of the styles of association that help sustain the public culture of a deepened democracy? What difference should the deepening of democracy make to the nature as well as the content of these ways people deal with one another: to the distinctiveness, inflexibility, and power of such habits of human connection? How can we challenge and change them when institutional reform, as it often will, proves inadequate? What relation between the delights and anxieties of life and the struggle over the organization of society will the deepening of democracy bring?

In a deepened democracy people must be able to see themselves and one another as individuals capable of escaping their confined roles. It is an experience we may have in personal love insofar as love escapes the deceptions of idealization and projection. However, it passes only fitfully into the tenor of everyday existence. To make this passage, it must draw strength from practical arrangements, such as those that moderate the contrast between task-defining and task-executing jobs as well as the rigid barriers among executory jobs. It must also be nourished by an education enhancing the imaginative powers of ordinary men and women, especially their power to imagine one another.

This indispensable attribute of the social life required by democratic experimentalism stands opposed to some of the styles of personal connection that continue to exert the greatest influence in contemporary societies. One of the most persistent of such styles has been the logic of patrons and clients: a species of association combining, in the same encounters, a bargain, a structure of individual subordination, and a reciprocal demand for loyalty or allegiance. Its defining trope is the sentimentalization of unequal exchange. Where it rules, in the relations between superiors and inferiors, or men and women, it undermines the basis of democracy in living experience. It does so by aggravating the tension between the requirements for individual self-construction and the claims of social solidarity. It forces us at every turn to choose between betraying other people and betraying ourselves, between fighting for freedom at the cost of betrayal and accepting self-suppression for the sake of our bonds to other people. A deepened democracy cannot end these tensions but it can moderate them.

The progress of democracy must bring about a change in the character as well as the content of the ways people deal with one another. It must make these habits of association more hospitable to the reconciliation of individual self-development and social solidarity. By so doing it reconciles the conflicting conditions for strong, independent personality – requirements of apartness from other people and engagement with them.

The advance of democracy must also diminish the blind, compulsive force of our habits of association, their take-it-or-leave-it quality, and therefore their clearcut distinctions from one another. It is one thing to be able to take much for granted in our relations with other people as we pass through the repetitious situations of practical life. It is another thing to have to act out, in each such situation, a set script, in the fear that every improvisation may be held a transgression. To make such directives more like cues we can reject than like orders we must obey is a spiritual requirement of deepened democracy.

Changes in the content and character of our habits of association depend upon continued institutional renewal. However, institutional reform is insufficient to produce them. A course of reform may, for example, diminish the inequalities that enable people to become patrons and clients. However, no institutions can keep people from covering persistent inequalities with the haze of sentiment and allegiance, the better to renew the roles of the client and the patron.

Institutional innovations like those that have been the subject matter of this book must be completed by stories people can tell, and begin to act out, about danger and opportunity in the reconciliation of self-development and solidarity. Such stories and their enactment require a progressive refinement of subjectivity, not the sacrifice of subjective awareness to a selfless civic virtue. We see these narratives of human possibility all around us in the most distinctive achievements of modernist high and popular culture as well as in the concerns of social and cultural movements like feminism.

This extra-institutional politics of personal relations must work together with the politics of institutions. Neither can achieve its objectives without help from the other. Each will find its work limited by the other's accomplishments and failures. We lack, however, an agent to orchestrate their collaboration, doing for it what the political parties have done for the narrower politics of governmental power. Thus arises the conundrum I earlier described about the agency of a politics that has become inclusive in its scope but skeptical and experimentalist in its assumptions.

It is not enough to challenge and change the hardened styles of personal encounter and connection. It is also necessary to establish a more open frontier between personal and political hope than the unconscious conservatism of an age of disenchantment is willing to allow. In two hundred years of democratic politics and culture we have learned the hard way how self-defeating and dangerous it is to seek in a blueprint for social improvement the cure for all the miseries of life. Humanity has rightly tired of crazed and armed crusades conducted in the name of all-or-nothing ideologies of social or national regeneration.

But how should we correctly understand the lesson of this experience? We are told that the world should continue to converge on a similar set of institutions and practices, and settle down to reconciling American-style market flexibility with European-style social protection. The doctrine of the humanization of the inevitable, within a framework of unchallenged arrangements, has become the watchword of chastened progressives everywhere.

Together with this narrowing of the horizon of transformative ambition goes an idea about the proper relation between the political and the personal. Politics must become little so that people can become big. The public world will belong to the resigned and benevolent manager, committed to secure basic decencies and efficiencies by negotiating conflicts of interest and of view. However, as the public world cools down, the private one will supposedly heat up. A restless testing of limits will continue, where it can produce the best effects and do the least harm, in the lives of individuals and communities of like-minded people.

The message of this book is that the assumptions of this teaching are false and that its implications contradict the requirements for the advance of the democratic cause throughout the world.

Our interests and ideals remain, now as always, hostage to the practical arrangements available to realize them. We can achieve our interests and ideals more fully only by reimagining and remaking the arrangements to which they are fastened. We can do so only piece by piece and step by step. The public culture in which such an experimentalist practice thrives leaves open the frontier between hopes for the self and hopes for society.

The language transformative politics needs to develop and deploy suggests what such an opening means. Political persuasion, in the service of democratic experimentalism, needs to include a visionary element as well as a calculating one. It must hold up the image of a reordered world in which people acquire different identities and interests as they seek to satisfy more fully the interests, and live out more fully the identities, they now recognize as theirs. It appeals from a narrower to a broader view of self-interest, and then from self-interest to self-respect, and then from self-respect to the hope of becoming bigger and more connected at the same time.

Institutional proposals gain some of their seductive force from their resonance in personal experience. Political prophecy speaks in a language of personal immediacy: a proposal to reorganize society becomes intelligible and authoritative through analogy to a compelling chapter of personal experience.

The more we succeed in deepening democracy, the less of a gap remains between thinking practically about problems and thinking prophetically about alternatives. A republic of citizens should become, little by little, a nation of prophets, seeking prophetic power in the genius of ordinary men and women. In its life, people should more easily be able to change their contexts, piece by piece, while doing their jobs, day by day.

Democracy must make a practical success out of social life while responding to the evils of oppression as well as the injuries of belittlement. It cannot, however, do its work without giving expression to the most important fact about us: that we are greater than the institutions and cultures we build. They are exhaustible. We, so long as we live, are not. Although they help make us who we are, there is always more in us than there is in them. We must deny them the last word, and keep it for ourselves.

II
A MANIFESTO

THE CONSTITUTIONAL ORGANIZATION OF GOVERNMENT AND THE LEGAL FRAMEWORK OF ELECTORAL POLITICS

No one genre of thinking, talking, and writing enjoys the privilege best to represent today a progressive, programmatic imagination. We can think discursively, prophetically, or poetically; systematically or by fragment and parable; with a particular context in mind or on a worldwide scale; linked to particular parties and movements or disconnected from them; extending actual experience or anticipating possible experience; for the here and now of immediate feasible changes or for the remote and speculative future of unborn humanity; with a wealth of empirical detail and justificatory argument or with nothing but the suggestive and dogmatic invocations of a manifesto. These forms have different uses. They complement one another. It is a mistake, for example, to oppose short-term and context-oriented proposals to the tentative exploration of long-term alternative futures, or moderation to radicalism, in programmatic thought. Any trajectory of cumulative structural change can be considered at points close to present social reality or distant from it. The direction matters more than the distance.

What counts is to populate our imaginative world with more such practices, and to free ourselves from the superstitious inhibitions that prevent us from doing so. The following theses amount to one such experiment in discourse. Although placed at an extreme limit of the repertory of programmatic genres, they address directly the problems that have been central in this book.

First thesis: On the history of democratic institutions

The dominant constitutional tradition in the West draws today upon two sets of arrangements and ideas. The first set consists of a preference for constitutional forms that fragment power, favor deadlock, and establish a rough equivalence between the transformative reach of a political program and the severity of the legal-constitutional and practical-political obstacles set up in the course of its execution. Both the system of "checks and balances" in American-style presidential regimes and the need to base political power upon broad consensus within the political class in parliamentary regimes exemplify this inhibiting preference. The second set of arrangements and ideas in the dominant tradition is the adoption of rules and practices maintaining society at a relatively low level of political mobilization. These practices gradually replaced the institutional devices of protodemocratic liberalism – the limits to the suffrage and the recourse to multiple levels of representation – that secured property against populism. Progressives must reject and replace both parts of this tradition.

Second thesis: On the constitutional arrangements of government

A constitutional style designed to accelerate politics and to favor the repeated and frequent practice of basic reform should combine a strong plebiscitarian element with a broad range of channels for the political representation of society. Example: A strong parliament coexists with a directly elected president with substantial powers of political initiative. But the standard hybrid form of presidential and parliamentary regimes (as in the constitution of the Fifth Republic) is replaced by a system that avoids weak government and the perpetuation of deadlock. It does so according to the following principles. First, reform programs enjoy priority over ordinary, episodic legislation: they must be agreed to, rejected, or negotiated quickly. Second, when, under such a system, president and parliament disagree on a reform program, they may agree to plebiscites or referenda. Third, if the political branches of government are unable to agree about the realization or the terms of popular consultation, or if the result of the consultation is indecisive, either the parliament or the president may call anticipated elections, but the elections must be simultaneous for both branches of government. The general principle is rapid resolution of impasse through direct involvement of the general electorate. The aim is to quicken democratic experimentalism by facilitating the repeated practice of radical reform: change in the formative institutions and practices of society as well as in the beliefs sustaining them. In many countries, with strong political parties and informed electorates, the reform of a parliamentary system of government can produce similar results.

Third thesis: On the reorganization of electoral politics

A sustained heightening of the level of political mobilization is required for the acceleration of democratic experimentalism in all fields of social life. The level of political mobilization is not a natural fact about a society or a culture; it is, to a large extent, an artifact, responsive to changes in the rules and instruments of politics. Among such changes are: public financing of political campaigns; expanded free access to the means of mass communication for political parties and social movements; multiplication of the forms of ownership of the means of communication; rules of mandatory voting; and changes in the electoral regime. Although a system of closed lists and proportional representation is usually most effective in strengthening political parties as the agents of structural proposals, the temporary adoption of majority elections may in certain countries help shake up a rigidified party system and reveal underlying progressive and conservative coalitions. A politics of repeated structural change is necessarily a high-energy politics. For the high energy to persist beyond interludes of collective enthusiasm it must find sustenance in arrangements friendly to the rise of popular political engagement. For the high energy to exercise a lasting productive effect it must leave its work inscribed in the institutional and imaginative order of the society.

THE ORGANIZATION OF CIVIL SOCIETY AND THE PROTECTION OF RIGHTS

Fourth thesis: On the conception of fundamental rights

Progressives should reinterpret rather than reject the idea of fundamental rights. There is a dialectical relation between the protection of individuals in a haven of vital interests and the capacity of individuals to flourish in the midst of a quickened experimentalism. The role of the rights is to assure people of the political, economic, and cultural equipment they need in order to stand up, go forward, and connect. Such rights must safeguard them against the insecurities that might tempt them to abandon their freedom. We must take the definition and assignment of this equipment out of the agenda of short-term politics so that we can broaden this agenda effectively. Thus, the relation of fundamental rights to the generalized tinkering of a deepened democracy is like the relation between the love children receive from their parents and the capacity of children to make and remake themselves through moral adventure.

People should inherit from society rather than from their parents: they should have a social-endowment account. Inheritance upon death or through gift should be limited to the patrimony required by a conventionally set standard of modest independence. The social-endowment account should include both a fixed and variable part. The variable part should increase by one measure according to a principle of compensation for special need, for physical, social, or cognitive disadvantage, and by another, countervailing principle according to a criterion of reward for special capability, through competition among individuals for increments to their accounts.

Education, continuing through a lifetime, rescuing people as children from the imaginative hold of their families, their class, their country, and their time, and giving them as adults access to a repertory of generic practical and conceptual capacities, is the most important enabler of individual and collective freedom. It is therefore the principal object of the social-endowment account.

In keeping with the experimentalist impulse, we should try out and compare different ways of composing the accounts and of restricting their use. Thus, some part may be received as cash grants from the government, and some part held as tradeable but not cashable stakes in productive assets. Some part may need to be spent in predetermined ways according to fixed rules, and some part may be available for choice among alternative uses and alternative providers. Moreover, if these inheritance-replacing arrangements impose a cost upon output and prosperity, let us find out what the cost is, and let us decide how much of it we want to bear for the sake of a form of life better equipping and connecting us. Let us redefine as social choice what would otherwise remain institutional fate.

Fifth thesis: On the protection of fundamental rights

Rights, especially social and economic rights, should not be viewed simply as resource-dependent schemes of social welfare and social insurance. Claims of right enter into conflict with particular social organizations or areas of social practice when (a) a structure of inequality or exclusion emerges in particular organizations or practices, threatening the effective enjoyment of rights and (b) the individual cannot readily challenge this citadel of privilege by the normal forms of economic and political activity available to him. We need a type of corrective intervention and reorganization that is both (a) structural and rights-defining and (b) episodic and localized. Examples: Intervention in a school system to correct the disfavoring of children with certain skills or disabilities; intervention in a factory to reorganize a system of work imposing extreme forms of hierarchy in the interest of control and surveillance rather than as a requirement of technical coordination and efficiency. None of the existing branches of government are entirely well suited, by reason of political legitimacy or practical capacity, to serve as the agents of such intervention. A new branch of government must be designed, elected or co-chosen by the elected branches. It should have budgetary and technical resources appropriate to its reconstructive responsibilities.

Sixth thesis: On the legal organization of civil society

A vigilant and organized civil society is indispensable to the advancement of democratic experimentalism. A disorganized society cannot generate alternative futures or act upon them. Disorganization is surrender to accident, to drift, to fate.

It is not enough to call for an intensification of voluntary association without reimagining and remaking the institutional context in which voluntary association takes place. We can call the spirits, but they may not come. There are two paths of institutional reform that can strengthen the capacity of civil society for independent self-organization. Call them private law plus one and public law minus one. Far from being mutually exclusive, they can complement each other.

Private law plus one accepts the conventional body of contract and corporate law as the basic framework for the self-organization of civil society. However, it supplements this framework by establishing a branch of government responsible for localized intervention in organizations or practices corrupted by entrenched forms of social exclusion or subjugation. The evil to be redressed by such corrective intervention is a social disadvantage people are unable to escape by the normal forms of political and economic action. Left unchallenged, such disadvantage prevents its victims from effectively exercising many of their other political and economic rights.

The work of the reconstructive branch of government is neither to promulgate general laws like a legislature nor to settle rights disputes among individual litigants like a traditional judiciary. Its work is to repair a localized obstacle to capable economic or political agency. To this end, the intervening branch may have to run the offending organization for a while, placing it in a kind of social receivership, the better to lift it past the threshold of acceptability. The new part of government may need to investigate, invest, and reform – but always with a focused scope and for a limited time. Thus, it must enjoy the political legitimacy that comes from being elected by the people or co-elected by political branches of government, and the practical capacity that results from having financial and investigative resources at its disposal.

Public law minus one means a public-law framework for the organization of civil society outside the state, around jobs, neighborhoods or shared special concerns (like health care or education). There would be a right to opt out of this framework and fashion alternative arrangements under certain conditions. These readymade public-law provisions should help establish a bias toward inclusive organization in civil society. However, they should remain free from any taint of governmental control or tutelage.

For example, the contractualist labor-law principle of complete freedom of the unions from the government may be combined with the corporatist principle of automatic unionization of everyone. Automatic unionization may sound coercive until you realize that the choice may be between unequal organization, reinforcing the advantages of the advantaged, and inclusive but democratic organization, creating a structure over which everyone can fight on relatively equal terms. There is internal democracy in such a unitary and all-inclusive labor-union system: different labor movements, whether or not affiliated to political parties, compete for position in this union system just as political parties compete for position in government. The same idea can be reproduced on territorial principles: a system of neighborhood associations, outside the structure of local government and parallel to that structure. In yet a third domain the principle can take a functional direction: the organization of civil society around certain shared concerns, such as education or health services. Associational depth and diversity are conditions of cooperative competition in production and of deliberative capacity in politics. They diminish the terrors of innovation by sustaining trust and containing risk. To promote them is the proper object of a body of social law expanding and shaping the space between private initiative and public policy.

People should be able to exit this public-law system of social organization and create alternative arrangements so long as two basic conditions are satisfied. The first condition is that those who withdraw be in a situation of rough equality relative to one another. The second condition is that they not use their power of exiting the framework to establish another little citadel of entrenched subordination.

THE ORGANIZATION OF PUBLIC FINANCE AND OF THE ECONOMY

Seventh thesis: On public finance and the tax system

Some significant element of indirect taxation has been shown to be necessary in most contemporary societies to guarantee substantial tax revenues and thus to ensure a high level of public investment in people. The least regressive of the indirect taxes, and the one least likely to distort and disrupt economic activities, is a comprehensive flat-rate value-added tax. On the secure basis of the revenue collected by this tax there should be two principal direct taxes. The first is a Kaldor-style consumption tax, taxing the difference between income and savings-investments, with a large exemption for a basic level of consumption and a steeply progressive scale. The second is a wealth tax, of which the most important part is heavy taxation of family gifts and inheritance.

In this way, we distinguish clearly the two targets of standard-of-living (for the consumption tax) and economic power (for the wealth tax) and address them directly rather than accepting the relatively confused and ineffective machinery of the income tax. The organizations of civil society described in the sixth thesis should be engaged in the allocation and supervision of public spending. At a later moment in the deepening of democracy, when, according to the ninth thesis, traditional unified property rights have given way to a system of fragmentary, joint, and residual rights in productive resources, taxation may cease to be the mainstay of public finance. Instead of taxing, the government may impose differential rates of return for the use of the productive resources of society. The semi-independent organizations responsible for broadening the decentralized allocation of social capital (ninth thesis) would pay such charges, recovering them from the firms and work teams who would be the ultimate resource users.

Eighth thesis: On the reform of the production system and of its relation to the state

The reformation of production along more experimentalist lines need not have democratizing consequences, but it offers democratizing opportunities. The most promising path to the realization of such opportunities lies in a growth strategy combining the following attributes: (a) within firms, the practice of production as learning and the softening of rigid contrasts between task-defining and task-executing activities; (b) among firms, cooperative competition – small and medium-sized firms, or decentralized divisions of large firms, simultaneously compete and cooperate, pooling financial, commercial, and technological resources; (c) between firms and governments, a wide range of forms of partnership, with decentralized, pluralistic, and socially inclusive forms of strategic coordination between government and business. To prevent such partnership from degenerating into collusion between bureaucratic and entrepreneurial elites and from falling victim to rent-seeking and dogmatism we need to diversify the cast of economic agents and to screen governments from particular firms while affirming, in novel form, the idea of association between public power and private enterprise.

Democratizing the partnership between government and business requires the development of a level of organization standing in between the state and the firms: competitive social funds and support centers. Enjoying broad independence, and subject to competitive pressure and financial responsibility, such funds would operate with the resources of an original endowment, supplemented by their own gains. Their task would be to associate private initiative and public power in a decentralized form, calculated to minimize bureaucratic prejudice and economic privilege while promoting experimental innovation in the institutional forms of market activity.

From the outset some of these organizations would be charged with taking a view beyond the short term, in the fashion of a public venture-capital business. A characteristic concern of theirs would be to invest in a productive vanguard capable of producing, in customized fashion, the materials and machinery the productive rearguard of the economy needs. They would also work to lift up this rearguard, helping it identify and assimilate better practices and more advanced technologies.

Ninth thesis: On property rights

The decentralized and democratized partnership between governments and firms described in the eighth thesis can in turn advance through the dismemberment of traditional property rights. The powers now brought together under the label "property" would be torn apart, step by step, and vested in different tiers of rightholders: governments, intermediate organizations, and firms. Democratic governmental institutions may mark the outer limits to inequality of benefit or position in the workplace, shape the alternative means for the decentralized allocation of capital, and set the basic underlying charge for the use of capital. The intermediate organizations – social funds and support centers – would coordinate access to productive resources under different legal regimes.

Under some such regimes the funds would have an arm's-length relation to their client firms: assigning resources, in exchange for debt and equity, to those with the best prospect of assuring over longer or shorter periods the highest rate of return. Under other regimes the firms would develop a more intimate relation to their client firms, as centerpieces of little confederations of cooperative–competitive businesses. The ultimate capital-takers and users – the client firms or the teams of professionals or workers moving in and out of the firms – would share with the intermediate organizations and with local governments or community associations joint residual rights in the businesses they established.

Thus, we qualify property rights to make them proliferate. We achieve more decentralization of economic opportunity as well as more diversity in the legal forms of the market at the cost of weakening the absoluteness of the command rightholders enjoy over the resources at their disposal. Different systems of contract and property law, amounting to alternative methods for the decentralized allocation of capital, come to coexist within the same economy. An active, informed society can then evaluate their respective merits for each sector of economic activity, their economic benefits and social costs.

We diminish the tension between private initiative and public control by changing their institutional vehicles. Moreover, we diminish it simultaneously in many different ways, the better to see and to judge the practical consequences of each way. By such devices we turn into recognized and replaceable artifice what had been mistaken for practical or conceptual necessity in the institutional design of a market economy. The result is neither "capitalism" nor "socialism" but the market economy made more inclusive, more pluralistic, and more experimental.

DEMOCRACY AND THE LEFT

Tenth thesis: On what it means to be progressive today

To be progressive today is to insist upon crossing the boundaries of the established institutional settlement in a democratizing direction. Anyone who accepts the established institutional framework as the horizon within which interests and ideals – including egalitarian ideals – must be pursued is not a progressive. The European social-democratic parties are not progressive. A pessimistic, socially concerned but institutionally conservative reformism is not progressive. The error lies in believing that the alternative to resignation is the total substitution of one "system" by another. Revolutionary reform – the part-by-part substitution of formative institutional structures and ideas – is the exemplary mode of transformative politics. The idea of revolutionary change has, by its impracticality, become a pretext for its opposite. The first nine theses give examples of revolutionary reforms crossing the frontiers of the established institutional settlement.

Eleventh thesis: On the interpretation
of the democratic cause

The democratic cause is the effort to identify and to realize arrangements exploiting the area of potential overlap between the conditions of material progress and the conditions of individual emancipation. Thus, it moves toward the generalization of experimentalism in social life. It subjects the institutional forms of representative democracy and of the regulated market economy to this same experimentalism. It is not antiliberal; it realizes liberal hopes by changing liberal forms. It refuses to sacrifice the plurality of human interests to a single-minded egalitarianism. It wants us to be less unequal and less disconnected from one another in ways that also make us bigger, energizing and empowering.

Twelfth thesis: On the social base
of the progressive parties

The progressive parties cannot accept the choice between clinging to the favored representation of organized workers in mass-production industry and redefining themselves as middle-class "quality-of-life" parties. By choosing the first path they sink into the defense of ever narrower factional interests. By choosing the second path they betray their transformative and democratizing mission. They must find in a program of structural reconstruction both the focus and the basis for an enlarged popular alliance. What makes this effort possible is (a) the internal or dialectical relation between the redefinition of interests and ideals and the remaking of institutions or practices and (b) the asymmetrical relation between social alliances and political alliances. Social alliances are built through the transforming work of political alliances and sustained by structural reforms that turn tactical convergences into lasting combinations of group interests and identities. However, political alliances do not take social alliances for granted; they have the development of social alliances as a task.

Thirteenth thesis: On the focus of institutional innovation and ideological conflict in the world

The democratic project advances through conflict: the inherited ideological divisions lose their living connection to real concerns and possible alternatives. They must then be reinvented. The conflict between statism and privatism is dying and being replaced by a contest among the alternative institutional forms of political, social, and economic pluralism. Representative democracy, free civil society, and the market economy can all take forms different from those they now assume in the North Atlantic world. The choice among such alternatives is fateful because it represents a preference not just for certain arrangements but also for the possibilities of individual and collective experience these arrangements sustain. The involuntary institutional experimentalism of the poor countries (that invent when imitation fails to work) sheds light on the suppressed opportunities for transformation in the rich countries. The albatross of state socialism has been lifted from the neck of the left. However, the attempt by institutionally conservative social democrats to reduce progressive politics to the reconciliation of social protection with market flexibility leaves democracy unrealized and fails in its own objective. The time for progressives to reinvent themselves by driving democratic experimentalism forward is now.

AN APPENDIX ON SAVING AND INVESTMENT

by Zhiyuan Cui

The possibility and desirability of alternative institutional arrangements linking saving and productive investment is the central issue of democratic experimentalism in the area of finance. However, contemporary mainstream economics has helped obscure this problem rather than illuminate it. Two flaws of the existing economic literature – both "neoclassical" and Keynesian – contribute to this obscurity.

The first defect lies in the accounting identity between saving and investment. The second defect concerns the view of the causal relation between saving and investment. The first flaw prevents us from addressing the second. Opening up any macroeconomics textbook (e.g. Dornbusch and Fischer, p. 44), you will find that saving and investment are equal within a country by definition. This idea has its origin in Keynes's *General Theory* of 1936.[1]

---

[1] Keynes remarks as follows: "Provided it is agreed that income is equal to the value of current output, that current investment is equal to the value of that part of current output which is not consumed, and that saving is equal to the excess of income over consumption – all of which is conformable both to common sense and to the traditional usage of the great majority of economists – the equality of saving and investment necessarily follows. In short:

This accounting identity is a useful tool for the National Income Account,[2] but it prevents economists from considering alternative institutional arrangements linking saving and productive investment. Only in the earlier period of industrial revolution, when saving and investment were usually done by one and the same individuals, did it make sense to follow Adam Smith: "What is annually saved is as regularly consumed as what is annually spent, and nearly in the same time too" (Smith, 1776, vol. I, pp. 337–8). However, with the development of the sophisticated financial institutions of the modern market, economy, saving and investment are usually done by different people, Keynes's accounting identity between saving and investment has become counterintuitive. Recognizing this counterintuitive nature of his definition, Keynes offers a substantive justification that is worth citing in some detail:

> The prevalence of the idea that saving and investment, taken in their straightforward sense, can differ from one another, is to be explained, I think, by an optical illusion due to regarding an individual depositor's relation to his bank as being a one-sided transaction, instead of seeing it as the two-sided transaction which it actually is. . . . But no one can save without acquiring an asset, whether it be cash or a debt or capital-goods; and no one can acquire an asset which he did not previously possess, unless *either* an asset of equal value is newly produced *or* someone else parts with an asset of that value which he previously had. In the first alternative there

---

Income = value of output = consumption + investment

Saving = income − consumption

Therefore saving = investment." (p. 63)

[2] Keynes was directly involved with the preparation of the first National Income Account for England (by James Meade and Richard Stone), which became the basis for the United Nations' recommendations for every country in 1948.

is a corresponding new investment: in the second alternative someone else must be dis-saving an equal sum. (pp. 81–2)

. . .

Thus the old-fashioned view that saving always involves investment, though incomplete and misleading, is formally sounder than the new-fangled view that there can be saving without investment or investment without "genuine" saving. (p. 83)

. . .

The reconciliation of the identity between saving and investment with the apparent "free-will" of the individual to save what he chooses irrespective of what he or others may be investing, essentially depends on saving being, like spending, a two-sided affair. (p. 84)

It is clear from this citation that, by the time the *General Theory* was published in 1936, Keynes had completely changed the view expounded in his 1930 *Treatise on Money* – that is, that saving and investment are not equal by definition. This change is more than a matter of definition for national income accounting,[3] for its consequence is to obscure the alternative institutional links between saving and productive investment. If our purpose is to understand institutional arrangements in capital markets, it is more useful not to define saving as equal to investment. As Gunnar Myrdal pointed out with regard to Wicksell's monetary theory (which Keynes was still to uphold in *A Treatise on Money*): "the idea underlying his [Wicksell's] whole analysis of the capital market is that investment and saving are not identical but that

---

[3] As a matter of definition, the identity between saving and investment can be accepted for limited purposes, such as constructing National Income Accounts. James Tobin once said that "respect for identities is the first piece of wisdom that distinguishes economists from others who expatiate on economics" (p. 300). However, we must go beyond this identity to explore institutional mechanisms linking saving and investment.

they can be compared. They can then in a given situation be found equal or unequal." (p. 88)

The point here is not to object to the saving-investment identity for national income accounting, but to argue that we should not be blinded by this identity from looking for better institutional alternatives for mobilizing saving for productive investment. Let me illustrate this point by discussing what Keynes calls the "dilemma of liquidity." On the one hand, initial public offerings of corporate stocks are useful for mobilizing saving for productive investment; on the other, secondary stock-market trading breeds wasteful, casino-like speculation. The dilemma arises because we cannot enjoy the first effect without suffering the second. In Keynes's own words:

> Of the maxims of orthodox finance none, surely, is more anti-social than the fetish of liquidity, the doctrine that it is a positive virtue on the part of investment institutions to concentrate their resources upon the holding of "liquid" securities. It forgets that there is no such thing as liquidity of investment for the community as a whole. (p. 155)
> . . .
> For the fact that each individual investor flatters himself that his commitment is "liquid" (though this cannot be true for all investors collectively) calms his nerves and makes him much more willing to run a risk. If individual purchases of investments were rendered illiquid, this might seriously impede new investment, so long as alternative ways in which to hold his savings are available to the individual. This is the dilemma. (p. 160)

Here, it is important to realize that if we were to take the accounting identity between saving and investment literally, the dilemma of liquidity would not exist at all. There is simply no waste in the financial casino, because nothing prevents successful speculators from reinvesting their gains in productive projects. At the end of the day, saving and investment are still equal by definition without saving having been diluted and wasted in financial casinos. However, in reality, relatively little real investment in the expansion of production and productivity is financed directly through stock markets. Corporations in all major Western countries fund almost all their capital expenditures – investment in plant, machinery, and inventories – internally, through retained earnings, in other words through profits and depreciation.[4] Since 1952, retained earnings have covered ninety-five per cent of capital expenditures. Since the early 1980s, through mergers and acquisitions, buybacks, and dividends distribution, more stock has been retrieved from stock markets than has been issued. As a result, new equity as a net source of finance is negative![5]

By going beyond the accounting identity between saving and investment and looking into the flow of loanable funds, we see that the potential for productive investment has indeed been reduced by the financial casinos. The accounting identity should not be understood to imply that all potential uses of loanable funds are equally productive. To justify such an implication, we would need to add two other crucial links to the chain of reasoning: that the established arrangements channeling saving into production approach the ideal of a market system that

[4] From the accounting perspective, retained earnings can be viewed simply as "corporate savings." So the dominance of retained earnings as the main source of finance does not change the accounting identity between saving and investment. However, if we really want to know how well stock markets mobilize public savings for corporate investment, the dominance of retained earnings is revealing: the mobilizing job is not well done! Moreover, the reliance upon retained earnings tends to perpetuate the existing economic divisions and hierarchies in the market, to the disadvantage of small and start-up firms.

[5] There is much statistical evidence, all based on official flow-of-account analysis, on the dominance of retained internal earnings as the net source of finance in all Western countries. See, for example, Colin Mayer (1997).

allocates resources to their most "efficient" uses and that there is no major, market-friendly alternative to these arrangements. These are empirical, not analytical claims. This book has argued that they are false.

Hence, Keynes's "dilemma of liquidity" is a real one. Our task as democratic experimentalists is to search for alternative institutional arrangements to reduce the detrimental consequence of this dilemma.

The equation of saving with investment obscures a problem of great practical interest: the way in which particular institutional arrangements can either squander or tap the productive potential of saving. One way of squandering this potential is so to centralize access to finance that a myriad of small or would-be businesses are denied the practical resources with which to begin and to expand. One means of tapping this potential is to create alternative devices for the commitment of retained earnings to productive projects. Yet another strategy is to popularize the business of venture capital: the long-term investment of funds in start-up firms, typically in exchange for an equity stake.

Contemporary experience offers suggestive although limited examples of both approaches. Remember, as an example of the alternative routing of retained earnings, the Meidner Plan of wage-earners' funds in Sweden. As described by John Stephens, these funds work in the following way. "Companies with more than 100 employees, which account for two thirds of all private employment, would have to transfer a portion (10–30 per cent) of their profits in the form of newly issued shares of stock to 'wage earner' or 'employee investment' funds administered by the unions. The transferred portion of profit would be new equity capital and would remain in the firm for investment. The voting rights of the stocks would go to the unions with the first 40 per cent split between the national and the local union." (Stephens, p. 189)

As an example of the popularization of venture capital, consider an experiment that has been underway in Canada for more than a decade. Starting from the first labor-sponsored venture capital project in 1984 – the Québec Solidarity Fund – labor-led venture capital funds now account for more than one third of venture capital in Canada. Established with tax credits and public seed money, the funds channel the savings of Canadian workers into small and medium-sized companies. The funds are independently managed and dedicated to ensure their investors high returns and diversified risks. Studies have suggested that the value of the tax incentives – worth some forty per cent of the funds invested – is paid back to the government in about three years, thanks to effects such as the increase of payroll taxes, as well as the diminishing of welfare payments, associated with the new jobs created.

A second way in which contemporary economics helps obscure the institutional issues in finance is its failure to resolve a conundrum about the causal direction between saving and investment. The neoclassicists hold that the causal direction goes from saving to investment; Keynesians, the other way around. As James Meade vividly put it, "Keynes's intellectual revolution was to shift economists from thinking normally in terms of a model of reality in which a dog called savings wagged his tail labelled investment to thinking in terms of a model in which a dog called investment, wagged his tail labelled savings." (p. 342)

According to the classicists before Keynes and the neoclassicists after him, high saving rates provide means for investment at low interest rates. Inversely, low saving rates make loanable funds more scarce, thereby raising interest rates and discouraging investment. In the long run, saving and investment are brought into equilibrium by interest-rate variation. That equilibrium interest rate is called the "natural rate of interest." Keynes's revolution in 1936 turned this classical saving-drive-investment theory upside down. For Keynes, investment decisions are made on the basis of future profit expectations. Investment spending, through the mechanism of the multiplier, increases total income and, thereby, the level of saving. In this sense, investment is a revolving, self-liquidating fund for the society as a whole: it is not constrained by the prior saving level. However, this important insight did not prevent Keynes from running into a crucial theoretical problem. Before the completion of the investment multiplier, how can the initial investment be financed if not by prior saving?

Keynes's answer is that banks will accept a temporary decline in their liquidity the better to finance the initial investment before the multiplier completes its work. This is why he insists that his "most fundamental conclusion" is that the investment market "can never become congested through shortage of saving" (Keynes, 1930, p. 222). But ever since Keynes published his *General Theory*, the critics, from Robertson (1936) and Ohlin (1937) through to Asimakopulos (1983) have argued that banks would not accept the reduction of their liquidity without high interest-rate compensation. In turn, high interest rates will increase the cost of capital and thereby discourage investment. At this point in the causal chain, the critics claim, saving comes back into the picture again as a determinant of investment, since without a prior increase in saving, banks' demand for high interest rates compensating their liquidity loss cannot be resisted.[6]

These debates on the causal direction between saving and investment in economics have reached a dead end. For, having failed to bring institutional alternatives into discussion, the Keynesian revolution is at risk of being totally reversed. Only by overcoming the obscurity perpetuated by mainstream economics – through the accounting identity between saving and investment as well as through the conundrum about the causal direction between saving and investment – can we begin to explore alternative institutional arrangements linking saving and production.

---

[6] Bridel (1987) and Dymski and Pollin (1997) are good surveys of the fascinating debates on the causal direction between saving and investment.

References in Appendix

Asimakopulos, A., "Kalečki and Keynes on Finance, Investment, and Saving," *Cambridge Journal of Economics*, vol. 7, 1983, pp. 221–33.

Bridel, Pascal, *Cambridge Monetary Thought: Development of Saving-Investment Analysis from Marshall to Keynes*, St. Martin's Press, 1987.

Dymski, Gary and Pollin, Robert, eds, *New Perspectives in Monetary Macroeconomics*, The University of Michigan Press, 1994.

Keynes, John Maynard, *The General Theory of Employment, Interest, and Money*, Harcourt Brace Jovanovich, 1953 (originally published in 1936).

Keynes, John Maynard, *A Treatise on Money*, Harcourt Brace, 1930.

Keynes, John Maynard, *The Collected Writings of John Maynard Keynes*, vol. XIV, Macmillan, 1973.

Mayer, Colin, "The City and Corporate Performance," *Cambridge Journal of Economics*, vol. 21, 1997, pp. 291–302.

Meade, James, *The Collected Papers of James Meade*, vol.1, edited by Susan Howson, Unwin Hyman, 1988.

Myrdal, Gunnar, *Monetary Equilibrium*, William Hodge, 1939.

Ohlin, B., "Some Notes on the Stockholm Theory of Saving and Investment," *Economic Journal*, vol. 47, March and June 1937.

Robertson, D.H., "Some Notes on Mr. Keynes's General Theory of Employment," *Quarterly Journal of Economics*, vol. 51, November 1936.

Tobin, James, "Comments," in Robert Pollin, ed., *Macroeconomics of Saving, Finance and Investment*, University of Michigan Press, 1997.

PROPER-NAMES INDEX

THEMATIC INDEX

accelerated politics, constitutionalism of
213–17
action
belief in efficacy of 221
capacity for, through voluntary
association 221
affirmative action, redress of racial
injustice and 128
agency and insight: democratic
experimentalism and ordinary
people 10–16
agrarian property, smallscale 38
agriculture, and economics 93
alliance, majoritarian popular, through
solidaristic political strategy 78
alternative pluralisms 27
antidualism, redistribution and 206–12
antidualist political economy
and "neoliberalism to the hilt" 70
antiexperimentalist illusions, and
alternative to neoliberalism
188–90
antinecessitarian beliefs, about
institutional change 244
antisaving thesis, and demand–supply
difficulties 158
association, and structure of civil
society 222
asymmetry thesis 14–16
authoritarianism
political 64
truncated liberalism as form of

politics in authoritarian hard state
68
in alternative to neoliberalism 137
North East Asian economies
dependency on authoritarian state
193
as shortcut to hardness of hard state
195
see also relative democracy

banks
and stable relationship with firms 46
multiplying channels between saving
and investment outside banks and
stock market 121
initial public offerings and financing
of production 153
bureaucratic dogmatism,
antiexperimentalism illusions and
188
business and government, rebuilding
relationship between 40
business unionism, as cooperative
devices for employers 224

capability
and social–endowment accounts
209
dialectic between safeguard and
capability 250
capital
global mobility of 32
and license to move freely 42

and investment outside banks and
stock market 121
initial public offerings and financing
of production 153
strategic coordination, and hard states
191–6
structural change, structural reform
monetary stabilization by exchange-
rate anchor and high interest rates
55–6
as change in the formative
institutional context of society 74
equalizing, and investment in
education 193
and energy level in politics 218
and nationalism 252–4
thinking structurally, with and
without structural determinism
20–24
structure fetishism 25–6
manifestations in history of social
thought 110
subversive opportunism, on deals inside
and outside national economy
47–8
supply response, unreliability of 156
surplus value, as proportion of wages to
value added in industrial sector of
national economy 170

tax-and-transfer
vanguard and rearguard in 35
conservative social democracy in
neoliberal vision 54
programs of, in conditions of
dualistic economy 83
and high level of savings 135
social entitlements and actions 182–3
distribution of rights, resources,
opportunities 207
taxation
and radical–democratic program in
reorganization of firms 50

raised, as alternative version of fiscal
adjustment 118
redesigned, in alternative to
neoliberalism 139–47
of consumption, and waste of
resources by individuals 140–41
progressive, and redistribution
through public spending 141–2
indirect, and collective deception and
self-deception 142
on wealth 144
inheritance, in alternative to
neoliberalism 144
of gifts and estates 146
redistributive, in alternative to
neoliberalism 146
internal saving levels raised and tax
reform 162
progressive, and compensatory
redistribution 166
and participation of wages in national
income 169
and short-term movement of capital
182
high tax take in ways friendly to
growth 183
and priority of public revenue
generation 184
of gifts and estates 208
and public finance 271–2
teachers, movement of in education 232
technological innovation, and practical
progress 7
temperament, affinities of, and tyranny
of circumstance 181
township–village enterprises, in China
106
trade
systems of clearing rules,
administered by international
organizations 85
fragmentation of trade within state
apparatus 196